FLY FISHING
—— WEST ——
YELLOWSTONE

FLY FISHING
— WEST —
YELLOWSTONE
A HISTORY AND GUIDE

BRUCE STAPLES AND BOB JACKLIN

STACKPOLE
BOOKS

Guilford, Connecticut

Published by Stackpole Books
An imprint of The Rowman & Littlefield Publishing Group, Inc.
4501 Forbes Blvd., Ste. 200
Lanham, MD 20706
www.rowman.com

Distributed by NATIONAL BOOK NETWORK

British Library Cataloguing in Publication Information available

Library of Congress Cataloging-in-Publication Data

Names: Staples, Bruce, author. | Jacklin, Bob, 1945– author.
Title: Fly fishing west Yellowstone : a history and guide / Bruce Staples and Bob Jacklin.
Description: Guilford, Connecticut : Stackpole Books, [2021] | Includes bibliographical references and index. | Summary: "Fly-fishing legend Bob Jacklin and well-known writer and fly historian Bruce Staples team up to write the compelling history of this area, which still remains the epicenter of fly fishing in the western United States. This book also includes fly patterns, past and present, as well as up-to-date information about these famous rivers, making this an indispensable reference for anyone visiting the region"— Provided by publisher.
Identifiers: LCCN 2021005055 | ISBN 9780811738255 (paperback) | ISBN 9780811768269 (epub)
Subjects: LCSH: Fly fishing—Montana—West Yellowstone—History. | Fly fishing—Montana—West Yellowstone—Guidebooks.
Classification: LCC SH456 .S73 2021 | DDC 799.12/409786662—dc23
LC record available at https://lccn.loc.gov/2021005055

♾™ The paper used in this publication meets the minimum requirements of American National Standard for Information Sciences—Permanence of Paper for Printed Library Materials, ANSI/NISO Z39.48-1992.

CONTENTS

ACKNOWLEDGMENTS

The subject of this book required researching many sources. First, we offer thanks to the Museum of the Yellowstone, the West Yellowstone Historical Society, the West Yellowstone Public Library, and the International Fly-Fishing Center.

Our appreciation goes to Cal and Jan Dunbar for sharing information, reviewing drafts of this book, and suggesting persons to contact. Jan's delightful book *It Is All True, or It Ought to Be* was a treasure trove of information on West Yellowstone's early days. Cal's friendship with the Don Martinez family provides the best view available of Don's skills and personality. Jan's passionate interest in preserving West Yellowstone's history and her generosity and enthusiasm in sharing it proved vital.

Charles Barnes graciously not only provided information on the operation of the Pat Barnes Tackle Shop, but also gave us family history items, suggested persons to contact for detailed information, and provided significant materials that enrich this book. Charles also shared memories of summers working in the shop from 1959 to 1980. Sam Eagle's two youngest sons, Joe and Wally, and Wally's son Dr. Kim Eagle provided information on their family and West Yellowstone history and photographs, as well as information on Eagle's Store. As with the Dunbars and Charles Barnes, we owe them a depth of gratitude. Wally Eagle also provided fascinating information on his family's relationship with Don Martinez, Charles Borberg, George Grant, Pat Barnes, Bud Lilly, and other fly-fishing icons.

To Jim and Lois Danskin goes appreciation for sharing incidents from their experience in the West Yellowstone fly-fishing business. Appreciation also goes to Craig and Jackie Mathews for relating the development of Blue Ribbon Flies and their exemplary efforts to preserve regional salmonid habitat.

Thanks and appreciation go to Paul Shea for allowing use of the Yellowstone Historic Center archives and to Denise Zdanski for allowing us to use materials within the Museum of the Yellowstone in West Yellowstone. Brad Sheppard, Bruce Rich, and Dick Vincent shared information on the status and management of westslope cutthroat trout and grayling in Montana's portion of the Greater Yellowstone region.

Thanks go to Gloria Kramer for sharing information on the Elk Lake Resort and her Selby parents and grandparents, and to Don Ryder for relating his fly-fishing experiences at the original Selby resort. To Bill and Loretta Chapman we give thanks for providing information on Bill's dad, Scotty. Jim O'Toole also graciously provided information on Scotty Chapman, his fly-fishing mentor.

We thank Sandy (Ebersole) Stradley for information on the Narrows Resort on Hebgen Lake and on her parents, Jack and Mickey Ebersole. The same thanks go to Shilo and Sheila Klatt, former owners of the Cliff Lake Resort, now Wilderness Edge Retreat; Jim Slattery for information on the Campfire Lodge and other resorts; and Kelly Galloup, owner of the Slide Inn.

To Arrick Swanson go thanks for providing information on establishing his business in West Yellowstone. Roland Whitman provided information on the history of

Picture taken at Parade Rest Ranch of Bud Lilly and the authors. No one knew the waters around West Yellowstone and their history as well as Bud. We are honored that he graciously shared that knowledge with us. (Bruce Staples collection)

his family, and Lorenzo "Buck" Goodrich and Ralph Moon shared their times in the Federation of Fly Fishers (FFF) Conclaves.

Thanks go to Bill Schiess for sharing experiences and thoughts on area stillwaters. Betty Webb gave information on her days at the Fenwick Fly-Fishing School and on her husband Tom Webb's connection to the school. To Fred Jacobi, Catherine Jacobi Uchiyama, and Arlene Jacobi Carlton go thanks for sharing remembrances of Yellowstone Park outings during the 1950s and for donating pictures.

We held several discussions with Bud Lilly, in which he passed on information not obtainable elsewhere. Not only were these discussions particularly informative for us, but within them Bud passed on incidents in his fly-fishing retailing experience that had not yet been revealed. We owe Bud much for revealing information that enriches our fly-fishing heritage and otherwise could have been lost.

Others that provided valuable information include Clayton Parman on the West Yellowstone lodging industry, Tom Carmichael on the Bob Carmichael–Don Martinez fly-tying relationship, Mike Atwell on the role of his family in West Yellowstone fly-fishing history, and Will Godfrey and Mike Lawson on their times in West Yellowstone. John Juracek provided information on his times in town. Some of his photos grace this book. John Harder described his experiences supplying Orvis flies and merchandise to West Yellowstone fly-fishing retailers. Harold Roberts gave thoughts on his experiences guiding for Pat Barnes and Bud Lilly, Al Troth on his tenure with Bud Lilly, Bud Morris on the Parade Rest Guest Ranch, Roger Porter on Jack Gartside fly patterns, and Jesse Riding on Dave Whitlock patterns.

René Harrop offered information on House of Harrop contributions to the West Yellowstone fly-fishing retail industry. Paul Stimpson gave information on his experiences in the regional fly-fishing industry and on Gary LaFontaine's interface with it. Laurie Schmidt provided information on the Wade Lake Resort. Dave Whitlock shared thoughts on his West Yellowstone experiences. Cici Ives provided unique information on West Yellowstone's early days.

Once again Dr. Roger Blew flew me around the West Yellowstone area in order to do some aerial photography. Thank you, Roger!

Several persons tied flies to be photographed for this book. We acknowledge the efforts of Gary Barnes, LeRoy Cook, Jim Fisher, Aaron Freed, Doug Gibson, Kelly Glissmeyer, Buck Goodrich, Al Jacobi, Bucky McCormick, Gerry Randolph, Paul Stimpson, Dave Whitlock, Chris Williams, Linda Windels, and the House of Harrop. We tied a few ourselves. Thanks goes to Jay Nichols, Stephanie Otto, Meredith Dias, Elissa Curcio, and Wendy Reynolds for help in producing this book.

INTRODUCTION

West Yellowstone, Montana, is sited in the midst of our country's most extensive and best remaining inland salmonid habitat. To the north is the Gallatin River drainage. To the west are the Madison River and Red Rock River drainages, and to the south is the Henry's Fork drainage. To the east lie the nearly pristine waters of Yellowstone National Park. Charlie Brooks estimated that there are 2,000 miles of high-quality trout streams in the Greater Yellowstone region of about 8,000 square miles. Within Yellowstone Park's 2,300 square miles are forty-five streams and at least forty lakes hosting trout populations. Nowhere else in our country is there a location surrounded by such an array of quality salmonid waters, and because of this a rich regional sportfishing culture was born and continues to thrive.

The Madison River in the fall is a stream of "many faces." Within Yellowstone Park and down to Hebgen Reservoir the river flows through beautiful meadows punctuated by riffle-and-run sections. Between Hebgen and Quake Lake, as pictured above, is a fast-water section as the river drops into the upper end of a canyon now under Quake Lake. The area is easily approached, and fly fishers congregate here throughout the season. (John Juracek photo)

As introduced brook, brown, and rainbow trout grew large and abundant in the cold, clean waters of the region, visiting anglers and the local angling retailers came to revere (and become increasingly protective of) these new fisheries. Because of the legendary fishing, personalities such as Barnes, Brooks (Charlie), Chapman, Danskin, Dunbar, Eagle, Jacklin, Johnson, Juracek, Lilly, Martinez, Mathews, Ritchie, Servatius, Sivey, and Swanson established in West Yellowstone.

Complementing this array of famed angling personalities came visiting outdoor writers to the area beginning in the 1930s. Through their books and articles, middle-class and blue-collar fly fishers became fully aware of the area's exceptional angling. The proliferation of outdoor magazine and newspaper articles around the second half of the twentieth century intensified the attention on the area waters and the great fishing. Bailey, Bergman, Brooks (Joe), Grant, Hewitt, LaFontaine, Schullery, Schwiebert, Sturgis, Swisher and Richards, Waterman, Whitlock, and Zern all wrote about how fantastic the fishing was around West Yellowstone. What other town can boast such an array of superb fly-fishing waters combined with nationally recognized and renowned homegrown fly-fishing personalities?

While West Yellowstone has a rich fly-fishing history, no one before has set down how it became perhaps the most hallowed fly-fishing destination of today. Uncon-nected pieces exist, and much history was in the memory of persons who lived to see the town's stature as such develop. When we approached Bud Lilly with the idea of collecting as much of that history as possible under one cover, he prefaced his encouragement and offer to help with the comment "You'd better hurry!"

That was nearly ten years ago, and we immediately began research and contacting persons, nearly all in or approaching elderly years, for information on the town's fly-fishing history and for discussion of nearby famed waters and important fly patterns created by not only West Yellowstone fly tiers but also visiting anglers eager to ply the famous waters nearby.

This book preserves the evolution of this fly-fishing heritage, the progression of its advocates, and the gifts that West Yellowstone has given to enrich fly fishing like few other communities. It also provides information that guides visiting fly fishers to favored locations on fabled streams and stillwaters and famed fly patterns originating from experiences on these waters.

Numerous magazines and books have covered these nearby waters, but we include some of the history associated with them as well. There has been even less informa-tion on local fly patterns. Blue Ribbon Flies' excellent books describing in-house fly patterns, interesting articles detailing Don Martinez's fly-tying accomplishments, and Charlie Brooks's descriptions of dozens of patterns in his superb books are all available. But there is much unpublished information on many fly patterns as well as none on others, so one of our major goals was to collect patterns, past and present, from local tiers and share some of their histories.

CHAPTER 1

BEGINNINGS

In 1870 President Ulysses S. Grant appointed Henry Dana Washburn as Surveyor General for the Montana Territory. Washburn led an expedition tasked with exploring the region that would become Yellowstone National Park. The expedition started on August 22, 1870, where the Yellowstone River exits the park, circled Yellowstone Lake, and followed the Madison River to exit what would become the park. A sign commemorates the Washburn Expedition's campsite near the confluence of the Firehole and Gibbon Rivers during the night of September 19, 1870. Here the idea of making the explored region a national park began.

Ferdinand Hayden's geologic surveys, also during the early 1870s, gained broad and specific scientific information that revealed the unique character of area's land and water. The national park idea became reality when President Grant signed into law, on March 1, 1872, the congressional act forming Yellowstone National Park.

The first written accounts of fly fishing in Yellowstone National Park came as early as 1875, many from US Army officers assigned with exploring and protecting the park. John Varley and Paul Schullery, in *Freshwater Wilderness*, document General William Strong's journal describing an 1875 encounter with Yellowstone Lake cutthroat.

The Lamar Valley hosts bison in large numbers. Fly fishers here must proceed with caution. (Courtesy of Acroterion)

1

This Red Rock Pass sign identifies the Continental Divide. Red Rock Creek in the Missouri River drainage is to the west, and the Henry's Fork in the Columbia River drainage is to the east. Stage lines traveled east from the Monida, Montana, railhead, through the Centennial Valley, and over the pass on a two-day journey to reach Yellowstone National Park and what would become the town of West Yellowstone. (Bruce Staples collection)

From about 1875 to the end of the century, reports of the park's extraordinary sportfishing grew and stimulated angling traffic. One of the visitors, Edward Ringwood Hewitt, considered by many to be the father of American nymph fishing, was the first of the major eastern fly-fishing writers to fish the Yellowstone River and nearby waters such as the Henry's Fork in Idaho's Island Park. He first visited during the early 1880s, at about age fifteen, and had angling we cannot imagine today.

A significant amount of support for park tourism came from the Northern Pacific Railway, which in the early 1880s built a branch line from Livingston to Gardiner, Montana. The State of Montana and the railroad realized that commercial benefits could result from tourism into the park.

In the late nineteenth century, non-mechanized travel limited impacts on the Greater Yellowstone area and its wildlife. Many primitive roads followed Native American trails built as trade routes and to access hunting grounds. In the southwest corner of the Greater Yellowstone area the Bannock and Shoshone peoples established the Bannock Trail. It began near Camas Meadows west of Idaho's Island Park region, skirted the south and east sides of Henry's Lake, crossed Targhee Pass, and proceeded into the Madison Valley, crossing the river at a site now under Hebgen Lake, then over Horse Butte. From here the trail went east, not far from the future settlement of Grayling, into the Cougar Creek vicinity, over the Gallatin Range south of the present Mammoth area, then east up Lava Creek to cross the Yellowstone River near Tower Falls. It then continued on through the Lamar Valley and over the Absaroka Range to the Clark's Fork Valley and access the plains.

This detail is significant because portions of the highway system around West Yellowstone follow parts of this trail. In West Yellowstone's origin, the most important road, now US Highway 20 and portions of the park's West Entrance Road, was built in 1873 by Gilman Sawtell from his ranch on Henry's Lake over Targhee Pass and into Yellowstone Park along the Madison River.

The Oregon Short Line branch of the Union Pacific Railroad was first into the region. By 1878 it pushed over Monida Pass, nearly sixty miles west of the future West Yellowstone site. Most visitors detrained at Monida, Montana, then used stage lines going through the Centennial Valley, over Red Rock Pass, around Henry's Lake, and over Targhee Pass to access the Greater Yellowstone area.

Harry Dwelle's Grayling Inn, sited where that stage line crossed the South Fork of the Madison River (a few miles south of present US Highway 20), was the first permanent structure in the area. Sawtell's road from Dwelle's to the park along the Madison River served for access.

Before the end of the century, reports of the park's extraordinary sportfishing grew. In general, visitors to the area would, unthinkable by today's sporting standards, kill and discard catches without regard for consequences. Thus waste was the first major negative impact of European-American sportfishing. Preservation of the unique area and concern over the absence of law and order prompted citizen organizations to lobby that the army be sent to the park. Much of the mistreatment of wildlife and fisheries diminished when US Army cavalry units arrived in 1886, tasked with stopping illegal activities such as poaching, unauthorized livestock grazing, and natural resources waste. Some soldiers were garrisoned at the Riverside mail station a few miles east of the future town.

In 1916 park superintendant Horace Albright began actions to replace the cavalry units with a civilian ranger force to continue fighting abuse and destructive acts to the

This 1913 photograph is probably one of the earliest of a day's catch on the Widow's Pool. Fishing here was allowed for a fee. Nowadays fish like these would be photographed then released to be enjoyed another day. (Bob Jacklin collection)

◀ Lillian Hackett Hanson arrived in Dillon, Montana, and began a seamstress business before marrying Bill Culver and homesteading on property holding what would become the Widow's Pool. (Bob Jacklin collection)

A panorama of the northeast area of the Red Rock Lakes National Wildlife Refuge. In the foreground is Picnic Creek and on the left is Culver Pond, fed by Picnic Springs. On the right is Widgeon Pond. The Centennial Mountains (Mount Taylor and Sheep Mountain) border the image on the far south. (Courtesy: James "Newt" Perdue / USFWS)

park and its wildlife. A misuse that continued in the park until 1917 was commercial fishing to supply table fare to area eateries. Outside the park in the Greater Yellowstone region no such protection was applied, so abuses, mainly poaching, continued.

Not all activities were of the illegal kind. Homesteading went on in many locations. Some homesteads would eventually offer famed fishing, and several would become destinations for anglers upon recommendation of West Yellowstone fly-fishing retailers.

Around 1900 homesteader Lillian Hackett Hansen, a Dillon, Montana, seamstress; her husband Bill Culver, whom Lillian later divorced; and her son Fred established a pond on Picnic Creek originating from springs on their property in the northeast end of the Centennial Valley. The pond was to provide water for cattle, and the Hansons stocked it with native cutthroat trout and grayling from nearby streams to be a food source. Next rainbow and brook trout were introduced and grew to large sizes. Lillian, now divorced from Bill, and Fred harvested and prepared the fish and sent them as table fare to Montana mines and Salt Lake City. Lillian and Fred also allowed sportfishing for rainbow and brook trout for a fee. In the fly-fishing community that pond is now known as the Widow's Pool; its official name is Culver Pond.

Nineteenth-century actions by European-American anglers, including the introduction of preferred exotic salmonids and the practice of "catch and kill," produced destructive impacts on native salmonids. Commercial fishing also reduced native salmonid populations. Many of the visiting anglers were influential persons from eastern states or England, who generally held salmonids and other sport fish residing in their home regions in higher esteem than native Greater Yellowstone salmonids. Brook trout, brown trout, Atlantic salmon, and even the rainbow trout of waters farther west had better sporting qualities, they proclaimed. Thus from these anglers came pressure to establish exotic salmonids in the region. The US Commission of Fish and Fisheries came to the park to define its fisheries and, of course, supported

the plantings, as such actions helped justify its existence. In Montana directly east, west, and north of the future town of West Yellowstone, westslope cutthroat, Montana grayling, and Rocky Mountain whitefish were the dominant salmonids. But the days of this domination were numbered.

The first significant stocking of park waters devoid of salmonids took place in 1889, opening the door to the introduction of exotic species. Brook trout were stocked in the upper Firehole River that year. About the same time, rainbow trout were released in the Gibbon River above the falls. Brown trout were released in Nez Perce Creek in 1890. Downstream drift from the more successful of these plantings would have a huge eventual impact on native salmonid populations. Not only the displacement of native species but also the hybridization between native cutthroat and introduced rainbow trout began.

Plans called for the introduction of brook trout into Glen Creek and the Gardner River above its falls, rainbows into the Gibbon above Virginia Cascades, brown (Loch Leven) trout into the Firehole River above Kepler Cascades, and Rocky Mountain whitefish into Twin Lakes and the Yellowstone River between the lake and falls (the Rocky Mountain whitefish failed to establish). Due to an administrative error, some eggs were not properly identified and therefore switched in destination. Thus brook trout were introduced into the salmonid-free Firehole River in 1889 and brown trout into the Gardner River. Gardner River tributaries received brook trout above the barrier falls, as planned. Brown trout were introduced into the Firehole River through their release in the salmonid-free Nez Perce Creek the following year.

Hiram Chittenden, in *The Yellowstone National Park: Historical and Descriptive*, offers numbers of fish released in the various US Fish Commission plantings in the park, including this number and location that catch the eye: "10,000 yearling lake trout in the Yellowstone River above the falls in 1890." Chittenden gives no specific location for this act. If his words are correct, location and the passage of time could be important in the following speculation. If placed nearer the falls, these fish most likely drifted downstream and out of the system. If placed near the lake, who can say where they ended up? But could this be the origin of the late-twentieth-century discovery of the lake trout in Yellowstone Lake? If the latter is true, it was for decades almost unnoticed and began a major abuse of native salmonids.

The reason why events taking place in Yellowstone National Park are important to understand is simple. Without the park's formation to preserve resident ecosystems and subsequent events in the surrounding area, the town of West Yellowstone as we know it would probably not exist and its fly-fishing heritage would be poorer. For area pioneering families, life was difficult. In particular, winter meant isolation, potential starvation, unattended medical emergencies, and little gainful employment. Forming a town could provide the means to reduce these conditions. The annual return of the tourist season, which increasingly included guiding and accommodating anglers, could provide the means for incomes and better physical living conditions. So the stage is set at the end of the nineteenth century for West Yellowstone to be formed.

Among the first individuals with a desire to establish in the area was S. P. "Sam" Eagle, who came first to Mammoth in 1903 from Pennsylvania. He found employment as a bartender, a table fare fisherman, and on occasion a fishing guide at the Fountain Hotel, successor to the Marshall House, in the Madison River drainage.

In 1903 architect Robert Reamer began construction of the Old Faithful Inn with the closure of the Fountain Hotel. It would become the only inn operating in the Madison River drainage within the park.

Tales of the superb salmonid population inhabiting the region spread among affluent visitors and regional business interests. For example, Frank J. Haynes owned the Monida-Yellowstone Stage Company. His company would soon be greatly impacted by the coming rail line. Nevertheless he offered in the 1902 edition of the Haynes Guide to Yellowstone Park: "[Dwelle's] Grayling Inn, near the western boundary of the Park, is situated on the South Fork of the Madison River, one of the most famous grayling streams in the West." The town of Grayling, holding the first post office in the region, was sited about fifteen miles northwest of the park's West Entrance in 1898 near its namesake Grayling Creek. This post office would operate for more than fifty years.

Somewhere in the East around 1904 or 1905, probably Connecticut, Donald Skillman Martinez was born. He would not live a long life, but his tremendous influence on the West Yellowstone area's fly-fishing heritage would begin in two and a half decades. William S. "Scotty" Chapman was born on July 20, 1907, in Westfield, Iowa, and would have few peers in knowledge of fly-fishing Yellowstone Park waters. In 1909 Lucinda Marshall Barnes gave birth to Antrim Earl Barnes Jr.; in the fly-fishing world he would be known as Pat Barnes.

Descriptions of the region's fabulous fly fishing began appearing in nationally distributed magazines. As angling pressure in the park increased, so did the waste of fish, as no creel limit was in place. Some of the most popular streams were in the Madison River drainage. Here was the Firehole, devoid of salmonids a dozen years before, now touted as a beautiful limestone stream (which technically it is not) hosting large brook and brown trout. In the smaller but equally picturesque Gibbon River, introduced rainbow trout prospered. In 1905 brook trout were introduced into the river above Gibbon Falls.

Below in the Madison River, exotic species continued displacing the native westslope cutthroat, and grayling grew to huge sizes and drifted downstream and into tributaries within and outside the park. In a few decades the westslope cutthroat, now the Montana state fish, would exist only in headwater streams of the drainage,

A trail ending at Lookout Butte provides a panoramic view of the Old Faithful area from the east. The Old Faithful Inn has hosted many fly fishers from the early twentieth century to the present day and is a national treasure. (Bruce Staples collection)

The Fountain Hotel succeeded the Marshall House. Here Sam Eagle found his first employment in the area. On its closure and demolition, construction of the Old Faithful Inn began. (Bob Jacklin collection)

◀ The Marshall House was the first hotel built in the Madison River drainage. Its site was near the Firehole River–Nez Perce Creek confluence. (Bob Jacklin collection)

FIRST HOTEL
YELLOWSTONE NATIONAL PARK
built and operated by
G. W. MARSHALL ----1879

and grayling would endure in the park only after their introduction into three lakes: Cascade, Grebe, and Wolf.

Brook trout prospered in the Gardner River drainage. Farther east, Yellowstone cutthroat reigned supreme in the Yellowstone River drainage but suffered from being discarded after being caught, having strains mixed during hatchery operations, and continuing commercial fishing. Hatcheries on Yellowstone Lake, beginning operations in 1902, were extracting eggs to a final figure of 800 million from resident cutthroat. Fortunately for Yellowstone Lake and Duck Lake above it, landlocked Atlantic salmon planted in 1908 failed to establish. Some of the plantings attempted and proposed for park waters seem hilarious, but indicate a misunderstanding of established ecosystems and a lack of appreciation of native salmonids.

Army administrators for the park set a legal catch limit of twenty fish per day from park waters, and in 1911 set eight inches as the minimum length for creeled fish. Thus began park sportfishing restrictions that would increase through the century as pressure on and understanding of the fishery progressed. Just outside the park, actions were taking place that would bring more anglers there to enjoy the excellent fishing its waters offered.

E. H. Harriman owned the Union Pacific Railroad at the turn of the century. Harriman had heard of the wonders of Yellowstone National Park and observed the Northern Pacific's branch line to Gardiner, Montana, meant to capture tourist trade through the park entrances. Noting the Northern Pacific's success, Harriman became involved in discussions on establishing a railway branch line from the south into the vicinity of the park. Tourist visits were climbing, and the shipping of cattle from Island Park ranches to market was increasing.

Frank J. Haynes, president of the Monida-Yellowstone stage line, accompanied Harriman into the park in 1905. This visit not only solidified the effort to construct a branch line to the west side of the park, but also resulted in Harriman's conviction to obtain an operating cattle ranch in the region that would also serve as a sporting retreat for family and guests. His death, however, left its purchase up to his widow.

In 1908 the Harriman family bought into the Thurburn ranch owned by the Guggenheims and other wealthy families since 1906. After ensuring that lodging space within the park could adsorb the anticipated increase in visitation from a railroad, the Harrimans ordered construction to begin, and the ranch, through which the Henry's Fork runs, became known as the Railroad Ranch. By November 12, 1907, the railroad was completed to the west boundary of the park. In June 1908 the first trainload of tourists arrived on the "Yellowstone Special." In 1909 Averill Harriman was the first in the family to visit the ranch.

Regional national forests were established by congressional action in the summer of 1908. The Madison National Forest contained land that was being inhabited at the West Entrance of Yellowstone Park. Forest surveyors defined a six-block town site north and adjacent to the rail line and along the park's west boundary. Lots within were leased to private citizens, and the leases remained until private ownership was allowed at the end of the next decade. A few businesses, including a first hotel of sorts, were established within the town site by 1908.

Culinary water was hauled to the town site from the Madison River until 1909, the same year commercial fishing ended in Montana. Demand for water for the railroad steam engines led to the need to obtain a more convenient water source, so the first

The Union Pacific Railroad's depot in town served travelers, including visiting fly fishers, until passenger service ceased in 1959. With respect to the outside world, the depot put West Yellowstone "on the map." (Bob Jacklin collection)

Sam and Ida Eagle with their partners, the Stuarts, opened Eagle's Store in 1908 before there was a town of West Yellowstone. Eventually the couples formed separate businesses. Eagle's Store endures to this day, offering, among other merchandise, fly-fishing retail items. (Courtesy Dr. Kim Eagle)

wells came into operation in 1909. Public schools would not come until 1915. The town site's post office was designated "Yellowstone," but that name was changed to "Riverside" by October 1908 to avoid confusion in sending mail to Mammoth. It was changed back to "Yellowstone" in 1910. Seeking employment, folks from other parts of the country came to work in town or for the railroad, or to become cowboys.

In 1908 a young adventurer from New Jersey arrived in Butte, Montana, worked in a local mine for a day, then sought work as a wrangler. This was Jim Jacklin. In six decades his grandson Robert would begin his ascent into a West Yellowstone fly-fishing legend.

After Sam Eagle arrived from Pennsylvania in 1903, he married Ida Carlson and they continued working at the Fountain Hotel for the Yellowstone Park Hotel Company. That same year, Alex Stuart arrived from Canada to work for the same company. He married company employee Laura Larson in 1905. In 1908

Looking east near Hebgen Dam shows how Hebgen Lake inundates much of the Madison Valley above. The river in the valley was of low gradient and an excellent host for native salmonids. Because of downstream drift and stocking, brown and rainbow trout gradually replaced the native cutthroat trout and Montana grayling. (Courtesy Bruce Staples)

the Eagles and Stuarts moved to the new town at the West Entrance. With Alex and Laura Stuart, Sam and Ida began the Eagle-Stuart Store, but wintered outside the area. Among the items offered in this variety store was fishing gear, including flies and tackle, mainly those preferred in the eastern states. In addition to his business and being postmaster, Sam Eagle was a conservation officer and in 1909 the first Montana state-licensed fishing and hunting guide in town. Eagle's Store exists into the twenty-first century and continues to offer fly-fishing items. The Eagles' progeny would play a significant role not only in developing the regional sportfishing heritage, but also in preserving those fisheries.

The stone railroad station, dubbed the "Terminal Depot," was completed early in 1909. Meals were offered in the nearby "Eating House." The presence of brook trout from local waters on the menu added familiarity for the easterner. Now the

combination of railroad and town site offered comforts, conveniences, and quick access for park visitors.

Permission had been obtained from the Forest Service in 1910 to build a road from Bozeman upstream along the West Gallatin River to the new town. Through this action the park's West Entrance would eventually surpass the North Entrance in terms of number of visitors. Wagon roads to town came from the southwest over Targhee Pass and also across Raynolds Pass and up the Madison River canyon. Thus the network of roads that would precede the modern highway network around West Yellowstone was established. With the coming of the railroad, stage line traffic west of the park decreased.

For several years Harry Dwelle's Grayling Inn had served as the only stage stop

Hebgen Dam, begun in 1909, changed the Madison Valley physical makeup forever and resulted in the same for its salmonid population. The dam endured, with repairable damage, the 1959 earthquake. The reservoir it forms is a world-class fishery. (Bruce Staples Collection)

with accommodations for tourists mostly coming from the Oregon Short Line Railroad station at Monida, Montana, to visit Yellowstone Park. Dwelle saw that the end of this stagecoach service was coming due to the Yellowstone Branch railroad, and that it would significantly reduce his business. In 1909 he sold the Grayling Inn to Frank Haynes and a group of wealthy eastern anglers (the property remains in private ownership). Fishing in the region remained the domain of the well-to-do, with many buying property from which to enjoy it. But the basis for the masses to later enjoy the region's angling loomed: An improved highway net and reliable automobiles were yet to come. Eventually even the rail lines would fall victim to these changes. The same was about to happen for the native salmonid population with the formation of Hebgen Reservoir.

Creation of a world-renowned fishery was probably the furthest purpose for an impoundment in Max Hebgen's mind. This dedicated and superb hydraulic engineer had the harnessing of Montana's bountiful running water foremost in mind. Hebgen, operating for the Montana Power Company, of which he was a vice president, evaluated sites in Montana and Idaho in which to establish power generation, flow regulation, and water storage facilities. Montana needed electrical power primarily to run an energy-intensive mining industry, to serve what was perceived to be a growing population, and for agriculture. Montana Power, a major political force in the state, held carte blanche in developing water resources.

About ten miles west of Yellowstone National Park, the Madison River ceased its slow meandering. As if deciding to plunge ahead to its fate, it picked up speed and flowed rapidly through a narrow, steep-walled canyon, the highest on the river. Behind it lay the broad, nearly flat valley. Company surveys revealed that the upper end of the canyon below the Madison Valley was ideal for a dam to form an upstream storage reservoir to regulate flows for hydroelectric facilities below. The company bought the site and began construction in 1909 of a dam to serve these purposes.

The dam was named for Hebgen, who did not live to see its completion. The resulting reservoir flooded most of Grayling, the original settlement in the upper valley. It also changed the character of the upper Madison River drainage fishery forever, and would become a world-renowned fishery. Within a few years of the filling it was planted with brown trout, supplementing those entering through downstream drift from the river above. Later rainbow trout established in the reservoir. All this was a death knell for the native westslope cutthroat and Montana grayling.

CHAPTER 2

1910–1930: A FLY-FISHING HERITAGE BEGINS

The automobile changed human impact in the Greater Yellowstone area. In answer to public and commercial interest pressure, congressional appropriations were in place by 1912 to improve Yellowstone National Park roads, and the first automobile entered the park from the new town on May 31, 1913. By 1913 the road up the West Gallatin River (now US Highway 191) was being used, and a road led to the Hebgen dam site and on down the Madison River (now US Highway 287). Horse-drawn stage line owners felt impending doom, so foresighted members began conversion to mechanization. Area roads were gravel at the time, but efforts were under way to pave.

Paving materials brought in by railroad were accumulating in town. An oil storage tank was built, and by 1914 paving into the park had begun from the West Entrance. In 1915 seven miles into the park had been paved, and the federal government authorized private automobile use there. Vehicle entry fees began at five dollars per day. For

Charlie Brooks named this section of the Madison River the "Beaver Meadows." The major fly-fishing attraction here is the run of brown and rainbow trout out of Hebgen Reservoir upstream to spawning areas. Beginning in late August and lasting past the closing of fishing season, this event offers a chance for catching a fish of the year. (John Juracek photo)

anglers detraining at the rail terminal, it was now possible to use the West Entrance Road and fish the fabled Madison River on arrival. The opening of Jesse Pierman's Madison Hotel within the new town around 1910 ensured lodging space. Other hotels were present, but none could be described as comfortable and convenient.

Frank J. Haynes, ever the promoter, told the world of the Madison River's salmonid treasure. In his *Haynes Official Guide: Yellowstone National Park*, twenty-ninth edition, 1915, there is a picture of Loch Leven (brown) and rainbow trout taken (and killed) with a fly rod. Below the picture his text reads: "The Rainbow and Loch Leven Trout of the Madison River have made this section of the park famous. It is not uncommon for an expert angler to land a six pound rainbow trout in this vicinity." Such flowery descriptions attracted anglers then as it would today.

In 1916 the Yellowstone Park Transportation Company switched from horse-drawn equipment to White Motor Company coaches after the coming of the railroad. These coaches were stored just inside the West Entrance and serviced in horse barns along the Madison River that were originally used to house stagecoach company horses. The barns remained for decades and became the landmark Barns Holes location for fishing the Madison River. The coaches brought tourists from the railroad depot in town to park accommodations and back, as well as transported them to the park's natural features.

The National Park Service was established in 1916, and within it Horace Albright became Yellowstone National Park superintendent in 1919. He would soon have influence not only on conserving regional fisheries and wildlife, but also on forming a civilian ranger force to replace army cavalry units. He also would have a major part in developing the town at the West Entrance.

Among other duties, US Army personnel stationed in Yellowstone Park had for decades protected fish populations by opposing market fishing, combating waste, and recommending against further introduction of exotic species into park waters. In

Sam Eagle fishing with a bamboo rod from horseback in the Barns area of the Madison River. The Barnes area is only a few miles from town, so an angler could be there within an hour. Horses provided transportation for fishing to many locations before automobiles came into popular use. (Courtesy Dr. Kim Eagle)

Before late-nineteenth-century plantings of exotic salmonids and the formation of Hebgen Reservoir, grayling populated most major streams in the upper Madison River drainage. It is uncertain whether they will reestablish in Yellowstone Park waters where reintroduction efforts are being conducted. (John Juracek photo)

their thirty-three-year tenure the army, within the limits of their mission, minimized waste and poaching of the park's fish and wildlife. They were replaced in 1917 by civilian rangers, much through Albright's efforts. Fortunately some of the first rangers, discharged men from army units patrolling the park, knew the area well. In the following year attempts were made to reinstate the army, but American entry into World War I guaranteed the future of the civilian ranger force.

Significant changes were under way in the region's salmonid population during the second decade of the twentieth century. Brown and rainbow trout were displacing cutthroat and grayling in the West Gallatin River. In some drainages brook trout dominated. With Hebgen Reservoir filled by 1917, brown and rainbow trout now had a refuge, and eventually magnificent browns and rainbows would ascend the Madison into the park to spawn mostly in lower reaches of the Gibbon River. Spawning runs from the reservoir also entered the South Fork of the Madison River and Cougar, Duck, and Grayling Creeks. Reared fish would either return to the reservoir or remain within the streams, bestowing upon them status as angling destinations. Commercial fishing was outlawed in the park by 1917.

Yellowstone Lake had long been the site of large hatchery and egg-collecting operations, and serious declines were being observed in its trout population. It hosted four hatcheries in which cutthroat trout spawn was collected annually for release into waters around the region and beyond, which reduced the number of trout available to replenish the stock in the lake. All plantings from these spawn outside western North America failed.

In those days, when little knowledge existed on the overall ecological picture, who could have convinced those managers that predators were responsible for the population declines in Yellowstone Lake? No one realized, or at least dared to suggest, that the ospreys, eagles, gulls, pelicans, cormorants, bears, otters, mink, and other predators had been there at least as long as the cutthroat they preyed on and that a natural equilibrium among all had been established. Humans, relatively new on the scene, were the guilty predators who within the past few decades caught and discarded trout, and had authorized, built, and operated the collecting stations which reduced the number of eggs needed to maintain the trout population. Thus human activities disrupted the natural equilibrium described above.

Further support for the fact that humans were responsible for the declines can be seen in the abuse at one of the primary spawning and habitation areas for Yellowstone Lake, its outlet. The use of Fishing Bridge as an easy place for thousands to waste fish was at its zenith in this decade. Hundreds of people would fish from the bridge or from boats anchored in the estuary. Caught fish were not returned to the water but allowed to die, their carcasses disposed of in garbage cans or left to rot along the shoreline.

Much of the park's hatchery operations were transferred to Trout Lake in 1911, and there they would remain well into the 1950s. Administrators had realized that the days were gone when fish taken to feed visitors would be a negligible loss. However, visions of unlimited salmonids, there for the taking, remained for the adjacent waters of Idaho, Montana, and Wyoming. Commercial fishing within Yellowstone Park ceased, but bag limits remained unsustainable.

Salmonid introductions in Yellowstone Park continued with the release of rainbow trout into the Firehole River in 1922. In 1928 brown trout were introduced into the Gibbon River above Gibbon Falls. These were preceded by the release of grayling into Grebe Lake in 1921. A thirty-year effort to enhance cutthroat populations in the Gallatin River drainage within the park began in 1923. Grayling were rapidly diminishing in the Madison River drainage, but originally fishless bodies, Grebe Lake and Wolf Lake, became their refuges. Adjacent Cascade Lake became a refuge for Montana grayling and Yellowstone cutthroat trout.

Through federal legislation enacted in March 1929 by President Herbert H. Hoover, the so-called Gallatin Addition to the park from national forest lands protected a petrified forest and provided further protection for fisheries in parts of the upper Gallatin River drainage. Hoover, an avid fly fisher, frequently visited the region's waters. During this time pressure to build storage dams and diversion tunnels within the park for downstream agriculture increased dramatically, but the US Congress, now generally protective of Yellowstone Park, quashed all of them. So, as the outstanding quality of park coldwater habitat and its hosted salmonids became protected and preserved, a basis for forming a fly-fishing subculture in the region was established.

In these times a fly-tying culture began developing throughout western Montana. Missoulian Jack Boehme operated a bar and angling establishment, a pattern often duplicated in Montana. Boehme adapted the Trude-style wing into his Picket Pin and Bloody Butcher patterns. In the same town wig-maker Franz Pott developed a line of woven wet flies that would become traditional for use by fly fishers throughout the state. These were among the first native Montana fly patterns created, and they would influence patterns created in West Yellowstone's fly-fishing future. Pat Barnes, at the age of eight, began tying wet flies in this Montana tradition. Presentation of wet flies would reign supreme throughout the state until Don Martinez arrived in

West Yellowstone in the early 1930s and introduced dry-fly fishing on a large scale to the Montana fly fisher.

Confusion resulted, particularly in postal service, in the name changes of the new town from 1908 to 1910. The new and permanent name, established mostly through the efforts of park superintendent Horace Albright, became "West Yellowstone" on January 7, 1920. The framework of infrastructure was now established to make major regional waters easily accessible. Continued improvements in roads, accommodations, eateries, facilities, and communication systems in town would come in this and future decades. The 1920s was the zenith decade for rail travel to the park. Total visitation to the park reached a quarter million.

But the jump in visitation by rail made certain facilities in town obsolete. Thus the railroad commissioned the famed architect Gilbert Stanley Underwood to design the West Yellowstone Dining Lodge, completed in 1925 just west of the Terminal Depot. This uniquely beautiful building went into service in 1926, not only doing its intended duty of feeding the rail travelers to the park's West Entrance for decades, but also becoming West Yellowstone's distinguishing landmark.

In June of the same year, a switchboard was installed in Eagle's Store and permanent telephone service came to West Yellowstone. Jay Whitman, the hunting and sometimes fishing guide, established his Conoco filling station that sold fishing tackle and licenses (the town's first agent). West Yellowstone became an official town in 1924. Lots established under Forest Service permits became deeded property. Where other lots went for deeded sale that year, costs ranged from sixty to seven hundred dollars. But more important, obtaining private title for land would guarantee the willingness of more businesses to locate there now that local control of police and fire protection was secured.

Major personalities that would play a part in the town's fly-fishing heritage around the middle of the century were born or came to town in the 1920s. Working out of various ranger stations, park ranger Scotty Chapman made it a lifetime goal to visit

Park ranger, fly fisher, fly tier, artist, and conservationist, Scotty Chapman was a multifaceted authority on fishing all Yellowstone Park waters. Working mostly out of Gardiner, Montana, he was assigned for a time to West Yellowstone. His nationwide reputation grew over time, with such fly-fishing luminaries as Ray Bergman and Bud Lilly honoring his knowledge. (Courtesy Bill and Loretta Chapman)

and fish all park waters. Hired in 1927, his credibility and generosity in sharing these experiences added significantly to the Yellowstone Park sportfishery knowledge pool. Scotty not only sampled the waters, but meticulously recorded his experiences. Soon after his arrival, he began tying flies. A practical fly tier, his simple creations would influence the works of many famed tiers.

Around the same time, Vint and Verna Johnson, a young schoolteacher couple, were fly-fishing waters around Montana and visited the West Yellowstone area during summers. They made a goal of entering the fly-fishing business there.

Young Pat Barnes began accumulating angling experience at the same time. His dad, a Milwaukee Road railroader, enjoyed fly fishing, while his mother, a bait fisher, favored grasshoppers. Both encouraged young Pat to supply trout for the dinner table. At the age of six, under his mother's guidance, Pat offered live grasshoppers to these fish. Three years later he caught his first fish on a fly in park waters on the Madison and began the transition from bait angler to fly fisher. He began tying flies around age eight and riding the Saturday excursion train to Butte, would slip away on arrival to Wilbur "Bugs" Beaty's Bug House to observe the wonders of fly tying. During trips to Missoula, Pat visited Jack Boehme's fly-tying operation and again absorbed all the information offered. All the while, he retained his interest in the attraction of grasshoppers for trout.

Pat bought his first fly rod in 1925: price, five dollars. He applied what he learned about flies and fly fishing during family excursions. One of his father's favorite locations was the Madison reach below Hebgen Dam. By now Lillian Culver's pool had a reputation for hosting very large brook and rainbow trout and was open to fishing for a fee.

Pat fished the Widow's Pool and other nearby waters in the 1920s. Later in the decade he tied flies commercially to help pay college costs while attending Western Montana College in Dillon. He thus accumulated the experience that would make him a beloved and revered icon in West Yellowstone's heritage. The best account of Pat's early years can be found in his memoirs, *Ribbons of Blue*.

Much more obscure than the events that brought Pat Barnes into the fly-fishing public eye were those that resulted in the same for his mentor, Don Martinez. Much of the information remaining on Martinez's origin comes from Cal Dunbar's accounts from befriending the family in the 1930s and 1940s. These notes have Martinez born into a family having some wealth, living in Connecticut, then studying limnology and entomology at Princeton University under Dr. Paul Needham. Cloudier accounts have him briefly in the Chicago-area realty business and fishing his way across the upper Midwest during the 1920s before coming to ground in the San Diego area. He developed into an excellent fly tier, acquired an interest in classifying aquatic insects, and became experienced in evaluating fly tackle.

In A. J. McClane's *Wise Fishermen's Encyclopedia*, Martinez offers that he had fly-fished throughout the western states by 1922, which seems remarkable for a person of about twenty years of age. Next he moved to Los Angeles and with wife Nola began a family. Son David, nicknamed Stuffy, was born in 1926, and daughter Mary, nicknamed Dinty, was born about 1929. From Los Angeles Martinez marketed flies to retail outlets around the country. His price was $1.50 per dozen.

Martinez became a mentor to fellow Los Angeleno Rae Templeton Servatius. Born in 1894 in Iowa, Rae was in the millinery business with her husband, Fred, in Los

Also in *Trout*, Bergman discusses several dry patterns originated or adapted by Martinez. These comments reveal Bergman's respect for Martinez's accomplishments in the art of the dry fly.

Later in the 1930s, Martinez began communicating with Preston Jennings, a renowned New York state fly designer and fly-fishing author on the nature of constructing fly patterns and aspects of their representation and presentation. Sometime in the mid-1930s, Martinez befriended Bob Carmichael in Jackson Hole, Wyoming. At the time, Carmichael was a US government fishing guide employed by Grand Teton National Park during summers. Like Martinez, he had ideas on dry-fly creation. With so much in common, and living in the same region, it seems predestined they would meet and combine fly-fishing ideas. They did, and the result was patterns that gained nationwide fame.

One Martinez/Carmichael pattern of great renown retained the grizzly hackle tip wings of the Adams, but was much more heavily hackled with brown and grizzly feathers. Thus began the practice

As a youth, Cal Dunbar befriended David "Stuffy" Martinez, Don Martinez's son. They fished waters adjacent to town, such as the South Fork of the Madison River shown above. In a few years Cal, above with a South Fork rainbow trout, would be tying fly orders for Martinez's shop in West Yellowstone. (Courtesy Cal and Jan Dunbar)

of heavily hackling dry flies for the generally more turbulent western waters. The new pattern had a body of blue and yellow macaw quill fiber and a tail of reddish brown spike feather. Carmichael named the fly Whitcraft for Tom Whitcraft, the fly-fishing Grand Teton National Park superintendent. Martinez tied the Whitcraft in quantity for his shop, for Carmichael's shop in Jackson Hole, and for eastern outlets for which he called it the "Quill Adams."

Fly pattern development was not the only area that Don Martinez pioneered. To him must go credit for conceiving the pin vise. The use of this vise is best described by Cal Dunbar, who first met Martinez around 1938. Cal, who provides much of the information on Martinez, relates:

In his working room bamboo rods dangled by their tips, a common practice to keep from taking a curve on setting, gut leaders soaked to enhance pliability, and the odor of mothballs permeated the air. His working area consisted of a card table, an occasional chair with one-half of a square metal typewriter ribbon box glued onto the left arm to provide a resting socket for the rubber tip of the hand (pin) vise rod. The hand vise, a Martinez development, consisted of a Thompson A vise jaw on an eighteen-inch stainless steel rod with a rubber tip on the end. He had vises in two sizes to fit large and small hooks. Don usually sat at the card table in the chair and tied. His method was: He held the hand vise in his left hand securely with the rod in his last two fingers. With his thumb and first fingers he spun the vise like a lathe. The hook in the vise jaw had its shank parallel with the vise and rod. With his right hand he manipulated the tying silk, body materials, and hackles. The materials were fed directly onto the hook from the spool and were cut only when each fly was tied wasting no material.

The pin vise is a predecessor of the rotary vise concept, so credit Martinez with another contribution.

Dunbar also offers that the Martinez family residing in West Yellowstone during summers in the late 1930s consisted of Don, his attractive blond wife Nola, their son David (called "Stuffy" by the family), and daughter Mary (called "Dinty" by the family). Mary became an excellent fly tier. Dunbar also offers a glimpse of Martinez's personality:

He was a complicated person. He was an elitist, affable to those he felt were deserving fly-fisherman but he could be curt and brusque to those he felt were wasting his time. He had great friendships with prosperous clients who were into serious fly-fishing and were his customers. He drank a lot, sometimes having local boys hustle him a can of tomato juice to his shop in the morning to help him meet the coming day. The heavy drinking probably hastened early death in his fifties.

Martinez was an Izaak Walton League founder and as such was one of the first conservationists in the Greater Yellowstone region. Pat Barnes, working summers for

Fly bins were central to Don Martinez's shop on Yellowstone Avenue. The shop also offered a variety of fly-fishing equipment. A young Pat Barnes is to Martinez's left in this photo. (Courtesy Pat Barnes Family)

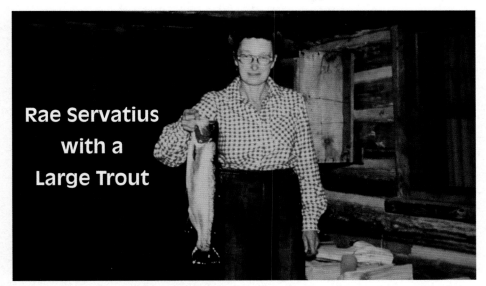

Rae Servatius
with a
Large Trout

"She was Don Martinez's agent," Bud Lilly said of Rae Servatius. Servatius was also one of the first female fly-fishing guides in the West Yellowstone area. She ran the Martinez tackle shop during the war years until it closed in 1945. Afterward into the 1970s she wholesaled Martinez shop flies to area retailers. (Bob Jacklin collection)

the US Forest Service nearby, frequented Martinez's shop. Martinez, realizing Pat's interest in fly fishing and conservation, hired him to guide in 1938, and also had him tying flies for the shop. Soon Pat was also tying flies for Dan Bailey, who had opened a shop in Livingston, Montana. Bailey saw potential in this Montana youngster and hired him to work part-time.

Another person Martinez mentored, Rae Servatius, ten years his elder, would go on to become his business partner and in a sense his successor. She was among the first of West Yellowstone's accomplished female fly-fishing figures. She and her husband Fred decided in the 1930s to spend summers in West Yellowstone. Rae's love of fly fishing led her to sell her Los Angeles millinery shop and begin a career in the motel business and fly-fishing retailing. She and Fred bought cabins on the north side of town to begin their motel business. Fred used the railroad for transportation back to Los Angeles. Martinez noticed Rae's determination, intelligence, enthusiasm, and perfectionist nature, and she soon began as a fly-fishing guide and fly tier for his shop.

Martinez was not the only person in town during the 1930s to be in the fly-fishing business. Vint and Verna Johnson, a Manhattan, Montana, schoolteacher couple, had also opened a fly shop around 1930. It was first in a corner of Fuller's Garage, according to Bud Lilly. Whereas Don Martinez's clients tended to be wealthy men, the Johnsons welcomed anglers of all kinds. Through their open and generous attitude, word spread in fly-fishing circles that the Johnsons would advise any interested angler on how to enjoy the region's fabulous fishing. The Johnsons soon befriended Jack and Mickey Ebersole, another couple who came to the West Yellowstone area to realize a dream based on the wonderful fishing.

Was it Vint Johnson's democratic attitude toward angling that first brought Ray Bergman to his tackle shop? For Johnson, sharing angling information grew to the point that he became the authority on the best locations in the area to fish, although he did not obtain Martinez's fly-tying reputation. By the early 1930s Bergman, then an outdoor writer, had heard of the famed waters around West Yellowstone and the regard visiting anglers had for them. He arrived in West Yellowstone not quite sure where to try these waters. In *Trout* he writes of Vint taking him to the Firehole River one September day (apparently in 1937). At the time, Scotty Chapman was stationed in West Yellowstone during the late 1930s. During his tenure as a ranger there, he gained a great deal of experience fly-fishing the Madison River drainage within the park, had a reputation for presentation and fly selection, and was famed for sharing information. Vint introduced Ray to Scotty for gaining information on fishing the fabled river. After Scotty suggested presenting small dry flies there, they visited the river and experienced success. Bergman went on to fish the Firehole River many times, and from these visits came his Firehole fly. As a result of his visits, much of the lore of the Firehole River began. Whether from reading *Trout* or *Outdoor Life*, Bergman's audience began to consider the Firehole and other waters around West Yellowstone as hallowed destinations.

One of Bergman's visits to Yellowstone Park, as related in *Trout*, was made to fish for grayling. In 1937 he contacted Vint Johnson to arrange a trip in Yellowstone National Park to pursue these fish. Again, Vint referred Bergman to Scotty Chapman, who recommended Grebe Lake for grayling. A September trip to Grebe Lake took place and was successful.

When in the summer of 1936 a twelve-year-old boy vacationing from the Los Angeles area with his family arrived at Vint Johnson's Tackle Shop, Vint noticed the lad's obvious fly-fishing interest. He offered the youngster information on equipment needs and where to fish. After the boy acquired rod, line, and reel, Vint offered him casting lessons and a gift of flies. This youngster was Jim Danskin. From this early day, a close friendship would develop between Vint as teacher and Jim as student.

In the late 1930s teenaged Bud Lilly plied local streams. Gaining fly-fishing experience that would serve him well later, he was fascinated by the response of trout to a fly. Like Montana fly fishers in general, Bud fished wet flies, especially Pott woven

Bergman, through advice from Scotty Chapman and Vint Johnson, visited several area waters. He and Chapman visited the "Tubs" area, shown here, of the Henry's Fork just below at the Big Springs–Henry's Lake outlet confluence. Bergman described the outing in his famed book *Trout*. (Bruce Staples collection)

Ray Bergman did much through the media of the day (1930s) to promote fly fishing in the region around West Yellowstone. In 1938 he authored the classic book *Trout*, which related some of his fly-fishing experiences in waters around West Yellowstone. (Bob Jacklin collection) ▶

Vint and Verna Johnson at their tackle shop on Canyon Street. Although they were mainly fly fishers, the Johnsons offered gear and advice to all anglers. Because of their open and helpful attitude toward all anglers, their shop was likely the most popular fly-fishing shop in town during their tenure. (Bob Jacklin collection)

wet flies. Only playing the game of baseball competed with his fly-fishing desire. With obvious relish he recounted an experience of a lifetime, that of batting against Satchel Paige and his barnstormers while playing as a youngster on his hometown baseball team. He credited the scratch single he managed in this encounter to Paige's amusement that a farm boy was needed to fill the team's roster. Bud eventually had enough talent to be noticed by Cincinnati Reds scouts, who he eventually took fly-fishing on local waters.

Fly fishers from other parts of the country were now converging on West Yellow-stone–area waters as roads and automobiles improved. Could it be that one of the fly fishers that "crowded" the West Gallatin for Bud and his dad in those days was an easterner from Brooklyn, New York? Dan Bailey began his summer fly-fishing visits to the region in the mid-1930s out of Ennis and Livingston. On his return east, he related his experiences on Montana streams to fellow fly fishers. The result was a literary flood of articles displaying and relating the quality of regional waters, those around West Yellowstone included.

In 1938 he made the move that would propel Montana's fly-fishing bounty fur-ther into the public eye with the opening of Dan Bailey's Fly Shop in Livingston. Soon his influence would reach from Livingston to West Yellowstone. It began with Bailey hiring Pat Barnes to tie squirrel tail streamers for the shop. Bailey also began supplying flies to Eagle's Store. Throughout the decade, Sam Eagle mentored his son Wally, taking him to local waters. By the end of the decade Wally was tying flies and befriended the Martinez family, which operated Don's Tackle Shop. Wally and Stuffy Martinez were fishing pals in those days.

Howard Back seemed like any well-heeled fly fisher coming to the Greater Yellowstone region in the 1930s. He was wealthy, refined, well educated, and possessed the finest fly-fishing gear and sporting clothing his era offered. Through working in the family insurance business and through friends at the Anglers' Club of New York, he learned of the Madison and West Gallatin Rivers and the Widow's Pool. So he made a 1936 pilgrimage to the Greater Yellowstone region, spending time during his initial visit on waters having the most media attention and easiest access.

Back returned to the Greater Yellowstone region in 1937 with a determination to experience the best it had to offer the fly fisher. He consulted with Scotty Chapman, who was stationed in West Yellowstone that year. Through his 1937 experience Back became more than appreciative of the region. He would do the area honor by writing *The Waters of Yellowstone with Rod and Fly* following the visit.

Back was among the first to give cutthroat trout their due as a sport fish, and he questioned cutthroat management practices by park personnel. He recognized the importance of Hebgen Lake to the fisheries in the upstream Madison River drainage, and beseeched the reader to adopt a conservative philosophy when fishing the region's waters. Back's book also offers among the first descriptions of fly-fishing in the park's southwest corner, an experience he relished through Scotty Chapman's advice. Most of all, Back's book provides a wonderful and pleasant glimpse of the fisheries within and bordering Yellowstone National Park in the days just before World War II.

This book was rediscovered decades later, and its value was realized. It was then published again, with contributions by Craig Mathews, Robert H. Berls, and Dan Callaghan, through Lyons Press in 2000. Back died in 1946 but through Craig's efforts would be given his due as an eloquent and sincere proponent of the Greater Yellowstone area's fisheries.

The Pat Barnes Cabin, originally built in the late 1930s by Sam Eagle, remains as Barnes family property and is totally habitable. The Barnes family lived here during the Pat Barnes Tackle Shop's tenure. (Bruce Staples collection)

Even less noticed than the visits by celebrities to the area was a visit in 1938 by an Arkansas Ozark Mountains teenager, Charles Brooks. Already a fly fisher, Charlie merely observed the Madison River during this visit. In the future he would write of this river with a reverence and love that matched Howard Back's efforts for regional fisheries. Likely this visit initiated Charlie's goal to relocate to this area with the best salmonids waters. Like Back, and Ray Bergman, he would also express in his future writings admiration and appreciation for Vint Johnson and Scotty Chapman. He became a wet-fly proponent for taking trout, more in line with the philosophies of Johnson than those of Martinez.

The guardian of the fabled Widow's Pool, Lillian Culver, died in 1936 and since has attained a legendary status in the fly-fishing world. All of West Yellowstone's fly-fishing businesses and many elsewhere honor her. Ownership of her waters passed on to family members, who continued access for anglers. Along the drainage below the Widow's Pool,

Howard Back's *The Waters of Yellowstone with Rod and Fly* vividly described personal experiences fly-fishing many regional waters. In this photo, Back displays a nice grayling likely caught in Red Rock Creek about 1938. (Bob Jacklin collection)

the establishment in 1936 of the Red Rock Lakes National Wildlife Refuge initiated protection of wetlands vital to the survival of trumpeter swans and other migratory birds. The refuge also protects salmonids residing in the Red Rock Lakes and their tributaries.

So the 1930s came to an end in the region, with the decade witnessing the beginnings of the modern era in West Yellowstone fly fishing. The first fly-fishing shops, and a variety of modern accommodations and services, were established. The first major fly-fishing personalities had arrived. Now it appeared that large numbers of fly fishers would soon descend on West Yellowstone, as the highway net was nearly complete, automobiles were coming into their own, and in June 1935 an airport had come to the west side of town. But World War II was looming, and its constraints on domestic fuel supplies, automobile production, and general construction kept the regional fisheries in the domain of the wealthy well into the next decade.

CHAPTER 4

1940–1950: DIMINISHING NATIVE SALMONID CONCERNS

With the beginning of the new decade, West Yellowstone offered three full-service shops for the angler: Charles Borberg's Trout Shop, Don's (Martinez) Tackle Shop, and Vint Johnson's Tackle Shop. In addition, Whitman's Service Station and Eagle's Store offered lines of merchandise for visiting anglers regardless of terminal gear.

The young town seemed on the way to becoming the fly-fishing center of its potential, even though visitations through the Yellowstone Branch of the Union Pacific Railroad were slowing. By 1942, after the country entered World War II, the number of Yellowstone Park visitors reduced to about a third of those in 1941. Gasoline rationing began impacting automobile travel, and significant infrastructure

Centennial Valley streams such as Red Rock Creek, pictured here, have held their native salmonid population better than other waters in the Greater Yellowstone area. Grayling, cutthroat trout, and Rocky Mountain whitefish remain in these waters, and brook trout were introduced decades ago. Magnificent scenery can be a pleasant distraction to fly fishers visiting valley waters. (John Juracek photo)

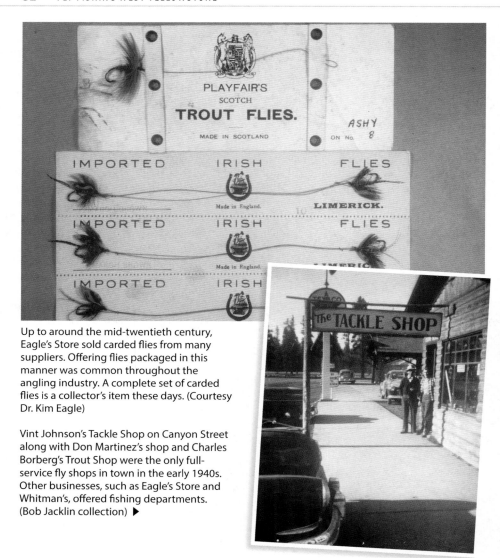

Up to around the mid-twentieth century, Eagle's Store sold carded flies from many suppliers. Offering flies packaged in this manner was common throughout the angling industry. A complete set of carded flies is a collector's item these days. (Courtesy Dr. Kim Eagle)

Vint Johnson's Tackle Shop on Canyon Street along with Don Martinez's shop and Charles Borberg's Trout Shop were the only full-service fly shops in town in the early 1940s. Other businesses, such as Eagle's Store and Whitman's, offered fishing departments. (Bob Jacklin collection) ▶

development in West Yellowstone waited until postwar years. Fly-fishing visits during the war returned to being a privilege of the well-to-do, but increasingly more of their visits were by automobile. For the lucky person with the means to travel to the region, visits to its waters resulted in solitude and an angling experience quality not seen since the early twentieth century. This lasted the duration of the war.

Montana's policy of supplementing exotic salmonids continued to diminish the number of westslope cutthroat in the upper Gallatin, Madison, and Red Rock drainages. Cliff Lake was a good example where a former westslope cutthroat domain had been hybridized by rainbow trout released by the Neely family. Montana grayling simply disappeared from many waters. There were, however, some significant conservation actions at the beginning of the new decade. One that would surely enhance fishery habitat was incorporation of Culver Pond (Widow's Pool) and McDonald

Pond into the Red Rock Lakes National Wildlife Refuge through purchase from the Lillian Hackett Hansen Culver family in 1941. Culver Pond was enlarged to its present size by moving its dam a half-mile downstream. Fishery operations in the park diminished during the war years, but rainbow and brown trout were sporadically released in the Gibbon River into the 1940s.

During the war the fly-fishing industry operated in good capacity serving well-to-do anglers, who consulted with Don Martinez to form strategies. The postwar years marked the beginning of the influx of middle-class anglers from other parts of society, and Vint Johnson's Tackle Shop served these individuals as well as anyone asking for angling equipment or fishing information. With Jack and Mickey Ebersole at the Narrows Resort, Johnson had built the largest boating operation on Hebgen Lake.

Jack Hemingway fly-fished most regional waters beginning in the 1940s. The Widow's Pool was among his favorites. During this decade many celebrated fly fishers were clients here. (Bob Jacklin collection)

For young Bud Lilly in Manhattan, high school years in the early 1940s were divided among hunting, fishing, and baseball. That he kept a fishing diary reveals the value he placed on outdoor experiences. That diary also included fishing information from his friends and thus helped cement in his famed memory facts on regional fly fishing.

By the early 1940s, Jack and Mickey Ebersol's Narrows Resort offered the largest fleet of boats on Hebgen Reservoir. By now the reservoir had gained a reputation as an outstanding salmonid fishery. (Bob Jacklin collection)

The Eagle family stayed on in West Yellowstone, braving its fierce winters. Eagle's Store offered merchandise from groceries to hardware to angling items. Sam Eagle operated the town post office year-round from the store. His son Wally, like most of the tiers Martinez hired, tied mostly Woolly Worms for Don's Tackle Shop.

In 1941 Pat Barnes, still tying flies for Dan Bailey, married Sigrid Bortveldt. She would go on to become not only a sought-after fly-tying and fly-fishing personality, but also a beloved and gracious West Yellowstone figure. Pat taught school in Helena during winters, tied flies, worked in the shop, and guided during summers for Martinez until 1942.

Martinez continued communicating with Bob Carmichael, Wayne "Buz" Buszek, and Preston Jennings. In 1940 when Jennings visited Dan Bailey in Livingston and fished in Yellowstone National Park, Martinez sent him a black Woolly Worm with a note that verified his scorn for wet-fly fishing but conceded that the fly is superbly effective. He also admitted that in the previous two years, it outsold all other patterns combined in his shop. Nevertheless, Martinez continued to create dry flies to simulate the life cycles of regional aquatic insects available to salmonids as food. Most of these dry flies adopted Edward Ringwood Hewitt's Bivisible hackling, which is light in front of a darker color to aid visibility. He proved their value during trips to area waters and recorded their ability to catch fish.

Based on his documentation on area waters, Martinez published his first "Fishing Guide" in 1939. By 1941 this free pamphlet was the most comprehensive document available on fly-fishing area waters, and it would become a model for future guides by Pat Barnes and Bud Lilly. Of Cliff Lake it proclaimed the 1941 version: "This is the best place we know for specimen Rainbow. Fish over five pounds are quite common."

In September 1941 young Cal Dunbar vacationed in West Yellowstone and fly-fished around the region for first time. He visited Don's Tackle Shop to obtain destination information and items, and from this visit came his first impression of the area and its fisheries. Jack Hemingway visited the Widow's Pool the same year. He also fished park waters including the Madison River and Grebe Lake.

Meanwhile, Martinez and Carmichael collaborated on evaluating tackle, seeking and evaluating fishing destinations, and designing fly patterns. Martinez continued to tie commercially for Carmichael. Later, Carmichael, in J. Edson Leonard's *Flies*, would describe their relationship and promote the patterns he and Martinez developed. By 1943 Martinez began giving his address as "Don's Tackle Shops, Jackson, Wyoming, and West

Don Martinez holds one of his pin vises with daughter Mary at his side. Martinez's pin vise is the forerunner of present-day rotary vises. Mary became an accomplished fly tier under her father's tutelage. (Courtesy Cal and Jan Dunbar)

Three Bear Limo

During the 1930s and 1940s, West Yellowstone motels provided shuttle services for client anglers to certain nearby fishing locations. The Three Bears Motel, still in operation, was one of these. This motel, expanded in size, remains a popular haven for visiting fly fishers. (Courtesy Three Bear Lodge)

Yellowstone, Montana." As the war advanced he spent more time in the Jackson shop, never to return full-time to West Yellowstone.

Rae Servatius, now Martinez's business partner, managed the shop, tied flies, guided clients, and operated what would become the Whispering Pines Motel. With purpose and determination she became an authority on fly-fishing local waters, then put her knowledge to good use when guiding Martinez's friends. Martinez's daughter Mary (Dinty) tied flies for the shop. By 1945 Servatius moved the shop, still known as Don's Tackle Shop, to her motel but soon closed it, preferring to wholesale flies well into the 1970s.

The end of World War II signaled the beginning of big changes for the town's fly-fishing industry. Normalcy meant abundant gasoline, improved roads, increased accommodations, and the resumption of private automobile production. Going back into the 1930s, periodicals featuring articles on fishing the region from Ray Bergman, Dan Bailey, and others targeted white- and blue-collar classes, those who bore the manpower brunt of the war. The anglers among these groups had not forgotten what they read, and soon they arrived to seek the regional coldwater treasure.

The war also released several fly-fishing personalities back to West Yellowstone. In 1946 Pat Barnes, returning from service, realized a long-standing dream by establishing West Yellowstone's first new major fly-fishing business. Pat's years working and guiding for Martinez, fine record in tying flies for Dan Bailey, and connections with well-to-do and accomplished fly fishers helped establish the business.

Pat and Sig Barnes lived seasonally in a cabin built before the war by Sam Eagle and bought by Pat's mother. In 1941 they honeymooned in it. The cabin, and a newer one off Boundary Street, remains in the Barnes family. The first location of the Pat

Barnes Tackle Shop and Guide Service was just east of Eagle's Store and where Martinez operated years earlier.

Martinez's lease had run out on the building while he was operating his shop in Jackson, and Rae Servatius had moved the wholesale part of the business to her motel. Pat, with his reputation for knowledge of area fly fishing since the 1920s, acquired this location just outside the park's West Entrance and began garnering his share of business. Now the revered routine the visiting fly fisher experienced for the next three and a half decades began emerging, that of Pat guiding and Sig tending the shop and tying flies. The Barneses were now on their way to becoming not only the primary fly-fishing retailer in the area, but also a major contributor to its conservation and fly-tying heritage.

The Sofa Pillow would not be the only major, popular fly pattern coming from the Pat Barnes Tackle Shop. The origin of another immensely popular fly has been the subject of discussions in fly-fishing circles for decades. The most credible examination of its origin comes from a feature Barnes wrote for the spring 1990 edition of *American Angler*. Pat and Sig were soon bombarded with requests for that "goofy deer hair fly." Soon it became referred to as the "Goofus Bug"; in Jackson Hole it was known as the Humpy. Another pattern Pat claimed as a favorite was the Hopkins Variant created in the 1940s by Don Hopkins.

Fly patterns would not be the only major contribution coming from the Pat Barnes Tackle Shop during the postwar days. Ever since childhood Pat had float-fished Montana's rivers, beginning with his parents, on family excursions, and later as a guide. Float fishing had continually demonstrated to him the advantage of covering extensive water. The reward would be quickly finding where fish are active in a given reach of river. This was never lost to Pat as he looked for ways to best satisfy his clients.

After hearing of the advantages of the McKenzie River boat, then made solely of wood, that was being used in Oregon, he traveled there to obtain one. In 1948 he put his purchase to the test and offered it for guided float-fishing trips on the

The building on Yellowstone Avenue behind Pat Barnes and friend was the final location of Don Martinez's shop. It became the first location of the Pat Barnes Tackle Shop in 1946 just after Pat returned from World War II. (Courtesy Pat Barnes Family)

The drift boat was Pat Barnes's gift to all fly fishers in the Greater Yellowstone area. Today no other form of boat for fly fishing exceeds the popularity of this type, whether being used by guides or by private owners. (Courtesy Bruce Staples)

Madison River. Other conveyances were being used at the time, but the McKenzie boat had distinct advantages including stability, durability, and handling. The high bow offered the person standing there a superb view of the upcoming river. It took a while for these "banana boats" to catch on, but within a few decades they became the dominant fly-fishing conveyance on western rivers.

In 1949 Pat added another layer of credibility to his angling contributions. In that year the State of Montana recognized outfitting of private parties for the purpose of hunting and fishing as a valid occupation and issued licenses for this purpose. Pat was the second such licensee to be recognized by the state. He was now the successor to Don Martinez.

After World War II the Martinez-Servatius partnership reduced to only wholesale merchandise distribution. Servatius distributed Martinez flies and some fly-fishing items such as leaders and lines to area retailers, mainly those in the park. The Eagle family, like many regional retailers, bought fly-fishing merchandise from Dan Bailey and eastern states suppliers to stock their store.

For Scotty Chapman, discharge from the Marine Corps meant back to being a park ranger, fly-fishing, painting, and attending his property near Gardiner, Montana.

Cal Dunbar was discharged from the Marine Corps in May 1946. Don Martinez read of it in the *Los Angeles Times* and asked Cal if he would tie an order of Woolly Worms, which were to be distributed to the Hamilton Stores outlets in Yellowstone

National Park. That was the last contact Cal had with Don. Martinez and his daughter Mary, working from Los Angeles, supplied flies for the shop through Rae Servatius.

Charles Borberg, a Billings, Montana, high school science teacher, had opened the Trout Shop around 1940 in a rented location at the north end of Eagle's Store. At the end of the war, Borberg hired George Grant to be its manager. Grant remembered that in Borberg's absence during the fishing seasons of his tenure, he would mail daily proceeds to him. There were no banks in West Yellowstone at the time.

For Vint Johnson, angling retailing after the war was short-lived. He died in early 1947. Verna, with help from their children, now ran the shop. Jim Danskin, receiving news of Vint's passing, returned that year to West Yellowstone with his bride, Lois. The Danskins offered their services to help Verna run the shop. She gratefully accepted, thus beginning Jim's association with the shop.

Late in the decade another personality arrived in West Yellowstone to play an important role in the town's fly-fishing heritage: Della "Tony" Sivey. Of pleasant disposition and honest nature, she soon became a part of the town's fly-fishing industry. As with so many Montana fly tiers, she offered a line of woven wet flies. In the next decade she would be tying and marketing her unique line of flies to the Johnsons and others in the Rocky Mountain West.

In 1947 a young woman from the East passed through West Yellowstone on her way to a California fly-casting competition. She marveled at the horses placed at hitching rails and the gravel streets with deep and numerous potholes so filled with water that later a drunken famed Pennsylvania fly-fishing instructor stumbled into one and needed help to be rescued. This woman was Joan Salvato, and in twenty years

Vint and Verna Johnson at their tackle shop on Canyon Street. The Johnsons offered all kinds of terminal gear from the shop. Outgoing, polite, and considerate, they set the standard for future fly-fishing retailers in town. (Bob Jacklin collection)

she would marry Lee Wulff then return to town to attend every Federation of Fly Fishers Conclave held there.

Bud Lilly returned from the navy in June 1946 and fished for about a month. He earned his applied science degree in 1948, then took his first teaching job in Roundup, Montana. However, Bud needed a summer job to supplement his salary. A friend, Norm Hansen, whose mother was the West Yellowstone postmaster, suggested they wash cars in town during the summer, so they set up shop and washed daily into the night. Now a family man, Bud heard from a friend that a local fly shop might be for sale.

After leaving the US Army Air Force at the end of World War II, Charlie Brooks was a Yosemite National Park ranger, accompanied by his new wife, Grace. By 1947 he was back in the air force, serving remaining time for early retirement. In 1948 he visited the Greater Yellowstone region and fished many of its waters. He took his first large fish from the Firehole River, a three-pound brown trout. This trout did more for fly-fishing knowledge than any fish caught from the river. It helped convince Charlie that he had found the best trout waters in the country.

GRANT'S RIFFLE
...a collection of thoughts, ideas, and memories

George Grant managed Charles Borberg's shop for a few seasons in the mid-1940s. He went on to publish two major books, *Master Fly Weaver* and *Montana Trout Flies*, along with a collection of essays, *Grant's Riffle*, and spent the remainder of his life protecting the Big Hole River. His elegantly tied flies are now coveted collector's items. (Bob Jacklin collection)

CHAPTER 5

1950–1960: MAJOR FLY-FISHING RETAILING CHANGES

Few Greater Yellowstone–area earthquakes were of the strength of the one that unleashed on the night of August 17, 1959. With its epicenter just northeast of Hebgen Lake's Grayling Arm and a Richter scale rating of 7.3, this monstrous event created the greatest natural change of historic times in the Madison River drainage. It was the second-most-intense twentieth-century earthquake recorded in the lower forty-eight states up to that date.

Hebgen Lake was tilted north such that ranches and homes that were once on the south shore were rendered hundreds of feet from the new shoreline. Conversely, many structures on the northwest shore near the dam were inundated. Charles Barnes remembers a rock slide blocking the highway into the park just beyond the West Entrance. Highway 191 was destroyed north of West Yellowstone, and the only way

Hebgen Reservoir's formation changed the native salmonid species makeup in the upper Madison River drainage, likely forever. Now magnificent brown and rainbow trout dominate its salmonid population. Only the sturdy Rocky Mountain whitefish remains from the original salmonid distribution. (John Juracek photo)

The August 17, 1959, Madison Canyon landslide impounded Earthquake Lake, which inundated a prime fishing section of the Madison River. "Quake Lake," as it is commonly known, is now a major angling location in the Greater Yellowstone area. (Bruce Staples collection)

into town was from Idaho over US Highway 20 or by air travel. Parade Rest Guest Ranch on Grayling Creek, near the epicenter, suffered severe damage. At the same time, the bed of the upper end of the lake rose, according to Charlie Brooks, about twelve feet while that of the lower lake beneath the dam fell almost as much. This tilting sent water surging over the top of Hebgen Dam four times. The dam held with considerable but repairable damage.

The original Wade Lake Resort, owned by Elliot family descendants, was destroyed but soon rebuilt. In Yellowstone Park, the Old Faithful Inn and some roads were damaged and thermal features were altered, some permanently so. But the changes above the canyon were minor compared to what happened simultaneously near its mouth. A massive amount of the north face of a mountain broke away and almost instantaneously dammed the river, which nearly dried up downstream. Earthquake Lake formed and quickly filled to nearly 250 feet in depth at the face of the dam and four miles in length. Tragically nineteen people were killed in Rock Creek Campground, buried by the slide, and another nine were killed in the immediate area.

Nearly all tourists left West Yellowstone, and damage caused by the earthquake totaled several million dollars. The Army Corps of Engineers was on-site immediately to stabilize the dam formed by the slide. Luckily, seepage of water kept trout alive in the river below. Hebgen Lake was drained to check the status of its dam.

The stabilized dam has held to this day, and the lake behind it, Earthquake Lake, has become a marvelous brown and rainbow trout fishery. For a few years after the event, relative solitude could be experienced on surrounding waters, as the number of visiting anglers slumped for fear of a repeat.

This picture reveals how Earthquake Lake fills most of the Madison River canyon. Charlie Brooks considered the canyon waters the best fishing location on the river and offered that it had a nearly unmatched population of giant stoneflies. (Bruce Staples collection)

By the 1950s westslope cutthroat trout no longer inhabited the Madison River or its major tributaries within Yellowstone National Park. Park managers observed this decline and finally understood that recreational anglers essentially became competitors with wildlife that depended on resident salmonids as a food source. The hatcheries along Yellowstone Lake and other places closed in 1957. Now emerging was the philosophy of managing waters according to their ability to host fish and without human interference. Part of this philosophy was that waters unable to sustain fish life would be honored as naturally unfit and not stocked. Proposals to eliminate bait fishing and to establish catch-and-release fishing on park waters were premature with respect to public acceptance and so were tabled. Fly-fishing-only was introduced on the Firehole and Madison Rivers in 1950 and 1951, respectively, and the following year on the Gibbon River below Gibbon Falls.

The stocking of trout in Slough Creek ended in 1954. The following year, the park ceased stocking brown and rainbow trout and Montana grayling in the Firehole and Madison Rivers, but even with the restrictive fishing regulation the rainbow trout population of the Madison River declined during the decade. Some rainbows planted in both rivers were old brood stock from Montana's Ennis hatchery. Their presence helped build the lore of both streams as producers of large trout. By 1959 Yellowstone Park waters were no longer stocked and artificial propagation ceased. Emphasis now for fisheries personnel was to research the park's salmonid populations and their habitat. In some places closures were established to protect fragile spawning habitat or vital wildlife areas.

Now only the Gallatin, Madison, and Red Rock River drainage headwaters outside Yellowstone National Park held westslope cutthroat. Minor Montana grayling populations existed in the upper Gallatin River drainage, and a fair population held on in lakes and streams of the upper Red Rock River drainage. Those in the Madison River drainage could be traced in most instances to upstream Wolf and Grebe Lakes.

In the early 1950s Montana Fish and Game stocked brown trout in Wade Lake and began stocking Yellowstone cutthroat trout in Madison River drainage lakes and streams formerly populated by westslope cutthroat. The same was done in Elk Lake and other waters outside the Madison drainage. Rainbow trout flourished. The official Montana state rainbow trout record, holding for thirty-six years, of twenty pounds came from Cliff Lake in 1952. In 1956 Montana cut back stocking brown trout after observing that natural reproduction was maintaining good populations. The same had been done with brook trout in 1954.

By 1950 no town in the Mountain West the size of West Yellowstone had a comparable number of fly-fishing retailers. Charles Borberg put his shop up for sale. Bud Lilly, still washing cars, and his wife, Pat, heard of Borberg's action and looked into this opportunity with an advantage. The shop was located in Eagle's Store, and Bud and Wally Eagle had been friends since their Montana State College days. Wally promoted him to family members, and with the Eagles favoring his acquisition, Bud entered the angling business, with Borberg's Trout Shop becoming Bud Lilly's Trout Shop. His first season, 1951, was trying, but with Pat at his side, he prevailed.

That same year, Wally introduced Bud to dry-fly fishing. This experience began his promotion of dry-fly fishing that would increase as the Trout Shop gained popularity. At the same time, the use of spinning gear crossed the waters from Europe

The Quake Lake Visitor Center looking east up Earthquake Lake. The upper end of the lake holds the best locations for fly fishing. (Bruce Staples collection)

and was making huge gains in popularity. Bud was aware of this, and like few in the West Yellowstone angling retail scene, saw the key to success would be to offer merchandise to meet the demands these changes would bring. Adapt he did, and the Trout Shop steadily gained ground. Although Eagle's Store maintained a line of tackle, making them a competitor, they at times passed merchandise on to Bud when his stock became depleted.

The Trout Shop was seasonal during these years, with Bud teaching school when in session. Likewise, Wally Eagle taught in Bozeman when school was in session and returned to help operate the family business when it was out. His father, Eagle's Store founder Sam Eagle, died in 1950. Sam, a West Yellowstone pioneer, was also the first in town to offer fly-fishing items for sale. His family would continue offering this merchandise year-round into the twenty-first century.

By mid-century the Pat Barnes Tackle Shop and Guide Service reigned supreme in the West Yellowstone fly-fishing industry. Located on Yellowstone Avenue, a stone's throw from the park's West Entrance, it became a destination for many fly fishers. Middle-class and blue-collar anglers began arriving in increasing numbers late in the 1940s, mainly by automobile. They demanded information, merchandise, and service, so a stop at West Yellowstone's retail angling shops became a tradition. Vint Johnson's Tackle Shop, now in the hands of his widow Verna and son Joe, continued to serve all comers regardless of terminal gear preference. Existing eateries and motels expanded and new ones came into business, and the first banking services were established. The entire town profited during fishing season.

The Union Pacific's Yellowstone Branch line did not fare so well, however. Passenger service ended in 1959, although freight trains ran several more years to serve the cattle and timber industries. Thus the unique and beautiful dining hall and the depot fell into vacancy and disrepair.

The Union Pacific Railroad ran passenger service to West Yellowstone each year until 1959. Seasonal service began not long after rails were plowed of snow in the springtime. A main reason for the end of rail service was the improved road system and more-reliable vehicles that allowed more middle-class anglers to travel to town and enjoy the nearby excellent angling. (Bob Jacklin collection)

In town, Pat Barnes carried on Don Martinez's mantle, offering fly-fishing merchandise almost exclusively in the 1950s. In those days Sig tied most of the flies sold in the shop. Pat and Sig were now the renowned fly tiers in town, and most of the flies they offered were tied on winter evenings in Helena. Fly fishers from the East would find in the shop an array of popular flies from their home waters. Pat offered that the Adams was his best-selling dry fly. Another pattern Pat claimed as a best seller was the H&L Variant, also a favorite of President Dwight Eisenhower. Other popular patterns sold from the shop during these years included the Sofa Pillow, Betty Hoyt's Improved Sofa Pillow, Goofus Bug, Royal Wulff, Woolly Worm, Martinez Nymph, and Pat's Weighted Nymph.

Pat Barnes's tenure in the West Yellowstone fly-fishing industry spanned from the Johnson-Martinez era to Jacklin-Mathews times. His shop not only competed with these shops, but also with Bud Lilly's Trout Shop and Jim Danskin's Tackle Shop. (Courtesy Pat Barnes Family)

Son Charles began working in the Pat Barnes Tackle Shop in 1959. His duties included shop maintenance, retailing, and guiding. He recalls cleaning up the shop in the aftermath of the 1959 earthquake. The drift boat concept his father Pat introduced brought increasing business to the shop, and Charles participated in guiding through its use.

Through the increased business, the Barnes family realized that conservation measures needed to be applied to retain the quality of the region's fisheries. "Catch-and-keep," as Pat called it, was now inappropriate in Montana sportfishing. Thus he practiced catch-and-release, which he learned from Don Martinez during the 1930s. From these days on, the Barnes family advised their clients that to retain the quality of the area's waters such a practice was necessary.

Rae Servatius maintained her Martinez family flies wholesale operation. Increasingly she was the only continuous connection to Don Martinez. Pat and Sig Barnes marketed her flies because of their mutual ties to Martinez. Bud Lilly became a new customer of Rae's as his supply of Martinez flies dwindled. Eagle's Store became one of her customers in 1951 and had begun offering flies from Dan Bailey the year before.

One of the last times Don Martinez returned to West Yellowstone was early in the decade. Bud Lilly remembers Don coming into the Trout Shop then. Martinez now operated solely out of his Los Angeles home. In 1953 A. J. McClane's *Wise Fisherman's Encyclopedia* appeared in print and contained Don's extensive contributions to the area's fly fishing and recommendations for appropriate fly patterns and tackle. That McClane had selected Martinez for these contributions over eastern fly-fishing writers is testimony to Don's renown as a western fly-fishing authority. In June of the same year, Don's article "The Right Dry Fly" appeared in *Field & Stream*. It revealed his depth of knowledge on dry-fly design, presentation, and the visual senses of a trout.

The fly-fishing audience of the day looked forward to more such analyses by Martinez, but he died in 1955. So in ten years the West Yellowstone fly-fishing industry lost three pioneers: Vint Johnson (1947), Sam Eagle (1950), and Don Martinez (1955). In 1957 Edward Ringwood Hewitt, the first of the renowned easterners to fly-fish Greater Yellowstone waters and describe his experiences, passed away.

Increasingly, Jim Danskin became part of Vint Johnson's Tackle Shop as the 1950s advanced. With Guy Hanson and others guiding, Jim spent time managing and soon acquired knowledge of effective fly patterns and became familiar with best merchandise lines and the best tackle for regional waters.

Sensitive and observant, Danskin quickly understood the need for guides to treat clients with respect and patience. He was proving to be a great match for the fly-fishing retail business with his personable manner, quick wit, and growing knowledge of area fisheries. When Tony Sivey began marketing her Bar-X flies in West Yellowstone, the Tackle Shop became one of her outlets. She proved personable and reliable in filling orders.

As with Bud Lilly and Pat Barnes, Danskin understood that fly fishing was undergoing a revolution with improved products and that soon demand for these products would grow. Like Bud and Pat, he also understood that customers wanted one-on-one conversations, "where to go" and "how to" advice. Dry-fly fishing was becoming more popular around the region, and the same was happening with respect to spin fishing. Thus Jim saw that Tackle Shop merchandise lines should offer items that would meet demands in both areas.

John and Della "Tony" Sivey first visited West Yellowstone in the late 1940s from Nebraska. As fly fishers, they marveled at the fly tying performed by fly-fishing retailers in town. Tony saw economic possibilities and by the mid-1950s began commercial fly tying with Bar-X Flies. The Siveys lived in West Yellowstone during summers and wintered in Butte, where Tony built a stock of flies for sale during fishing season. She had observed the popularity of Pott wet flies, and thus concentrated on a line of wet flies, for which she obtained a patent. Each fly was carded, on which proclaimed "The Make Fish Take!" and "THE FLY WITH INSEXAPPEAL!" She guaranteed her flies for the life of the hook.

Guy Hanson, above with wife Ethel, was a highly respected guide for Vint and Verna Johnson, the Jim Danskin Tackle Shop, and the Narrows Resort. He and Ethel were a beloved couple in West Yellowstone. (Bob Jacklin collection)

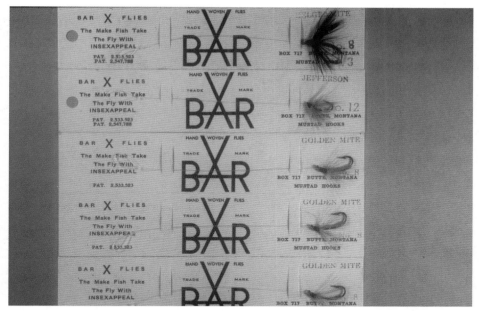

Tony Sivey's Bar X-Flies were carded for sale, as were most flies sold up to the mid-twentieth century. Woven nymph patterns were a twentieth-century tradition in Montana begun by Franz Pott's Mite series in the 1920s. (Bob Jacklin collection)

Tony's woven adult stonefly patterns were best presented wet because their material bulk wasn't very buoyant. Woven nymphs and stoneflies would not be the only flies she would become famous for tying. The famed Bitch Creek Nymph, which remains extremely popular in the West, came from her tying vise.

In the early 1950s Bud Lilly performed most of the Trout Shop's guiding, but as the business grew it became necessary to remain in the shop and associate with customers. Thus he hired individuals he judged suitable to be fly-fishing guides. Such persons would have to be knowledgeable, intelligent, and sensitive.

Al Troth, another young schoolteacher, arrived from Pennsylvania. Bud got to know Al, a superb fly fisher and an extraordinary fly tier. His Elk Hair Caddis was proving effective; Bud observed its potential immediately and began promoting it through the shop. He hired Al as a guide in 1955. Al, also an experienced photographer, stayed on with Bud to 1973. In this time he guided on all of the area's major waters and would be the first of Bud's guides to go on to greater renown. After 1963, Al guided occasionally for Bud but also for Pat Barnes, and he did photography for Bud's mail-order catalog. In 1973 he moved to Dillon, Montana, to establish his own business.

Several persons who would contribute to West Yellowstone's fly-fishing heritage came to the area in the 1950s. Catherine Jacobi Uchiyama remembers Jack Horner arriving unannounced to stay at the Madison Junction Campground and fish the Madison, Firehole, and Gibbon Rivers. Into the campground would come his Jeep pickup with a camper-shell living quarters. He would stay as much as several days until he heard of better fishing prospects elsewhere. Cal Dunbar with his bride, Jan, returned in the mid-1950s to the region. In the next decade the Dunbars began efforts to preserve the town's fly-fishing heritage. Scotty Chapman, working out of

Mammoth, returned to West Yellowstone to fly-fish the Madison River drainage. He befriended Bud Lilly, and Bud remembers Scotty canoeing the Madison and Firehole Rivers and Grayling Creek to learn more about them.

None of the visits discussed above would ultimately result in as much information and understanding of trout behavior as that generated by Charlie Brooks. Still a US Air Force officer, he visited and fly-fished regional waters in 1948, and he did so three times in the 1950s while on leave. During the first, in 1952, he relied mainly on popular regional patterns but soon began creating wet flies for area waters. He concentrated on park rivers. With much experience on the Firehole River, he soon called it the best dry-fly stream in the country. Outside the park he praised the Henry's Fork, the South Fork of the Madison River, the Widow's Pool, and the river in Madison Canyon. His praise for the latter applies before the earthquake.

Also in 1952 Charlie met Sid Gordon, who was doing research for an angling book. This encounter did much to advance his fly-fishing research. Gordon's book, *How to Fish from Top to Bottom*, was published in 1955, and Charlie considered it the most valuable purely fishing book. He began collecting and cataloging insects like Don Martinez had done previously but on a broader scale, and correlated this information with water hardness and fish-size information. He befriended Verna and Joe Johnson and became a customer of their shop. He discussed Don Martinez only occasionally in his works and does not mention visiting the Pat Barnes Tackle Shop, Bud Lilly's Trout Shop, or Eagle's Store. Nevertheless, in his later writings he honors Martinez for establishing the Woolly Worm in trout fishing. Charlie would also pay homage, like so many others, to Martinez's Black Nymph.

During his 1958 visit, Charlie went beyond merely collecting aquatic insects. Through scuba diving, he investigated regional stream bottoms to observe aquatic insect life. He created specialized patterns after observing these insects, and increasingly these were wet flies. On leave again, Charlie revisited the area in 1959, but the August earthquake and aftershocks ruined his fishing. Earthquake or not, he was convinced that he had found the best inland trout-fishing waters.

West Yellowstone fly-fishing professionals increasingly became aware that there were limits to the numbers of trout that could be removed without degrading their abundance. Almost without exception the major fly-fishing retailers in town were well-educated persons and many themselves educators. Each could foresee that a culture separated from the old "catch and keep" was the only way that populations could hold up and secure the future of their businesses. Customers thus were exposed to a catch-and-release ethic by shop personnel, guides, and literature. From this decade on, West Yellowstone fly-fishing professionals would be in the forefront of advocating conservation and education with respect to maintaining trout populations at natural capacity.

As any wise businessman would, Dan Bailey publicized the waters closest to his Livingston business. However, West Yellowstone, being essentially surrounded by high-quality waters, was attracting a larger share of business. Bailey saw this and realized the advantage for his business not only to supply merchandise to West Yellowstone retail outlets, but also to promote applying conservation efforts to the waters surrounding town. To this day most West Yellowstone fly-fishing retailers offer quality fly-fishing merchandise marketed by Dan Bailey's Fly Shop.

1960–1970: A FLY-FISHING GOLDEN AGE BEGINS

The 1960s marked the beginning of widespread concern in the local fly-fishing industry for the well-being of regional salmonid populations. The first major impact of this philosophy in the Greater Yellowstone area was to the park. Increasingly, but not without controversy, allowing nature to take its course there began winning over human manipulation. Now began "natural regulation," meaning the maintenance of natural associations and restoration of original (pre-European-American manipulations) conditions to preserve native species including salmonids.

Jack Anderson, beginning as park superintendent in 1967, championed the new management philosophy. He oversaw fishing regulation modifications to protect all aquatic species and expanded research to ensure their preservation. The first

Yellowstone Lake is now in a recovery mode from the effects of lake trout introduction and the ravages of whirling disease. Sustained management efforts hopefully will return its much-abused Yellowstone cutthroat trout population to numbers approaching those of its late-nineteenth-century past. (John Juracek photo)

Jack Anderson, as park superintendent, had an entire ecology protection approach. Within it he established restrictive fishing regulations and data collection meant to reveal the status of park fisheries. In the photo, taken during the 1975 FFF Conclave in West Yellowstone, are Pat Gartland and Bob Jacklin with Jack Anderson on left (Bob Jacklin collection)

catch-and-release fishing regulation, for Grebe Lake grayling, was applied to park waters in 1969. Anderson furthered resources to increase enforcement policies begun by his immediate predecessors.

The moderate earthquake frequency seemed to increase early in the 1960s. With this came increased heating of groundwater coming into the upper Madison River drainage. Experienced anglers, Charlie Brooks among them, noted that since the 1959 earthquake the Gibbon seemed to be silting while the Firehole was warming. As the decade passed, fewer large fish, those to which abundant dissolved oxygen was so vital, were encountered through most of the Firehole. Park fisheries biologists had no answers at the time. The large mayflies, those Bud Lilly encountered during his first dry-fly-fishing experience in 1950 on the Firehole with Wally Eagle, diminished rapidly as the decade passed. To this day the Firehole remains a destination fishery, challenging and beautiful, but with respect to hosting large trout, it is a shadow of its former self. Nevertheless, more trout inhabit it than in past decades.

Trout Unlimited came to Montana mainly through Dan Bailey's efforts. As a national director, he with other Montana fly-fishing professionals formed Montana TU in 1962. Bud Lilly became the first president, and Jim Danskin and Pat Barnes were active members. Montana TU had reason for concern because in the Madison River below Hebgen Lake, catch rates were dropping from overharvest and larger trout were becoming more difficult to encounter. The lake's Utah chub populations, released by careless bait anglers, also threatened its fabulous trout population.

For Bud Lilly, Pat Barnes, the Eagle family, Jim Danskin, and Dan Bailey, it was a bad dream coming true. Remembering Don Martinez's warning, they saw that they

West Yellowstone streets were famed for early-season mud, late-season dust, and enduring potholes until paving began in the 1960s. Side streets were paved nearly twenty years later. (Bob Jacklin collection)

◀ In 1963 expanded business demanded the move of the Pat Barnes Tackle Shop to this location farther west on Yellowstone Avenue. Bob Jacklin located here in the 1980s. (Courtesy Pat Barnes Family)

were partly at fault for not working for restrictive kill regulations earlier. The remedy became obvious to these professionals, but their problem would be convincing state fish and game commissioners and scientists that restrictive changes were necessary. In 1969 the Montana State Legislature appropriated in-stream water to preserve the Madison River salmonid fishery, demonstrating recognition of its economic value. Montana Power then altered its water release policy in coordination with other agencies in efforts to protect Madison River salmonids.

In the 1960s new infrastructure, such as bridges, rest areas, and highways improved to handle increased traffic, gave the region the overall appearance surviving today. Canyon Street, Yellowstone Avenue to the park's West Entrance, and Highway 20 in town were paved, but side streets would not be paved until 1988.

State Highway 87 from US Highway 191 skirting the north side of Henry's Lake, going over Raynolds Pass, and then continuing north to cross the Madison River

Gracious, engaging, and knowledgeable, Sigrid Barnes ran the Pat Barnes Tackle Shop when Pat was out guiding. Fly tying was another of her functions not only at the shop but also winters in Helena, where she and Pat built a stock for the upcoming season. Here she uses her treadle machine to wind materials on a hook. In a sense her machine was a forerunner of the rotary vise, as was Don Martinez's pin vise. The Goofus Bug was her "signature fly." (Courtesy Pat Barnes Family)

downstream of the 1959 landslide site was paved. Nearby, a famed destination for fly fishers, the Slide Inn, came into being. Highway 287, nearly destroyed by the 1959 earthquake, was rebuilt to serve as the main route from West Yellowstone to the Madison Valley. In 1965 the new airport just north of town began operations. West Yellowstone incorporated in 1966 and on May 23, 1969, received the Union Pacific's dining hall, depot, and other buildings. The dining hall became the town's convention center and would play a major role in its fly-fishing heritage.

Recovery from the 1959 earthquake and resulting Madison Canyon landslide moved quickly as the decade passed. Throughout, Rae Servatius kept the Don Martinez influence alive by supplying flies to retailers in Yellowstone National Park and in town. The increased demand for services and merchandise also brought need for Pat Barnes to acquire more space. Thus in 1963 he moved to a larger building on Yellowstone Avenue across from Eagle's Store.

Up to now, Pat had done all the guiding chores, but with expanded business he hired guides and reigned supreme in town for float-fishing regional streams. Pat and Sig issued their first fly-fishing map and Waterborn Flies catalog in 1964. Son Charles began guiding in 1969, occasionally tied flies, and took part in shop operations.

Leon Chandler, representing the Cortland Line Company, became a cherished friend and reliable supplier. His son, Kim, guided summers for Pat while attending college. Pat and Sig now enjoyed renown as fly tiers, and for Pat it was time to fill a void in the flies he offered from the shop. To take full advantage of demand, he needed not only a supply of tried-and-true patterns but also new patterns to keep up with the new offerings coming from competing tiers.

A dream came true in 1961 for Jim Danskin. Verna Johnson, wishing to sell the Tackle Shop, gave Jim first-refusal rights. He accepted her offer, and the business became Jim Danskin's Tackle Shop. The Danskins lived in a small apartment at the rear of the shop. Jim retained Verna's lines of merchandise and her suppliers, increased the number of guides working for the shop, and began expanding the business. Anglers such as Mike Lawson and Paul Bruun, as well as Bob Jacklin, repeatedly express appreciation for Jim and Lois's friendly and helpful manner.

Next Jim established fly-fishing schools, staffed by his guides, at local dude ranches. Parade Rest Ranch became his largest client. His philosophy was that his

◀ Jim Danskin's shop came into being in 1961, succeeding Vint Johnson's Tackle Shop on Canyon Street. Jim extended the Johnsons' reputation for quality merchandise, outstanding service, and honest information. (Bob Jacklin collection)

Lois Danskin stands in the doorway of the Jim Danskin Tackle Shop. All West Yellowstone fly shops had dedicated wives who helped in many ways to keep the shops running profitably. (Bob Jacklin collection)

Jim Danskin continued the Johnsons' fine reputation for the length of his shop's tenure. Jim mentored young anglers aspiring to enter the industry, just as Vint Johnson had with him. (Bob Jacklin collection) ▶

shop's reputation was reflected in the conduct of its guides. The guides he featured had to be intelligent, knowledgeable, and personable.

When Jim took a turn at guiding or was absent on business, Lois ran the shop, and like Sig Barnes, Verna Johnson, Pat Lilly, Rae Servatius, and Tony Sivey became a renowned and beloved West Yellowstone fly-fishing lady. Tony became a large supplier of flies for Jim and others beginning in 1962 until 1979, when she left the area. On doing so, she sold her stock of flies, materials, and equipment to Bob Jacklin.

The late 1960s also saw the beginning of major West Yellowstone fly-fishing schools. In 1969 Bud Lilly offered a fly-fishing school out of the Trout Shop in coordination with the Fenwick Rod Company. Jim Green and Lefty Kreh were among the first instructors, along with Greg Lilly and other Trout Shop guides. The arrangement lasted only a year, with Fenwick planning its own school.

As with Pat Barnes and his family, the 1960s began for Bud Lilly with the realization that local trout populations could not withstand the number of fish creeled by an increasing number of anglers. With the Trout Shop's business expanding, he increasingly advocated catch-and-release. In conversations, Bud's convincing and forthright manner convinced customers of the need for this philosophy.

The Trout Shop remained seasonal until 1970, with the family returning to Bozeman, where Bud taught school, for winters. Now it was becoming a family business. Son Greg joined the guide ranks at age sixteen, and the younger children, Mike and Annette, were introduced to catch-and-release fly fishing. Increasingly Pat Lilly tended the business operations. Bud became the public figure, greeting anglers, advising where to fish and what to use, arranging guide services, and on occasion guiding himself. Some days he was swamped with these activities, so he passed customers on to Greg. Bud envisioned going into retailing full-time. In 1965 he secured space on Hansen family property on the northeast corner of Canyon Street and Yellowstone Avenue, constructed a building there, and moved from rented space in Eagle's Store, establishing Bud Lilly's Trout Shop in 1966.

This act was the beginning of what Bob Jacklin refers to as the "fifty golden years of the town's fly-fishing industry." With increased space, Bud expanded his lines of merchandise and made associations with the great contemporary fly-fishing personalities. For Greg, beginning in the mid-1960s, guiding went on about six days a week until it was time to return to school at Montana State. Will Godfrey guided for the Trout Shop from 1965 through 1967. Afterward he opened the first full-service shop on the Henry's Fork in 1969 at Last Chance.

Now with the discovery of regional fisheries came the first of public personalities. The float trip Bud took writer Ed Zern on through the middle Madison during an early-July giant stonefly emergence resulted in the largest brown and rainbow Ed had caught up to that time. When Vince Marinaro came to the region he showed, much

Bud Lilly with a customer in front of the Trout Shop in the 1967. The Totem Café just north on Canyon Street is the site of Don Martinez's first fly-fishing shop in town. (Bob Jacklin collection)

to Bud's bemusement, more interest in studying aquatic insects than in fishing. Renowned fly tier Helen Shaw and her husband came to fish in 1962. Ernie Schwiebert arrived in 1965, and Bud took him to all of the area's famed streams. Schwiebert immediately wrote praise for the Firehole in a *Field & Stream* article titled "Strangest Trout Stream on Earth: Firehole River in Yellowstone National Park," the most detailed presentation of the river and its fishery up to that time.

Numerous fly tiers appeared at the Trout Shop trying to convince Bud to feature their creations. In 1969 Dave Whitlock arrived eager to learn, displaying impressive creativity and an engaging personality. Bud gave him a chance to create patterns for regional waters. He also promoted Bob Jacklin's fly-tying ability and offered his patterns in the shop. He featured Charlie Brooks's wet flies and also promoted Stan Yamamura of Idaho Falls, who was in those days eastern Idaho's most renowned fly tier. Although Bud promoted creations from individual tiers, wholesalers, mainly Dan Bailey, provided the bulk of the Trout Shop's flies.

Bud and Pat Lilly in the Trout Shop. Note the spinning lure display on the wall behind them. This would soon change as the Trout Shop became one of the premier fly-fishing retail destinations in the West Yellowstone area. (Bob Jacklin collection)

Bud admits that the mail-order catalog was his biggest business venture. The first catalog was issued in 1969. In addition to merchandise descriptions, Bud included in the catalog an outlook on regional waters for the upcoming season. Soon fly fishers around the world would anticipate receiving *Bud Lilly's Tackle Catalog and Handbook for Western Trout Fishing*. Bud also saw the value in offering fly-fishing art at the Trout Shop. Scotty Chapman was known as one of the best artists specializing in park scenes, and he and Bud maintained a friendship that centered on fishing and artwork.

Scotty was not the only fly-fishing ranger. Scotty Bauman was also an avid fly fisher, whose favorite waters included the Firehole and Madison Rivers. Alfred Harold (Shakey) Beals, a San Diego furniture sales executive, was a seasonal ranger stationed at the West Yellowstone ranger station during those days. Famed for his knowledge of the Madison River fishery along the West Entrance Road, Bud Lilly often consulted with Beals on the river's fishing conditions. Nick Nicklas, tying for Blue Ribbon Flies, created a fly, the Shakey Bealy, in his honor.

Cal Dunbar had a history of visiting West Yellowstone as a youth during family vacations and fly-fishing the area's waters. He and his new wife, Jan, returned for a visit two decades later and observed that the West Yellowstone pace of life was more attractive than that in Jan's home state of Utah or in the Bay Area of California, where Cal was employed. They moved to town in December 1961 and opened the

Dave Bascom's *Wretched Mess News* lampooned the West Yellowstone fly-fishing community for years. Likely inspired by *Mad* magazine, its humor has no equivalent in the fly-fishing community. Many anglers eagerly awaited upcoming editions. (Bob Jacklin collection)

Food Roundup market. Almost immediately the Dunbars became involved in the town's government and in preserving its history.

West Yellowstone was soon to meet a most unusual character in Dave Bascom. A San Francisco advertising agency owner, Bascom had a passion for fly fishing and had heard from friends of West Yellowstone's reputation as the center of the country's best fishing. It took little time for him to arrive and buy a home in the Lonesomehurst subdivision. Soon upon his arrival in 1961, everyone in West Yellowstone discovered Bascom's sense of humor. Out came his *Wretched Mess News*, which for two decades lampooned the local fly-fishing industry. In 1965 his sense of humor and Bud Lilly's wit combined to produce the Tackle Foundling Society Parade, meant to celebrate the fishing season opening. It illustrated that the Old West was still alive in West Yellowstone.

In these days a sense of camaraderie existed in the West Yellowstone fly-fishing retail community. For example, if a shop's guiding schedule was full and new requests for such services were received for a given day, owners called other shops to see if vacancies existed in their schedule. If such vacancies existed, customers asking for such services were recommended to shops with vacancies.

Bob Jacklin, living in New Jersey, would soon find his dreams of living and fly-fishing in the Rocky Mountain West coming true. He read the praises of Yellowstone National Park waters in sporting magazines, and renowned personalities, including Lee Wulff, reinforced these accounts. Now in his early twenties, he had fly-fished waters in his native state, tied flies commercially, developed taxidermy skills, supported stream conservation projects, and worked in the fishing tackle industry. He became, and remains, a Theodore Gordon Flyfishers member. With the exception of time spent with the 389th United States Army Band, most of his life had been directed toward fly fishing and fly tying.

Only five days out of the US Army, Bob journeyed west in 1967 driving a Volkswagen Beetle. Arriving at Madison Junction Campground, he almost immediately began fishing the Firehole, Gibbon, and Madison Rivers. He met Ed Mueller while fishing the Firehole, and their friendship bloomed into a professional association. Bob was not aware that West Yellowstone existed, and Ed took him there to meet Pat and Sig Barnes, the Eagle family, and Bud and Pat Lilly.

Bob returned home in autumn of that year, setting his pattern for the rest of the decade: home to New Jersey in autumn to attend college, then return in spring to enjoy the region's great fly fishing. His experiences these first seasons began

Bud Lilly was the first to employ Bob Jacklin. He worked as a Trout Shop guide and fly tier, and taught in Bud's fly-fishing school. Through this employment he increased his store of knowledge on area fisheries. Bob was photographed tying along with his flies in several Trout Shop catalogs. (Bob Jacklin collection)

the accumulation of his vast store of knowledge and deep appreciation for regional fisheries. In 1968 he met Jim Danskin, and another friendship would evolve into a professional association. In an action that would become significant in the future, Bob, as would Bud Lilly, Pat Barnes, Cal Dunbar, and Jim Danskin, joined the newly formed Federation of Fly Fishers (now Fly Fishers International) in his first season fishing area waters. By 1970 he had secured employment as a guide and fly tier for Bud Lilly's Trout Shop.

In 1961 Charlie and Gracie Brooks bought land on the Montana side of Targhee Pass, and there built their home. Charlie, a confirmed hunter of large trout, concentrated on presenting nymphs, having observed that trout feed primarily on them. His observations of the stomach contents of salmonids taken from higher-gradient area waters confirmed the importance in their diets of stonefly nymphs.

Curious, determined, and intelligent, Charlie intensified research to improve his presentation of stonefly nymph patterns. He frequented riffle-and-run water, mostly on the Madison River. At first, he fished mainly by himself to gather information on both fish and aquatic insects. After arriving in 1961, he began a practice new to observing nymph behavior. He fashioned a watertight face mask and breathing tube, and with Gracie's help observed, while submerged, the behavior of stonefly nymphs she presented by rod and reel.

Charlie noted the importance of placing nymph patterns as close to the stream bottom as possible. He compared the behavior of these patterns to that of live stonefly nymphs and discovered a significant difference that would forever alter nymph fishing: Artificial nymphs roll around their long axis due to the impact of uneven

Charlie himself recommended that everyone in range wear a hard hat while he was casting heavily weighted nymph patterns. He is doing so here on the Madison River just above the US Highway 191 bridge. (Bob Jacklin collection)

Regional fly fishers hung the moniker "Old Monochrome" on Charlie Brooks as he fished singularly to strengthen his store of knowledge on stonefly nymphs and their relationship to trout. But after observing the fishing success of his dress and demeanor, they adopted both. (Courtesy Ralph Moon) ▶

currents on the line and leader, whereas drifting live nymphs tend not to roll. He saw that the Woolly Worm was such an effective imitator of stonefly nymphs because it was tied in the round. This observation would impact the manner in which he tied flies and would be key to successful presentation. While submerged, he also observed the behavior of trout in holding water and what made up the best such water.

The Madison River fascinated Charlie. It was full of large trout in fast, deep holding water throughout its reach below Hebgen Lake, and these waters contained an abundance of large stoneflies. He began observations in the Barns Holes area. Here and in other faster, deeper waters he observed that stoneflies outnumbered most other aquatic insects. Increasingly he became a presenter of large, heavily weighted nymph patterns in deep, swift waters. In shallower reaches of the Madison he observed that caddisflies outnumber stoneflies and mayflies.

Parman, remaining at the motel, continued to make school attendance arrangements while his wife, Maxine, prepared breakfasts and lunches. The Parmans used their own vehicles to provide a shuttle service to the school from the Sleepy Hollow in town.

Phil Clock, CEO of the Fenwick Rod Company, had arranged for the Fenwick Fly-Fishing School to be sited at the east side of Targhee Pass. Clock bought the property, sold lots, and built small ponds and a headquarters building. He rented the building, some land, and ponds to the school for a dollar a year. Frank and Gladys Gray, the school headmasters, established a curriculum and hired casting instructors. The first of these were from Jim Danskin's and Pat Barnes's shops, including Bob Jacklin and Ed Mueller. Bob doubled in presenting aquatic entomology classes. All employees advocated catch-and-release fly fishing.

All of the major fly-fishing retailers in town promoted catch-and-release and protection of spawning areas, and offered advice on handling and releasing fish. In 1968 Charlie Brooks, Cal Dunbar, Bud Lilly, Bob Jacklin, and Dick McGuire formed Southwest Montana Fly-Fishers (SWMFF) to promote fisheries conservation. Charlie credited McGuire with knowing the middle Madison River better than any other angler. Charlie, and later Craig Mathews, also credited McGuire for major contributions on establishing a catch-and-release regulation and fisheries management on this part of the river. In fact, McGuire's knowledge helped form the basis of Dick Vincent's renowned study on the impact of stocked fish on Madison River wild fish. The Federation of Fly Fishers (FFF) would succeed SWMFF and go on to play a huge role in West Yellowstone's fly-fishing heritage.

As the 1960s progressed, outdoor writers began arriving in droves. Many of them not only sought information for publishing, but also brought warnings that the same fate could befall Greater Yellowstone waters that had befallen those in the eastern states and other parts of the world: the overharvest of salmonids, particularly those of larger sizes. Coming was an era where scientific and pseudoscientific elements would increase angling effectiveness. Complementary to these would be the introduction of new equipment that added further potential for successful fly fishing. The potential for salmonid depletion was clear to West Yellowstone fly-fishing retailers. So the 1960s ended with West Yellowstone on the threshold of a new fly-fishing era.

CHAPTER 7

1970–1980: THE GOLDEN AGE EXPANDS

Broadscale support for the preservation of Greater Yellowstone region fisheries developed as the 1970s advanced. Park fisheries management was first, instituting programs based on the ecologic and economic value of maintaining a wild fishery in equilibrium with available natural resources. Public opinion favoring maintenance of wild fisheries in Montana was not far behind.

Throughout the 1970s the size of Firehole River trout appeared to diminish, due almost solely to its warming waters. As the river's waters warmed through the summer, its tributaries would become important havens for fish stressed due to reduced levels of dissolved oxygen. In the autumn, the canyon below Firehole Falls continued

Beautiful to behold, and originally devoid of salmonids, the Firehole River is a unique and treasured fishery. Charlie Brooks called it "the finest dry fly stream in the nation." Thoughtfully, Yellowstone Park authorities close sections of it to human entry, thus protecting delicate thermal features that are national treasures. (John Juracek photo)

to host a few run-up spawning trout from Hebgen Lake, but the days such as those when Wally Eagle introduced Bud Lilly to large Firehole River trout were gone.

Grayling, thought to be extinct in the upper Gallatin River drainage by 1978, were occasionally caught in the upper Gibbon River. A minor plant of westslope cutthroat below Gibbon Falls in 1979 and 1980 failed to establish, as did a plant of grayling in Canyon Creek below Gibbon Falls about the same time. In the Madison River, catches of cutthroat trout were rare and possibly attributed to mistaken identity.

At the beginning of his tenure as park superintendent in the late 1960s, Jack Anderson observed the increasing visits to Yellowstone National Park and recognized the necessity to manage park resources through an approach that protected its entire ecology. He championed restrictive limits that would not detract from fishing being a quality experience yet would ensure the future of native species.

Anderson and his staff began research programs intended to observe the status of park fisheries. Angler surveys and free volunteer fishing reports provided catch-rate data, species distribution, and angler acceptance of fishing conditions. In 1973 many roadside fisheries and some in the backcountry of the park became subject to a catch-and-release regulation. West Yellowstone fly-fishing retailers, including Bud Lilly and Bob Jacklin, lined up to support this regulation. Fishing Bridge and the nearby marina were closed to fishing in 1973. In 1975 a maximum length of thirteen inches and a two-fish creel limit were applied for Yellowstone Lake cutthroat trout to protect mature fish. The same year, based on Bob Jacklin's recommendation, the park general fishing season, with some exceptions, would now open on the Saturday before Memorial Day.

Anderson was one of the organizers of the first Wild Trout Management Symposium held September 25 and 26, 1974, in Yellowstone National Park. The symposium, sponsored by the US Department of the Interior and Trout Unlimited, continues to this day and provides a forum for fisheries professionals, anglers, politicians, educators, writers, and conservationists to gather to discuss the state of salmonids.

Anderson retired in 1975, having gained much acclaim for promoting restrictive regulations and advocating management policies to preserve park fisheries. These restrictions resulted in a temporary decline in angler visitation, but eventually as more fish and those of larger size populated park waters, angler use increased. Anderson's successor, John Townsley, continued these restrictions and expanded them where necessary.

Respect for the Madison River trout fishery had gone beyond the Montana angling community. Protective action came from the state legislature and from the private sector. No entity in the private sector had more impact than Montana Power, which regulated flows from its reservoirs in a manner as beneficial as possible for the Madison's trout population. Nevertheless, an ongoing decline was observed in the river's trout population. Montana Fish and Game Commission studies were begun, with basic information provided by Dick McGuire, to determine the cause. A study performed for the Commision by Dick Vincent would have a global impact on fisheries management.

Vincent's study began in 1967 to investigate the impact of spring flows on the trout population in the river below Hebgen Lake. When significant population improvement was observed in only one of the two study areas, it became obvious that another variable was affecting the results. That variable was that one study section of the river had been stocked with hatchery rainbow trout for ten years, while the other had never been stocked. Vincent and his colleagues observed that without planting in the one study

Fishing Bridge as it appeared in the mid-twentieth century when fishing was allowed from its deck and from boats, which crowded the Yellowstone River outlet. Garbage cans were filled and banks littered with discarded trout. (Bob Jacklin collection)

Fishing Bridge today, with fishing from its deck and boats in the estuary prohibited. Now resident cutthroat trout spawn uninterrupted and the bridge serves as a fish-viewing location. (Bruce Staples collection)

section, its wild trout population increased by 180 percent and the average size of the wild trout also increased. This result demonstrated that the food and living space available to trout in a stream (and stillwater) is limited, and when trout are released into a body of water, its wild population will tend toward an "availability equilibrium." Cease introducing trout, and the wild trout population will move toward a natural equilibrium. As a result of Vincent's and other studies and with public support, Montana ceased stocking hatchery trout in all its blue-ribbon streams in 1972.

By 1973 angler use on the Madison River from Ennis to the Yellowstone National Park boundary had more than tripled since 1952, with fly fishers, having primarily a catch-and-release ethic, making up most of the increase. No boat use for fishing had been allowed on the river from McAtee Bridge upstream since 1971. When a decrease in the size of the trout caught on the Madison below Hebgen Lake was observed in the middle of the decade, a two-mile section of the river from Squaw Creek to Wolf Creek was closed for five years, beginning in 1977, to assess angler impact. Results of this study indicated that even under a catch-and-release regulation, anglers impact trout mortality, and mortality in the closed section decreased dramatically, especially for larger trout.

These results led in 1977 to an eventual catch-and-release, artificial-fly-or-lure-only regulation on the river upstream of McAtee Bridge. Even stricter regulations were applied to the heavily fished Madison River from Ennis Lake up to McAtee Bridge: a three-fish limit, one over eighteen inches. From McAtee Bridge to Quake Lake, catch-and-release fishing with artificial flies only and lures was applied. Improvement in fishing on the river was observed almost immediately.

When the great fly-fishing boom came to West Yellowstone in this decade, at least eight retailers were offering merchandise to anglers. The parade of fly-fishing personalities in West Yellowstone grew. Kazuhiro Ashizawa, the Japanese Lee Wulff, came to fish. Secretive and private, Frank Matarelli came seasonally from the San Francisco area. He frequented the Madison River along the park's West Entrance Road but socialized little. Maggie Merriman conducted a fly-fishing school during the 1970s. Al Caucci and Bob Nastasi arrived in town to collect information for their detailed book *Hatches*. Like Swisher and Richards's *Selective Trout*, *Hatches* offered detail not yet seen in the fly-fishing world.

Jack Gartside, another former teacher, arrived in the early 1970s. A unique character possessing unlimited fly-tying talent, he hitchhiked early in the summer from Boston, Massachusetts, to reside in the Baker's Hole and Madison River campgrounds and in the next decade Blue Ribbon Flies' basement. His pet cat came via airline. Gartside frequented fly shops in the area and attached himself to fly fishers and retailers for meals and rides to favorite fishing spots. Soon fly shops in the area were featuring his elegant flies.

Ross Merigold fell in love with the middle Madison River in the 1950s. Affable, generous, and observant, he began guiding there in the mid-1970s from a Slide Inn cabin. His season-long experiences on the Madison resulted in vast fishing knowledge of the river and famed fly patterns. Paul Brown, another schoolteacher, also became a local personality. Wally Eagle returned permanently to the family business in 1980. Scotty Chapman had retired from the park ranger force in 1960. From his ranch adjacent to Gardiner, Montana, he continued to ply regional waters and produce superb artwork.

Baker's Hole Campground, on the river at the lower right, holds a special place in West Yellowstone fly-fishing history. The river here meanders in and out of the Montana–Yellowstone Park border, making fishing licenses for both places necessary. David "Stuffy" Martinez and Wally Eagle rode their bicycles from town to fish here, and Jack Gartside camped here for entire summers. Access to the Madison River is convenient, as shown in the photo. For several decades anglers have gathered here to enjoy seasonal fly-fishing events. (Bruce Staples collection)

Bud Lilly launched his Celebrity Flyfisher program and specialty fishing clinics, and fished local waters with Lee Wulff and Arnold Gingrich. Dave Whitlock's elegant fly patterns graced Trout Shop fly bins and its catalog. The shop was now a year-round operation, with mail-order sales sustaining business during winter. Bud's Catch-and-Release Club, introduced in 1974, became immensely popular as anglers scrambled to have their names posted in the shop and purchase pins that proclaimed their skills, with the proceeds donated to the FFF and Trout Unlimited. Gone was the 1950s Lunker Club.

Whether from Darwin Atkin, Jack Gartside, Doug Gibson, House of Harrop, Bob Jacklin, Craig Mathews, Al Troth, or Dave Whitlock, elegant patterns were given center stage in the Trout Shop and its catalog. Bud proclaimed Al Troth's Elk Hair Caddis was his all-time favorite. Such actions did wonders for sales from an audience eager to know what their icons used. Through the Orvis Company, John Harder supplied flies from iconic regional tiers to the Trout Shop. On occasion other tiers, including the House of Harrop and Doug Gibson, tied orders directly for the shop. Fly tackle dealers and authors lined up for Trout Shop endorsements of their products and the chance to advertise in the shop's catalog. The family expanded the Trout Shop in the early 1970s to include an art gallery featuring works by local artists and craftsmen. One group of note was Scotty Chapman's paintings of regional scenery. Scotty's artistic genes found a home in son Bill, who went on to do the cover illustration for the 1975 Trout Shop catalog.

By this decade Mike and Annette Lilly were of age to join eldest child Greg in the family business. Annette became Montana's first licensed female guide in 1973. Later Bonnie, Greg's wife, and Lynn Corcoran joined her, giving the Trout Shop a huge advantage over other town retailers who had no female guides. Mike Lilly went on to establish himself not only as a top guide, but also as a model in generosity and diplomacy that would enhance the image of Greater Yellowstone fly-fishing professionals. Even competitors spoke well of Mike's capabilities and generosity.

For Pat and Sig Barnes the 1970s were an extension of the 1960s, with business expanding appreciably. The national reputation of the shop could be seen in its celebrity promoters. Pat retired from teaching in 1971 and devoted more time to the shop. Fly-tying help was enlisted outside the family because Sig was able to satisfy only half of the climbing demand for Waterborn Flies (Pat's trademark). Al Troth and Mike and Sheralee Lawson were contracted to help meet the demand, and Rae Servatius also supplied flies. The quality of Waterborn Flies and fly-tying material coming from the shop was always top grade.

Up to 1963 Pat had done most of the guiding himself, but now the shop employed seven guides. After graduating from Montana State University in 1973, son Charles guided during summers for the rest of the decade. Now everyone was using the McKenzie River boats that Pat introduced back in the late 1940s. A particularly

Bud Lilly in the Trout Shop discussing with a customer the use of the streamer pattern held in his right hand. Bud, though not a fly tier himself, was adept and knowledgeable in helping others select the right fly for a given time and place. (Bob Jacklin collection)

busy time was during the giant and golden stonefly emergence season beginning in early June on the Henry's Fork and ending in early August on the Yellowstone River.

Pat began his own fly-fishing school in the 1970s as demand for fly-fishing instruction began to surpass that available through other local schools. Pat and Sig took part in the fly-tying demonstrations at all three FFF Conclaves held in the 1970s. So beloved were they that clients gathered enough money to send them on a trip around the world, which included a visit to India to evaluate tying materials and to New Zealand to fish. Further trips to New Zealand followed. By the end of the decade, retirement was on their minds. They had been in business thirty-five years.

Jim Danskin's busiest guiding times extended from the late 1960s through the 1970s. During this period his guide staff included his son John, Bob Jacklin, Guy Hanson, George Weary, Jim Vermillion, Seldon Jones, Doug Pope, Bill Mason, and Mike Lawson. Bud and Lu Morris's Parade Rest Guest Ranch featured Danskin guides until 1979. Joe Brooks had been a client there; his last visit was in 1971, the year before he died. Bob, Bill, and Mike (also formerly a schoolteacher) would go on to open their own shops. Jim hired Mike in 1974 with intent to be a Henry's Fork specialist, but service demand on the Madison River meant Mike spent much time there. To be sure, camaraderie existed among area guides regardless of which shop they worked for.

After guiding for Bud Lilly (1970–1972) and Jim Danskin (1973), Bob Jacklin had gained almost unmatched experience. He, Greg Lilly, and Charlie Brooks were instructors for Bud's fly-fishing school; Lefty Kreh instructed there briefly at its beginning. While with Jim Danskin, Bob became a major participant in the Fenwick Fly-Fishing School. Bob had established a reputation as a sought-after guide and fly-fishing instructor, schooled in diplomacy, of a professional outlook, and

Jim Danskin, personable, generous, and honest, was beloved and respected in the West Yellowstone fly-fishing retail and beyond scene for decades. He fished area waters not only for pleasure but also to gain information to pass on to customers. Jim especially enjoyed drift-boat fishing on the Madison River. (Bob Jacklin collection)

Charlie Brooks teaching fly fishing on the Firehole River for Bud Lilly's fly-fishing school. The three major instructors for Bud's school were Charlie, Greg Lilly, and Bob Jacklin. (Bob Jacklin collection)

knowledgeable of the merchandise best suited for the area. He not only guided for Danskin, but on occasion ran the shop. He kept meticulous records on fly fishing and on his experiences teaching, guiding, and merchandising, and began accumulating materials on the history of West Yellowstone.

Bob came to town with a reputation as a superb fly tier. Late in the decade, Lee Wulff would present him with a letter of authenticity attesting that his dressings of the Wulff series of flies were "tied true to pattern and of the highest quality." So elegant were Bob's Atlantic salmon fly dressings that some were featured in Joe Bates's *Atlantic Salmon Flies and Fishing*, published in 1970. His versons of traditional wet fly patterns appeared in Joe Brooks's *Trout Fishing*, published in 1972, and in Joe Bates's *Fishing: An Encyclopedic Guide to Tackle*, published in 1973. Bob was one of two fly tiers to participate in the first fly-tying demonstrations held during a FFF Conclave (Jackson Hole, 1968). A stalwart member of the Federation of Fly Fishers, he continued demonstrating his tying skills at FFF Conclaves into the next century. He also applied his fly-casting skills to instruction during the conclaves.

All of these experiences provided encouragement to open a shop. Located on Madison Avenue across from the high school, Bob's shop began as a seasonal operation. It was small, with a log exterior and a trailer attached on the east for living quarters. Bud Lilly had been operating his Trout Shop on a year-round basis for several years, and Pat Barnes and Jim Danskin held well-deserved reputations for excellent service. Thus it was a challenge to start a business that must compete with three major shops owned by renowned figures.

Bob stayed in West Yellowstone year-round, making ends meet through taxidermy, fly tying, and his musical skills with drums. In 1977 he served as president of the town chamber of commerce. With encouragement from Cal Dunbar; Frank Gray; Herb Perry, the famed Hollywood music producer and avid fly fisher; and Tony Sivey,

Bob Jacklin's first shop was small, with attached living quarters. He maintained the shop through the winter months with the help of outside income sources. During West Yellowstone's long winters, Bob got plenty of exercise keeping the entrance free of snow. (Bob Jacklin collection)

Pat and Sig Barnes at the Tackle Shop. Here Sig is using her famed treadle sewing machine to tie flies. Fly fishers would come from all over to purchase Sig's custom flies and observe her in the act of tying. (Courtesy Charles Barnes) ▶

an open and forthright personal demeanor, and a share of the Fenwick Fly-Fishing School, he began to build a renowned business.

The Fenwick Fly-Fishing School expanded its classes. From a basic three-day course, it offered a five-day "graduate level" course covering such topics as aquatic entomology, tackle selection, fly tying, and knot selection in detail. All instructors and employees followed Phil Clock's lead in advocating catch-and-release fly fishing. The school was free for local anglers and served dinner to attendees Mondays through Wednesdays, making it one of the great bargains in fly fishing. Gary Borger, Mel Krieger, Gary LaFontaine, and Paul Brown were added as instructors. Borger and Krieger moved on to establish Fenwick schools in California and the Midwest, respectively. Tom Webb, a teacher from California, became an instructor at the school after guiding for Bob Jacklin and Bud Lilly. Tom's wife Betty, another schoolteacher, frequently worked there. Fenwick also gave a free evening class during the 1970s at Madison Junction, with Bob Jacklin and Frank and Gladys Gray instructing.

In the early 1970s Joe Brooks stayed at the Parade Rest Ranch and enjoyed fishing the Madison River. Here he casts a new-model Fenwick glass fly rod during the 1970 FFF Conclave held at Sun Valley, Idaho. Cal Dunbar and Bud Morris are in the background. (Bob Jacklin collection)

By the 1970s the FFF Conclave had become an international event. Its organizers sought locations offering not only attractive surroundings but also opportunities for quality fly fishing. When the FFF approached the West Yellowstone town council about holding a conclave in town, an enthusiastic response resulted. Bud Lilly, Cal Dunbar, and Bob Jacklin immediately began promoting the benefits of hosting the 1974 conclave. The town had bountiful lodging and restaurants, all major services, and the centrally located convention center. Thus the first of many conclaves was held there.

This first conclave was so well attended that it was repeated in 1975 with an even larger attendance. Many of the renowned personalities who attended in 1974 returned in 1975, with Arnold Gingrich being featured. The conclave returned to West Yellowstone in 1978, but without Gingrich, who passed away in July 1976.

An arrival in these days that would become permanent and have another great impact on the town's fly-fishing community happened about mid-decade. Venturing from Michigan, where he had acquired considerable fly-fishing and fly-tying experience and a strong conservation ethic, Craig Mathews had read of and absorbed word of the wondrous waters surrounding West Yellowstone. Seeking to escape overbearing law enforcement duties, he came to West Yellowstone with his wife, Jackie, during Septembers and Octobers to fly-fish. Craig's elegant array of patterns caught Bud Lilly's eye. Being a superb judge of fly pattern marketability, Bud was already offering flies from several suppliers. Now Craig's creations were added to those offered in the Trout Shop and through its mail-order catalog.

Fly-fishing experiences and appreciation for the region's quality waters during those vacations quickly spun their magic, and Craig interviewed for the job of West Yellowstone Chief of Police. For Cal Dunbar and other council members this was unexpected good fortune, as previous holders and other candidates were nowhere

Ernie Schwiebert, one of the country's foremost fly-fishing writers and conservationists, participated in many FFF Conclaves in West Yellowstone. He publicized the quality of regional waters through his many books, magazine articles, and personal appearances. (Bob Jacklin collection)

◀ Lee Wulff visited the iconic waters around town, usually when attending FFF Conclaves. Here he tries his luck on the Madison River. (Bob Jacklin collection)

near as well qualified. The city council welcomed Craig into the job, and Cal reflects that Craig, three years in that position, was one of the best chiefs of police West Yellowstone ever employed. Jackie held the job of police dispatcher. They intended to stay only two years in these jobs, and for a while the absence of resources appeared to make that a practical limit. This lack of resources might have driven away lesser spirits, but Craig and Jackie were now living their dream of being in the midst of the best inland trout fishing in the country.

They visited all the regional waters. The middle Madison River and the Firehole became favorites. They became familiar with aquatic insect activity and the best tackle for area waters, and developed seasonal fly-fishing techniques. Now Craig was creating fly patterns based on his local water experiences. John Harder recalls Craig tying thousands of flies for the Orvis Company in those days.

At the end of the decade, Craig was guiding for Bud Lilly in addition to tying flies for the shop. But in his and Jackie's minds was the beginning of a new business. They planned and organized that business as the 1970s ended and named it Blue Ribbon

Craig and Jackie Mathews opened Blue Ribbon Flies in 1980 after serving the city of West Yellowstone in law enforcement and exploring regional waters, and Craig tying an almost countless number of elegant flies and guiding. (Courtesy Terry Middleton)

Charlie Brooks, perhaps the most prolific writer on waters around West Yellowstone, was a unique personality equally famed for the number of fly patterns he created to simulate regional aquatic life-forms. In later years he willingly and enjoyably shared his fly-fishing expertise with anyone interested. (Bob Jacklin collection) ▶

Flies, inspired by the blue-ribbon trout streams surrounding them. Jackie designed their logo that would become so well known in the fly-fishing world.

For more than a decade, Charlie Brooks could claim at least one hundred days fishing each year, 85 percent of this time presenting nymph patterns. About this time Gracie Brooks wrote an article for *Flyfisher* magazine titled "I Married a Brook Trout," a delightful account of the life a spouse could expect if married to an intense fly fisher. Local shops and fly-fishing schools sought Charlie out to teach fishing. By the end of the decade, thousands of his flies had been sold from area fly shops.

Charlie's *Larger Trout for the Western Fly Fisherman* appeared in 1970. Here he presents a collection of more-or-less general thoughts and offerings ranging from presentation of fly types, stream character, equipment selection, aquatic insects, and the effects of weather. His *Nymph Fishing for Larger Trout*, with superb illustrations by Dave Whitlock, was published early in 1976. His discussions on conservation, destined to become more important later, emerge here. Late in 1976 came *The Trout and the Stream*, in which he discusses in more detail the relationship between trout and stream and methods of nymph fishing. His release of three major books in such a short period of time has no equivalent in fly-fishing literature to date. From these books a following emerges, and magazines present several articles, mostly excerpts from his books. He is now the literary spokesman for West Yellowstone, its first nationally recognized writer. It is Charlie's literary shining hour.

Charlie was approachable, but difficult. In 1974 a change came to his life. He suffered a major heart attack, so severe that almost overnight he lost nearly seventy pounds. Recovery meant much-reduced wading in cold regional waters. He still fished, but not with past vigor. Increasingly he became absorbed in conservation and the history of the region's waters. In 1976 he along with Bud Lilly, Ron Marcoux, Dan Bailey, and others formed the Montana Trout Foundation with the goal of preserving trout resources.

Charlie's personality mellowed as the decade wound down. He became more personable and humorous, while remaining approachable. In 1979 *The Living River*, an ode to the Madison River, was released. Certainly, his books and articles increased the flow of fly-fishing traffic into the region, and as offered by Bud Lilly in *A Trout's Best Friend*, promoted some controversy. Thus through Charlie's books and Swisher and Richards's *Selective Trout*, the waters surrounding West Yellowstone climbed to their pinnacle of fame.

A new outdoor literature facet, *Fly Fisherman* magazine, appeared in 1969, with fly fishing its only subject. It promoted the Greater Yellowstone region's fly fishing in almost every issue. Other magazines followed, and eventually overenthusiastic articles brought Bud Lilly to comment on the increase in the size of fish in the area brought on by writer exaggerations.

CHAPTER 8

1980–1990: AN INTERNATIONAL REPUTATION GAINED

Broadscale support for the preservation of the Greater Yellowstone region's fisheries matured during the 1980s. The diminishing quality of coldwater fisheries across the country was behind this acceptance. For West Yellowstone, at the center of the growing regional fly-fishing industry, the 1980s would be a decade of changes.

In 1983 the park issued nearly 168,000 free fishing permits. This was down from 220,000 in 1978, which was attributed to new stringent regulations. However, as public attitudes moved to favor conservation, the number of permits issued increased. Surveys also revealed that angler satisfaction climbed through the decade

Once the realm of grayling, cutthroat trout, and Rocky Mountain whitefish, the Madison River now offers brown and rainbow trout with an occasional brook trout. There are many Yellowstone Park walk-in approaches to the river from its origin at the Gibbon-Firehole confluence downstream to its exit at Baker's Hole. (John Juracek photo)

This view looking east reveals how close the fires of 1988 came to West Yellowstone. A ride into the Barns Holes skirts the western edge of the fires. Nearly three-quarters of the land in the Madison River drainage was burned. (Public domain)

and revealed that fish size and catch rates also increased. Further research revealed that park waters were being maintained close to their hosting capacity for salmonids.

In 1983 the most comprehensive book yet addressing the park's coldwater fisheries, *Fresh Water Wilderness* by John Varley and Paul Schullery, beautifully illustrated by Michael Simon, was released, furthering public interest. A Montana study completed around mid-decade found another indication of esteem for a wild trout fishery. This study indicated that the average angler expenditure per trip to the region was about $100. With 320,000 estimated trips per year to area waters, and using the $100 average, an annual income of about $32 million came from enjoying its wild fishery.

The 1988 Yellowstone Park fires were the most damaging event of the decade. No wildfire event of this scale had taken place within the park in recorded history, and human management was its cause. For about a century, policy was to control fires for maintaining scenery. Doing so seemed good business, but a huge tinderbox accumulated. A fire began along the west boundary of the park and spread east. By the time the fires ebbed, about 800,000 acres had burned.

Seventy percent of the Madison River drainage burned. Early in the next decade, technical observations revealed that salmonid populations in the Madison were stable throughout the decade, even with the fire. After years of selected closures and restrictions, the size of trout in the Montana reach of the Madison River increased.

Some of these restrictions remain in place today. Montana, however, keeps the reach of the Madison above Hebgen to the park boundary open to sustenance fishing for salmonids. Whether this depletes much of the autumn run has not been determined. Regardless, the Madison River remains perhaps the most visited stream in the region.

The spectacular angling opportunities surrounding West Yellowstone wove their magic on the Federation of Fly Fishers as the new decade began. When the federation expressed interest in moving its headquarters to town and establishing a museum, West Yellowstone donated land just east of the Union Pacific depot for the buildings. The federation commenced fundraising for the complex that was to house the International Fly-Fishing Center (IFFC) and held its 1981 conclave at the convention center.

Spirits were high, with offices, casting ponds, and a museum being planned. President Jimmy Carter, fly-fishing in the area, took part in the ground-breaking ceremonies. He and his wife Rosalyn borrowed float tubes from Bob Jacklin, who wrote their fishing licenses. With two Secret Service agents in tow, they fished Hebgen Reservoir with Bob during the August gulper activity. Rosalyn caught the only trout during the trip.

Major television networks provided national coverage for the 1981 conclave. The 1982 and 1983 conclaves followed in the convention center.

By now efforts to acquire funding for the complex had failed, and the project seemed in jeopardy. It was possible that the FFF might leave town. Seeing that such a loss would have a negative economic impact, the city council, of which Cal Dunbar and Bob Jacklin were members, made a proposal on Bob's suggestion.

Joan Wulff fishing the Madison River. A premier fly caster and fly-casting instructor, Joan fished all of the area's major streams during her West Yellowstone visits. Personable and considerate, she was always welcome. (Bob Jacklin collection)

Bud Lilly contracted Dave Whitlock to supply flies for the Trout Shop, and his flies graced the shop's catalog for many years. Dave also became a fly-fishing fixture during FFF Conclaves from the 1980s forward. (Bruce Staples collection)

Bob Jacklin's shop at the location previously occupied by the Pat Barnes Tackle Shop on Canyon Avenue. The shop suffered a propane explosion in February 1990. (Bob Jacklin collection) ▶

The convention center stood vacant much of the year. By hosting the FFF offices and museum, much of the building would have a continuous purpose as well as be maintained and heated. So for a dollar a year and agreement to heat and maintain the building, the town offered the convention center to house the IFFC. The city library and offices remained there, and events such as local high school graduation ceremonies continued to be held. The FFF accepted, and during its 1984 conclave held dedication ceremonies at the convention center. Jan Dunbar gave a fascinating verbal account of its history. In 1984 Bud Lilly was appointed the first IFFC director, and Ralph Moon the museum curator.

During the decade, the federation faithfully maintained much of the building through the efforts of Lorenzo "Buck" Goodrich, a stalwart proponent for maintaining ties between the FFF and West Yellowstone. The federation held conclaves in their

Author Sylvester Nemes, renowned for promoting soft-hackle fly patterns, fished waters around West Yellowstone and for decades participated in fly-fishing events held in town. Syl openly shared information on presenting these fly patterns. (Bruce Staples collection)

Ralph Moon was the lead curator for the Federation of Fly Fishers' (now Fly Fishers International) museum in its first location, West Yellowstone's Union Pacific dining hall. Ralph was also instrumental in bringing several annual FFF Conclaves to town. (Courtesy Ralph Moon) ▶

new home in 1985, 1987, and 1989. Buck chaired or cochaired the first two of these and was a major factor in the last.

A significant retailing addition resulted from this series of FFF conclaves in the 1980s. Arrick Swanson came from Albuquerque, New Mexico, with his family to enjoy some of the great regional fishing. As a youth he had camped and fly-fished small New Mexico streams with his father, Ken, and by 1974 had entered fly tying. Through Charlie Brooks's literature, he began studying aquatic insects to learn their life-cycle behavior and to create fly patterns that would best simulate them. With family members he came to fly-fish West Yellowstone–area waters and to attend the 1980 FFF Conclave. Here he learned even more about the town's fly-fishing industry.

As a teenager in 1982, Arrick began tying commercially through Arrick's Fishing Flies, operating out of his family's Albuquerque home. By the late 1980s he would leave home to live in West Yellowstone and work seasonally for Bob Jacklin. A Montana licensed guide, Arrick guided during summers and tied flies in the winter, an oft-repeated sequence for many persons aspiring to enter the local fly-fishing industry.

By 1993, with his father Ken partnering by providing financial backing and office management, he opened Arrick's Fly Shop. Its first location was in town across from the old high school on Madison Avenue. Not long after, the Swansons moved the shop across the street. Arrick began guiding out of the shop that year, while Ken ran the shop. They also began a long record of contracting fly tiers, although Arrick continued tying flies for the shop. In 1999 Arrick and Ken moved the shop to its current

During his high school and college years, Charles Barnes worked summers in the Pat Barnes Tackle Shop. It was common for shops in town to employ student family members to help operations. Charles's duties included guiding clients on area waters, and through this he became an authority on seasonal selection of waters to visit and an advocate for salmonid conservation. (Courtesy Charles Barnes)

Canyon Street location. It is now a major player in the West Yellowstone fly-fishing retail scene, offering complete fly-fishing services.

By 1980, it had been a thirty-four-year run for the Pat Barnes Tackle Shop. Pat, just past seventy years of age as the decade started, still relished the unfolding of the fly-fishing season. Now he and Sig could see there were places left to visit and things to do beyond their business. They had been approached in the 1970s about selling the business and declined, but now retiring looked attractive.

When Bob Jacklin offered to buy their business, including inventory, they accepted his offer in 1982. Bob would continue Pat's mail-order and wholesale businesses. Some of Pat's guides would work for Bob, and Pat himself would do the same on occasion. Pat and Sig remained active in the local fly-fishing culture, to which they had contributed so much.

Now Pat had time to fulfill one of his goals. He had always enjoyed presenting hopper patterns to trout, and so began putting into action his thoughts for a hopper pattern display to commemorate this appreciation. The display became a reality later in the decade, with about 120 patterns featured. Pat's son Charles now owns this display.

Arrick Swanson and his father Ken began Arrick's Fly Shop in 1993 at a Madison Avenue location. In time they moved to this Canyon Street location, now a full-service fly shop. (Courtesy Bruce Staples)

Bob Jacklin's shop in winter. Not only are winters extreme in West Yellowstone, but fly-fishing business dwindles to a slow pace. This is the time of year when town fly-fishing icons are on the show circuit, touting the superb fishing the upcoming season will offer. (Bob Jacklin collection)

Bob Jacklin was now in the forefront of regional retailers advocating catch-and-release and the protection of the regional fisheries' habitat. Thus his business began its ascent to world renown.

Bob also had become a cog in the West Yellowstone business community, serving as president of the town chamber of commerce in the mid-1970s and on the city council from 1982 to 1989. His "Beer Float Trip" of the 1970s and early 1980s was a celebration of fishing in the area. Its purpose was to take local business leaders down the Madison for a day of relaxation and camaraderie. On occasion good fishing was experienced.

Besides business, music, and fly-fishing acumen, Bob had other talents, including taxidermy. When Bud Lilly observed that the preserved Yellowstone Park record lake trout needed repair, he recommended that Bob be tasked with the job. That trout, a forty-two-pound behemoth taken from Heart Lake, originally was preserved in the 1930s. Restored by Bob, it resides in the park's Fishing Bridge Visitor Center.

The years 1981 and 1982 would see other major changes in West Yellowstone fly shop ownership and employees. Greg Lilly left the Trout Shop in 1981 to attend the University of Washington. Jim Danskin retired and sold his shop to Doug Miller out of Denver, who renamed it the Artful Angler. Brad Richey, who guided for Bud Lilly in 1978 and 1979, and Dan Hull, who also guided for Bud, managed the shop. Brad guided on area waters, beginning a stellar record for knowing how to approach these waters. Brad and Dan departed the Artful Angler in 1981 and began Madison River Outfitters. The Artful Angler closed.

Rick Welle would become a long-tenured guide for Brad and Dan. Madison River Outfitters was first located in a custom log building on the west side of Canyon Avenue. Retail business expanded to include outdoor wear and equipment as well as several renowned fly-fishing tackle lines. Guide service business also increased. In 1988 Brad and Dan acquired property on the east side of Canyon Street and moved to that location and expanded the shop.

Jane and Bud Niess had run the Slide Inn since 1974. Now their daughter Nancy and her husband Kevin Conlan took over operations. Ross Merigold still made the Slide Inn the base of his guiding operations. He lived at the inn during fishing season to enjoy the nearby river and during non-fishing times to create fly patterns suitable for fishing there. With uncommon generosity he shared his fishing experiences with others.

In 1980 the Woodstream Corporation bought the Fenwick Rod Company. The fly-fishing school soon closed, with Bob Kelly the last manager. The Clock family offered some former school land for subdivision, but retained most of the ponds and the school buildings. Famed fly tier Gary LaFontaine, a rising star in the fly-fishing world, came to test local waters. Some of Gary's first writings, appearing in *Fly Fisherman* magazine in the early 1980s, described his experiences on the Yellowstone and Madison Rivers. The spring edition of that magazine featured Ernie Schwiebert's second Firehole River article. In addition to her Nine Quarter Circle Ranch fly-fishing school, Maggie Merriman conducted free Saturday-evening casting lessons in town beginning in the mid-1980s. Bob Jacklin was doing the same on Sunday evenings and continues to do so.

In 1980 Bud and Pat Lilly's daughter Annette left with her husband Barry Schaplow to manage his family ranch, and son Mike was on the way to being an attorney. Bud and Pat finalized their decision to sell the shop and related businesses. In 1982 Fred Terwilliger and Jim Bonnet became the new owners, with Bud staying nearby to advise,

The Parade Rest Ranch has a colorful history as well a lengthy record of hosting dignitaries, famed fly fishers, politicians, corporate executives, and media icons. To this day it offers comfortable accommodations, fishing guide services, and a fly-fishing school. (Bruce Staples collection)

Greg Lilly, Bud and Pat's eldest child, built his own reputation as a knowledgeable and gentlemanly guide, teacher, and fly-fishing icon. After leaving the Trout Shop, he went on to establish other fly-fishing industry businesses. (Bob Jacklin collection)

meet customers, and help during the transition. Operating the shop and succeeding Bud, however, did not work out. In 1987 the business would pass on to Jim Criner, a former Boise State University head football coach. Bud, now living in Bozeman, remained active in West Yellowstone fly-fishing circles. Almost immediately upon retirement, Bud and Pat Lilly formed their Western Rivers Club for keeping in touch with friends. Their son Greg got back into the fly-fishing world as a partner in the River's Edge in Bozeman with Dave and Lynn Corcoran; both Corcorans had guided for Bud during the 1970s. Greg stayed there until 1988, then left to begin Greg Lilly's Fly-Fishing Adventures in Orange County, California. He was now the only family member in the fly-fishing retail world.

Another shop of legend, Blue Ribbon Flies, began business on Canyon Street in West Yellowstone for the 1980 season. Here Craig and Jackie Mathews wholesaled primarily flies, with local shops and outdoor corporations being major customers. They employed as many as thirty tiers at a time. One, Nick Nicklas, began tying for them in 1983 and continued to do so for decades. Included among Blue Ribbon Flies tiers were some physically challenged persons recommended by the State of Montana. Craig still guided for Bud Lilly in those days and continued to supply the Trout Shop, along with other local shops, with elegant fly patterns. When President Jimmy Carter came to town in 1981 with fly fishing in mind, Bud appointed Craig to be his guide. That same year Blue Ribbon Flies released their first mail-order catalog. About four hundred copies of this first issue, featuring fly patterns for various water types, were mailed to prospective customers.

As with so many others who would become a major part of the West Yellowstone fly-fishing community, John Juracek, a degreed fisheries biologist, arrived from outside the area. He had finished working for the Wyoming Game and Fish Department, but had seasonally fished waters around town since the mid-1970s. As with Craig, he brought an ability to tie elegant and impressive flies. In May 1982 John moved to town and became a tier for Blue Ribbon Flies, marking the beginning of a fruitful twenty-year partnership with Craig and Jackie that would result in famous fly patterns, coauthored magazine articles and books, and the making of Blue Ribbon Flies into a fly-fishing industry household name. Increased business resulted from catalog distribution and a growing reputation of Blue Ribbon Flies for product quality. This led to expanding the size of the shop to house employees and enlarging operations in 1984.

Jack Gartside began associating with the shop late in 1980. Eventually, through Craig's and Jackie's hospitality, he resided in Blue Ribbon Flies' basement during fishing seasons. With Craig he began the movement to post point of origin of flies sold in the shop. The idea caught on across the fly-fishing industry, proclaiming "Made in America." Gartside had relied on others for transportation, but now received an elderly Volkswagen van from Craig. He customized it with his own touch of paintings and dolls hanging in the windows. Sight of the van proclaimed that Jack Gartside had arrived.

Then, with encouragement from the likes of the L.L.Bean company, Nick Lyons, and John Harder, then with the Orvis Company, Blue Ribbon Flies entered the retail world in 1984 and became a year-round business. Each year business expanded, with Craig, Jackie, and John increasingly becoming associated with regional fly fishing. They came to realize the need to protect and preserve the Greater Yellowstone area's coldwater fisheries. Not for business purposes alone had Don Martinez, Bud Lilly,

Pat Barnes, Jim Danskin, and Bob Jacklin traveled down the same conservation road. Clearly the region held the best remaining coldwater fisheries in the country, and now they cried for protection. Craig was a member of the Southwest Montana Fly-Fishers beginning early in the 1980s. He and Jackie took part in the formation of the West Yellowstone Flyfishers, also in the early 1980s.

The 1980s would be a decade of sorrows with the passing of several West Yellowstone fly-fishing personalities, more than in any decade to date and to follow. The first of these was perhaps the most regretted. Pat Lilly had been ill with respiratory complications for a few years. There were moments of hope, but her battle with lung cancer ended on April 14, 1982, in Bozeman. "She had been the family's directing spirit," Bud declared in *A Trout's Best Friend*. Loved by all, she was the rock of the business, managing through thick and thin, doing finances, keeping the books, ordering stock, and evaluating merchandise. During the latter years of operating the business, the shop's art gallery was her special passion. Accolades for Pat rolled in from all over. In town, the IFFC dedicated the Pat Lilly Memorial Art Gallery. She was laid to rest in a Manhattan, Montana, cemetery. As expressed in *A Trout's Best Friend*, her stone held the epitaph "Our Strength."

Within six weeks of Pat's death, perhaps Montana's most widely known fly-fishing personality, Dan Bailey, died. Soon after his passing, Montana governor Ted Schwinden proclaimed August 14 as Dan Bailey Fishing Day. All West Yellowstone fly-fishing retailers operating after mid-century had ties to Bailey, whether through merchandising, exchanging fly-fishing information, or conservation matters.

Vernon (Pete) Hidy, who attended FFF Conclaves during the early 1980s and fished area waters, died in 1983. Rae Servatius died in 1984. Her passing left Pat Barnes, Cal Dunbar, and Wally Eagle the best sources of information in the area on Don

Dan Bailey's Tackle and Fly Shop in Livingston, Montana, is a hallowed business in fly-fishing lore since 1938. From it Bailey supplied West Yellowstone and surrounding areas for decades with quality flies, fly-tying materials, fishing tackle, and equipment for resale. (Bruce Staples collection)

Martinez. The mantle of connection to Martinez passed on to Bob Jacklin, who purchased Pat Barnes's business.

In 1984 Don Hopkins passed away. A lumber industry executive who frequented waters around the region, Don was generous, conservation minded, and knowledgeable, and was held in great esteem because of his direct involvement in conservation and fly-fishing basics. Ray Bergman named the Hopkins Variant in his honor and praises him in *Trout*. Pat Barnes also praises him in *Ribbons of Blue*, and Bud Lilly does the same in *A Trout's Best Friend*. Hopkins mentored Wally Eagle in dry fly-fishing in the early 1940s. Bob Jacklin remembers him as a fly-fishing gentleman.

The following year, Jack Anderson passed away. Under his watch as superintendent, modern fishing regulations and enlightened fisheries management became permanent in Yellowstone National Park. Dave Bascom died in 1986. His greatest contribution was to remind us that fly fishing was meant to be fun.

Charlie Brooks had not been in the best of health since his 1974 heart attack. Now diagnosed with cancer, he published on. Charlie had mellowed much in the early 1980s. Gone was the confrontational manner and contentious spirit. He still defended his theories and experiences, but now with humor, consideration, and diplomacy.

To Cal Dunbar goes much of the credit for making West Yellowstone the fly-fishing center it is today. He participated in local government and for decades worked tirelessly to bring angling events and renowned personalities to town. A longtime grocery retailer in West Yellowstone, he and wife Jan preserved much of the town's fly-fishing history. (Courtesy Cal Dunbar)

Fishing Yellowstone Waters was released in 1983, describing Charlie's Yellowstone National Park fly-fishing experiences. In terms of fishing available waters in the park, the book is limited to those close to the beaten path. Only in discussions on the Lewis River and Slough Creek does he delve into more-remote waters, which Craig Mathews helped him approach. But the waters Charlie discusses are addressed in his usual thorough, enjoyable, and knowledgeable manner. One can see in this book that a bit of the old confrontational streak remains, but for good reason. Firehole River discussion is centered on his observation of warming waters from geothermal inflows and their impacts on aquatic life, and he blasts park fisheries management for not researching these impacts. Time has proven Charlie right, as the increased influx of geothermal waters has compromised the numbers of large resident trout and all but eliminated some of the major aquatic insect emergences of old.

Next came Charlie's *The Henry's Fork*, released in 1986, paralleling what he offered for the Madison in *The Living River*. He was considering doing the same for the Yellowstone River, but knew he was running out of time. In any case, the information that Charlie passed on about regional streams remains the most detailed available and will never be obsolete as long as these waters do not change in character and quality.

Charlie died on October 30, 1986, at the age of sixty-five. For the fly-fishing world, his relatively early passing is tragic because with a decade or two more of life, he would have made more contributions. The same could be said for Don Martinez, Bob Carmichael, and Vint Johnson, all of whom died before reaching sixty years of age.

Next to pass away was the architect of Yellowstone National Park as we know it. Horace Albright died in 1987 at age ninety-seven. Few had matched him as a visionary and effective administrator. He was instrumental in the formation of the National Park Service, and oversaw establishment of much of the basic infrastructure we see today in Yellowstone National Park. Albright Falls, on a Bechler River tributary, now preserves his name.

As the end of the decade approached, one more passing rocked the fly-fishing world. Ross Merigold died falling facedown into the Madison River near the Slide Inn on September 9, 1989, while fishing with friends.

Bud Lilly's life took a new turn late in 1985. Annette, Greg, and Mike were away pursuing careers. He needed a consuming interest and found it through the IFFC, where he met Esther Simon, a FFF executive. Their working relationship grew deeper, and they married in October 1985. Bud now had a new family and the encouragement needed to stay involved in conserving regional coldwaters. With the IFFC in operation, he channeled his efforts into the Greater Yellowstone Coalition, founded in 1983. It was also time to publish his fly-fishing experiences. With Paul Schullery he

This plate established on the south bank just above the Reynolds Junction bridge commemorates Ross Merigold's love and dedication for the Madison River. Ross's knowledge of fly fishing the Madison below Quake Lake and his willingness to share it is legendary. (Bruce Staples collection)

produced *A Trout's Best Friend*, published in 1988. That same year, Bud was honored as *Fly Rod & Reel* magazine's "Guide of the Year."

The influence of Swisher and Richards's *Selective Trout* on fly patterns matured in this decade. In West Yellowstone fly bins featured the mayfly life-cycle patterns demanded by visiting fly fishers. Present were emergers, stillborns, cripples, and spinners, all in forms laying low on or near the surface. The same variety held true for caddisflies, with larva, pupa, emerger, adult, and spent patterns featured. Then came a turn for midges, with pupa, adult, and even mating cluster patterns being offered. Even damselflies, craneflies, and terrestrial insects did not escape attention.

Things were simpler for the large stoneflies, with nymph and adult patterns having been offered since the 1940s. Sofa Pillows, Bird's Stonefly variations, Jugheads for adults, Bitch Creek and Montana Nymphs, Soufals, and Brooks Stones still ruled the roost, but gave ground to Bob Jacklin's adult stonefly patterns and Blue Ribbon Flies' natural adult and nymph stonefly patterns. Fading from the scene were Pott patterns, Tony Sivey's Bar-X patterns, and George Grant's artfully woven stoneflies. The same happened to Don Martinez's mayfly patterns and many of the Catskill patterns. But as John Juracek points out, these new patterns filled gaps in the availability of imitations for life cycles of important trout food forms. Contributions made by John and Craig Mathews to the days' ever-expanding array of fly patterns were featured in their book *Fly Patterns of Yellowstone*, released in 1987.

Fly-fishing literature played a huge role in bringing enthusiasts to the area during the 1980s. Writers such as Dave Whitlock, Ernie Schwiebert, and Charlie Brooks contributed much. Dave attended all FFF Conclaves held in West Yellowstone during the decade to conduct fly-tying demonstrations and fly-fishing clinics. Charlie's books bridge the gap of not only describing fly patterns, but also offering details on usage. In many cases he identified specific places where his patterns are effective. This approach brought fly fishers to the area, but created tension as relative crowding resulted at times in cherished fishing locations. Magazine articles promoting such fishing locations did the same.

As the next decade reached its midpoint, a new media, the personal computer and the World Wide Web, arrived. Advertisements and information that could be placed on the web had another huge impact on the local fly-fishing industry.

CHAPTER 9

1990–2000: INTENSE CONSERVATION EFFORTS REQUIRED

In 1996 the US Fish & Wildlife Service relinquished all its fisheries-related activities to the National Park Service. Cooperation and proper application of resources by all agencies was needed because of the ecological peril looming in Yellowstone Lake. First came verification of the lake trout population. Surveys showed that the population was widespread and that spawning was concentrated in West Thumb. Next came investigations that found that the lake trout came from a different body of water.

Somewhat distant from West Yellowstone compared to upper Madison River drainage waters, Yellowstone Park's northeast corner waters nevertheless attract fly fishers from town. Increased tourist traffic dictates a long day of travel beginning almost at first light to reach these beautiful waters in a timely manner. The Lamar River, approachable and scenic, is one of these streams. (John Juracek photo)

Like so many investigations in this era of increasing technical excellence, scientific investigation determined that the source of these fish was not Yellowstone Lake. It worked by analyzing the lake trout inner ear structure that grows like a tree ring. This structure is principally formed of calcium carbonate but also contains strontium, which chemically behaves much like calcium but is much less abundant. Elemental analysis was performed on lake trout inner ears to observe the calcium-to-strontium ratio. Assuming no change occurs in this ratio, it is characteristic of a given surrounding. If the ratio remains constant throughout the inner ear structure and is about the same as the environment from which the fish came, it is likely that the fish has spent its life in a given locale. If, however, the early-life calcium-to-strontium ratio is different from that of its locale later in life, this is strong evidence that the fish was born and spent time in a different locale.

Such an anomaly found in the inner ear structure of some lake trout taken from Yellowstone Lake suggests that the fish spent the earlier part of life elsewhere. This inner ear ratio during early life is nearly the same as the ratio typical of Lewis Lake lake trout. Thus there is technical validity that these fish were transplanted from Lewis Lake, but it does not totally rule out that the lake trout could have been present in Yellowstone Lake for a much longer time.

Fish are the main staple of the lake trout's diet, and juvenile cutthroat trout tend to reside in deep water, exactly where lake trout reside. Adult cutthroat trout tend to cruise the shallows in search of food. Here they are more vulnerable to predation by birds and other animals than lake trout dwelling almost entirely at depths. Lake trout spawn at medium depths and are thus out of reach compared to cutthroat trout, which spawn in the springtime in tributaries and are thus much more available to predators.

As a seasonally abundant food form diminishes, the numbers of birds and other animals that prey on them must also diminish. Regardless of the origin, the presence of lake trout in Yellowstone Lake is a potential disaster for the segment of the ecosystem depending on cutthroat trout as a major food form.

By 1995 another potential peril to Yellowstone Park salmonids was confirmed as the New Zealand mud snail was observed in the Madison River drainage within the park. It was found upstream of the Firehole River's Kepler Cascade and above Gibbon Falls. Mud snails are transportable by birds and other animals and even on the clothing of anglers. They displace native food forms on which salmonids rely, and appear indigestible by them. As if there were not enough peril to Yellowstone cutthroat trout resulting from the presence of lake trout and the New Zealand mud snail, whirling disease was identified in 1998 in Yellowstone cutthroat residing in the lake near the Fishing Bridge area and in lower Pelican Creek.

Yes, natural threats to the park fisheries have emerged, but the peril does not stop here. Man himself seems to refuse to recognize the sanctity of Yellowstone National Park. Even in the early 1990s, dams were being proposed within it; one was proposed for the Yellowstone River just below Yellowstone Lake. In addition, geothermal drilling was proposed in the Firehole River drainage. Superficially valid attempts will continue for narrow economic gain that will negatively impact the quality of the Greater Yellowstone region's salmonid fisheries.

Nevertheless, fishing in park waters during this decade resulted in the best returns yet documented, with the restrictive management policies begun a few decades before having borne fruit. The successes and errors in fisheries management of and perils to park fisheries are summarized in *Yellowstone Fishes* by John D. Varley and Paul Schullery. Released in 1998, this book was an update of *Freshwater Wilderness* published by the same authors fifteen years earlier.

Adjacent Montana drainages would experience some of the perils that Yellowstone National Park fisheries were undergoing. In 1994 whirling disease was discovered in the Madison River below Quake Lake. It appears to have originated in hatcheries and particularly infects rainbow and cutthroat trout as well as their hybrids. It is spread by interfacing hosts, with pelicans being particularly suspect. Such a dire discovery gained national alarm and attention for the river. The rainbow trout population in middle and lower reaches quickly plummeted by about 75 percent due to this malady. Thus this part of the Madison would become mostly a brown trout fishery for the remainder of the decade, when rainbows would begin to return to their former numbers.

Predictably, whirling disease is considered to be the major threat to Montana's cutthroat and rainbow trout populations. It was also found in the Gallatin River drainage, mainly in the West Fork and East Gallatin River. As a result of this malady in so many popular and economically important rivers, the concerned public formed the Whirling Disease Foundation. Based in Bozeman, Montana, the foundation has the goal of raising resources to fight and eradicate the disease.

As if this were not enough peril for the Madison River, the New Zealand mud snail was identified there in 1994. Like the whirling disease parasite, it appears to be

Lakeview, Montana, is headquarters for the Red Rock Lakes National Wildlife Refuge, which hosts quality fisheries including Odell and Red Rock Creeks and the legendary Widow's Pool. No services are offered at Lakeview, but information on travel and habitat conditions are generously given. (Bruce Staples collection)

transportable by other life forms, including man. It is relatively new in our country, thus little research has been performed on it. But information is accumulating, and the fly-fishing public has become active in efforts to control it.

Certainly whirling disease in the Madison River was the major event in Montana coldwater fisheries during the decade. It was serious enough to obscure the fact that westslope cutthroat, the original native trout of the river, could be found naturally residing in only the upper reaches of a few tributaries: Cabin, Hyde, and Standard Creeks.

In Montana's Centennial Valley, native grayling remained in Lower and Upper Red Rock Lakes in the Red Rock Lakes National Wildlife Refuge. These fish continued to travel up suitable tributary streams to spawn during springtime, then returned to the lakes in late summer. These streams, principally Odell and Red Rock Creeks, also functioned as rearing waters for juvenile grayling that would descend to replenish stocks in the lakes. Native westslope cutthroat trout were gone from waters in the valley, replaced by Yellowstone cutthroat trout originally obtained by Montana Fish, Wildlife & Parks from Yellowstone Park hatcheries. This acquisition was likely less expensive than trying to maintain the native westslope cutthroat population. Refuge administration continued efforts to acquire surrounding private lands and recondition them to become more suitable for migratory waterfowl habitat and secondarily for waters within to be more suited to host salmonids. Efforts also intensified in the decade to better preserve the refuge's coldwater fisheries, particularly for grayling that were diminishing so quickly elsewhere.

By now the waters around West Yellowstone had become mainly destinations for middle-class anglers. As reliable air travel expanded, affluent and celebrity anglers

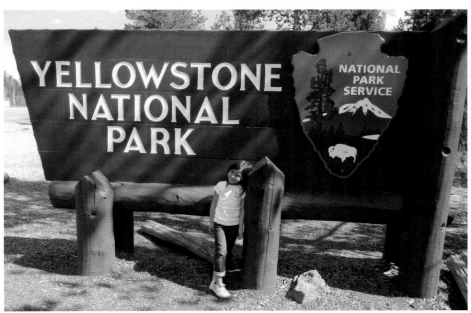

The Yellowstone Park West Entrance sign proclaims to the world that West Yellowstone is the park front door. At times lines of visiting traffic can extend back to the Canyon Street–Yellowstone Avenue intersection. (Bruce Staples collection)

increasingly tended toward far-flung locations. Exceptions would be those well-to-do persons who maintained residences in the region. Angling pressure almost anywhere on the West Gallatin River had increased significantly due to the growth of the Big Sky Resort that spread along Highway 191. Dave Whitlock, who back in the 1960s enjoyed solitude while fishing regional waters, predicted that regional waters would experience a visitation boom. His observations were coming true. What would be the effect of crowded conditions on the quality of a fly-fishing visit?

As the decade began, another change in the local fly-fishing industry was brought about by removal of the statute requiring a base of operations within Montana. This meant that after obtaining required permits for public land and specific waters, anyone, resident or nonresident, could declare themselves a guide. Most visiting anglers, however, turned to the nationally advertised shops in town to obtain reputable guide services.

None of these changes, however, would eventually be as far-reaching as those begun in this decade by the personal computer and the internet. The advent of electronic media revealed contributions to Montana's economy by those in its fly-fishing industry and increased efforts to recognize these individuals as well as those who contributed to its fly-fishing subculture. Fly fishing adds significantly to the state's economy, so such persons are readily honored.

This was a basis for honoring the state's fly-fishing pioneers. Former governor Ted Schwinden had established Dan Bailey Day back in 1982. The 1990s were about four months old when Governor Stan Stevens declared that Saturday, April 28, would be Pat Barnes Day. Across Montana people were encouraged to go fishing on this day. It was a fitting tribute to the man known in the Montana fly-fishing community as "The Old Pro."

At age eighty, the Old Pro could be seen fishing the Madison, Missouri, and other regional rivers. His family had operated the Pat Barnes Tackle Shop for thirty-six years, the longest tenure of a family to do so in West Yellowstone up to that time. Even beyond the boundaries of the state, he was still called on to relate incidents in his rich and lengthy fly-fishing experience.

Pat continued to tie flies, notably those that made the name Waterborn Flies revered. At first the fly patterns he and Sig created seemed of a smaller scale, but the Sofa Pillow became perhaps the most popular adult stonefly pattern of the era. The number of variations it fostered is living proof of its renown, and it remains in demand.

Pat's contributions of great impact included introducing the drift boat and being an ardent conservationist. Few persons had done more to advance the popularity and enjoyment of Montana fly fishing than Pat. More honors came for Pat when the book *Ribbons of Blue* was released in 1997 to honor his contributions to fly fishing. Pat died in Helena on August 29, 1997, at the age of eighty-eight. In his honor, the Missouri River Chapter of Trout Unlimited, based in Helena, changed its name to the Pat Barnes Chapter.

In West Yellowstone another change came about around the middle of the decade with the departure of the FFF office to Bozeman and the IFFC to Livingston. This took place after a successful conclave was held at the convention center in 1991.

It would be the last conclave held in town until 2004. The FFF/IFFC move from West Yellowstone was claimed to be necessary for economic reasons, but

The Union Pacific dining hall. This beautiful building was built to serve meals to tourists arriving on the Yellowstone Branch of the Union Pacific Railroad. Since closing of the branch passenger service, the building has served as the town convention center. (Bob Jacklin collection)

organizational politics played a role. In West Yellowstone the IFFC was not open through the winter months, whereas it would be in Livingston. Thus the move would make it a year-round destination and increase the potential to acquire more funding.

For Bob Jacklin, the decade began on an unexpected note when a propane explosion leveled his shop on the evening of February 12, 1990. That evening Bob was attending a Montana Fish, Wildlife & Parks meeting with Dick Vincent and others at the local high school one block north of his shop. The resulting fire was extinguished by the next day, and merchandise was found blown across the street to the depot and onto the roofs of adjacent buildings.

So on that cold February evening, Bob lost irreplaceable portions of his fly and fly-fishing equipment collections and what would appear to be his livelihood. But being a person with an unusual measure of focus, purpose, and energy, he resolved to be in business for the upcoming season. Within days he gathered his resources, then went with credit card in hand to Bozeman to purchase office and display equipment.

In the months that followed, Bob set up a temporary business in the Horseshoe Café building to be ready for the 1990 season. At the same time, he began efforts to rebuild the shop on Yellowstone Avenue. As a result of his determination and purpose, he was back in business for the 1991 season with a new and larger shop featuring an expanded line of merchandise and a second story featuring a fly tier's loft. The grand opening was held as the Montana angling season began in May of that year.

Almost without missing a beat, Bob's guide service continued through the trying times, then expanded its reputation for excellence as the decade progressed. Bob continued guide services to the Parade Rest Ranch and on occasion to other regional guest ranches. He maintained other activities outside his business, including meeting the increasing demand around the fly-fishing world to present destination

This was the result of a propane explosion in Bob Jacklin's shop on the night of February 12, 1990. Merchandise and structural items were blown across Yellowstone Avenue and onto adjacent buildings. (Bob Jacklin collection)

Bob Jacklin's shop rebuilt after the February 1990 propane explosion and as it appears today. The expanded shop has fly-fishing merchandise on the lower floor. The upper floor is devoted mainly to fly-tying items and activity. (Bob Jacklin collection)

information on Greater Yellowstone fly fishing, to conduct fly-casting clinics, and to take part in prestigious fly-tying events.

Bob never forgot the local fly fisher and continued through the decade with his summertime Sunday-evening free fly-fishing classes at the convention center as well as providing spontaneous instruction to answer fly-tying questions. Neither did he waver in his support of the FFF or in preserving West Yellowstone's fly-fishing heritage. He participated in the FFF's 1991 conclave and was active in the federation throughout the decade, particularly in its fly-tying and fly-casting activities.

Bob's new shop was across Yellowstone Avenue from the convention center and the IFFC, and this location near the West Entrance did much to bring the fly-fishing public from all parts of the world to see the newest shop in town. With increasing business, his wife Sharyn began working in the shop in 1992 and continues to do so. In a manner similar to that of Pat Lilly, she works in the background merchandising, keeping finances and records, and arranging guide services. Bob introduced her to fly fishing, and she became accomplished to the point of advising customers on the purchase of appropriate merchandise and offering advice on what fly patterns to present when and where on area waters.

Supporting conservation organizations was a way of life for West Yellowstone fly-fishing retailers, and Bob Jacklin was no exception. His support for Trout Unlimited continues to this day. When the Madison-Gallatin Wild Trout Fund began as a response to the discovery of whirling disease in the Madison River, he was there to support it. The same happened when the River Network was established as a national organization to understand, protect, and restore rivers around the country, and also to acquire properties that would guarantee public access at useful locations along those rivers.

It was more than good business sense for all West Yellowstone fly-fishing retailers to support efforts to conserve and protect local waters, and it was expected that they would do so by the fly-fishing public they served. The culture of conservation begun by Don Martinez and Scotty Chapman and expanded by Pat Barnes, Bud Lilly, the Eagle family, and Jim Danskin was now for Bob Jacklin, Craig Mathews, John Juracek, Brad Richey, and Arrick Swanson to sustain.

Ever conscious of the need to protect Yellowstone National Park, Blue Ribbon Flies joined the Yellowstone Park Foundation in 1996. Founded to work in concert with the National Park Service to protect the park from commercial and subsistence incursions through the support of individuals, corporations, and other organizations, the foundation works to protect the national park philosophy as well. After serving on the foundation's governing board for nine years, Craig and Jackie Mathews were given emeritus status. In this decade Blue Ribbon Flies also became very active in the Greater Yellowstone Coalition, which addresses protection of the entire Yellowstone ecosystem.

Conservation actions were only one facet of contributions coming from Blue Ribbon Flies. Some information on the behavior of area aquatic insects had been offered in print—for instance, Charlie Brooks had offered detail on such in *The Living River* and *The Henry's Fork*, and Swisher and Richards had made some contributions in *Selective Trout*—but large gaps remained in the subject. Seeing this, Craig and John Juracek collected information from many sources as well as their own experiences and that of their employees and published *Fishing Yellowstone Hatches* in 1992. The book was an in-house effort, and it offered the greatest detail yet under one cover on the behavior of local aquatic insects and their importance to trout. Doctorate-level entomologist Dan Gustafson provided detailed help.

Next to be published through Blue Ribbon Flies was *The Yellowstone Fly-Fishing Guide* by Craig with Clayton Molinaro in 1997. In the format of the guidebooks that were becoming so popular in the fly-fishing industry, it included maps for all waters, hatch charts, and details on accommodations and other services.

As with other renowned fly shops in town, Blue Ribbon Flies provided guide and educational services for area resorts. Its staff also came into demand to discuss the

Over the years Blue Ribbon Flies employed many accomplished fly tiers such as Bucky McCormick. Many went on to establish fly-fishing businesses or direct fly-fishing operations at resorts. (Bruce Staples collection)

Craig Mathews tying at Blue Ribbon Flies. Staff tiers often demonstrated their techniques during business hours. Craig took a turn at the tying bench on occasion and would give the patterns he created to admiring onlookers. (Courtesy Terry Middleton) ▶

wonders of Greater Yellowstone angling and the shop thus created destination programs for the park and southwestern Montana waters. Like West Yellowstone's other famed shops, Blue Ribbon Flies continued to attract famous clients.

At Blue Ribbon Flies, most flies continued to be stocked through in-house tying efforts. This was in the manner begun by Don Martinez and continued by Pat and Sig Barnes and Bob Jacklin. The Lilly family, on the other hand, contracted many of the Trout Shop's flies to renowned tiers and wholesalers, as we have seen. Blue Ribbon Flies still had several persons on its tying staff in the 1990s, and through working closely together, they satisfied demand and offered new patterns. Weekly tying staff brainstorming sessions were unique and fostered creativity.

Some renowned fly fishers were Blue Ribbon Flies customers over the years. Both Craig and John remember well discussing fly-tying techniques with Frank Matarelli, who also offered fly-tying ideas and thoughts on the design of fly-tying tools. Matarelli came from the Bay Area and bought a home in West Yellowstone from which to fish each season. Paul Brown, another schoolteacher and excellent fly tier, participated in and tied flies for the shop until his death in May 1997. His ashes were placed in the Madison River at the Barns Holes.

Bud Lilly stayed in Montana, actively supporting conservation actions. In 1993 his son Greg returned to Montana to accept an R. L. Winston Rod Company sales and marketing position in Twin Bridges. But Greg, possessing his dad's enthusiasm for helping others enjoy fly fishing, wanted to be closer to it, so in 1995 began Greg Lilly's Fly-Fishing Services to offer outfitting, guiding activities, and a fly-fishing school. These activities developed into the Healing Waters Fly-Fishing Lodge, begun in Twin Bridges in 1996. Greg would operate this establishment into the next decade. Not far away in Three Forks, Bud's mother, Violet, had been running a small hotel but died in 1994, so Bud and his wife Esther took it over. With remodeling and marketing it became Bud Lilly's Anglers Retreat in 1995.

Back in West Yellowstone, Jim Criner sold the Trout Shop to Dick Greene and Barbara Klesel in 1994. Greene and Klesel continued all Trout Shop services, including Madison River and Henry's Fork float trips, guided walk-in trips for Yellowstone National Park, and other guiding services on request. Madison River Outfitters expanded to offer various outdoor lines. They also offered guided trips, specializing in drift-boating the Madison River throughout the season and walk-in trips to the Firehole, Madison, and Yellowstone Rivers and special locations in the park on request.

Now the old camaraderie, so evident in the days when Bud Lilly, Pat Barnes, and Jim Danskin were the local icons, returned to the established shops. This feeling

Since the early 1980s, Madison River Outfitters on Canyon Street has offered guide services and quality merchandise for all popular outdoor activities, including fly fishing. (Bruce Staples collection)

was mainly expressed in universal support for conservation actions to sustain local salmonid fisheries. It was obvious to all the local retailers that presenting a united front was more than just good business—it was necessary to preserve quality in area waters, the largest concentration of coldwater fisheries in the country.

The revolution in fly tying that had immersed local fly tiers in the 1980s took a different turn in the 1990s. In the 1980s efforts concentrated on filling gaps in life-cycle stage simulations for aquatic and terrestrial insect food forms, but now efforts centered on introducing new materials and tools. John Juracek, a renowned West Yellowstone participant in these changes, notes that the use of synthetic materials expanded mightily in this decade.

Z-Lon, introduced by Blue Ribbon Flies, is a good example of one of these materials of local origin. It was first created as a rug fiber that would not absorb moisture. But when discontinued by the DuPont Chemical Company, much of it was acquired by Blue Ribbon Flies and would soon come to have many uses in fly tying, from dubbing bodies and forming wings to forming shucks and other body parts for small emerger patterns. It would prove ideal for patterns for low-gradient local waters in reaches of such streams as the Firehole, Gibbon, Lamar, and Madison Rivers and for the numerous stillwaters.

Perhaps the most unlikely material, closed-cell foam, would come to use because of the abundance of waters with higher gradients such as the West Gallatin, the middle Gibbon, and the middle Madison. The first really popular pattern made of this material would be the Blue Ribbon Foam Beetle, a creation of the 1980s. The use of closed-cell foam for such patterns as stoneflies, hoppers, and large attractors began to catch on.

Another material that came into widespread use was Mylar strips of various color. These were added primarily to streamer wings and nymph wing cases. Bill Schiess's Light Olive Crystal, which made use of Mylar chenille, became a particularly favorite damselfly nymph pattern on Henry's Lake, Grebe Lake, and the Graben Lakes.

Books on the use of these new materials would soon follow. *Fishing Yellowstone Hatches* and *Fly Patterns for Yellowstone*, both produced by Blue Ribbon Flies, would feature popular regional flies using these materials. Thus the fly-fishing culture centered in West Yellowstone became a major contributor to the use of synthetic and new natural materials.

CHAPTER 10

2000–PRESENT: A NEW CENTURY

The West Yellowstone fly-fishing industry led in public acceptance of restrictive angling regulations throughout the area. When Montana Fish, Wildlife & Parks (MFW&P) adopted "hoot owl" closures as in-stream water temperatures on certain streams approached lethal levels to salmonids, little objection resulted in the West Yellowstone fly-fishing community. When in 2017 MFW&P required for all anglers an aquatic invasive species (AIS) sticker for a minimal fee, the West Yellowstone angling community accepted this without reservation.

Some concern remains among the local fly-fishing retail community over the apparent decrease in the average size of trout in the Madison River below Quake Lake. Jim Danskin and Bob Jacklin had observed that during the 1950s on into the 1970s the average size of trout in the middle Madison was sixteen inches and now

The Yellowstone River within the park hosts the largest stream-borne population of Yellowstone cutthroat trout on earth. Above the lower falls only this salmonid populates the river. Its population is gradually returning to past numbers as management efforts in the lake above appear to be reducing the number of introduced lake trout. (John Juracek photo)

it is about thirteen inches, despite restrictive regulations. Bob and Jim held concern because due to the number of large fish killed up to the 1960s and the warming climate, the gene pool for large fish may have collapsed to the point where fewer fish with capability to grow large are present.

Montana fisheries management policies now aimed at restoring native salmonids. Beginning in the 1950s, Yellowstone cutthroat were introduced and periodically supplemented in many waters, simply for economic reasons. Their introduction has ceased, and westslope cutthroat, originally native but absent for decades, are now being released on an experimental basis through MFW&P operations.

By 2001, all native salmonids in Yellowstone National Park were subject to catch-and-release regulation. By 2004, 169,000 days were spent fishing in the park, making it more popular than ever, and more visitors entered from West Yellowstone's West Entrance than any other. By the middle of that decade, a catch-and-release regulation was applied to Firehole River brown trout.

However, three potentially devastating conditions emerged. First was the widespread 2007 drought in which water temperatures reached the mid-seventies in many streams. Park fisheries managers temporarily curtailed fishing from early afternoon to early morning, with wide support from the angling public. Summertime drought is common in this region of relatively sparse precipitation, but combined with the two other events described below to which area salmonids would be exposed, the potential for their reduction loomed.

Second, for Yellowstone cutthroat trout inhabiting Yellowstone Lake, the lake trout introduction became disastrous to the park ecology. Thus park fisheries management personnel increased their efforts to physically remove significant numbers of lake trout from the lake. "Judas Fish," which held an implanted radio responder with a trackable signal, were particularly effective in revealing spawning locations. The resulting action is ongoing, with thousands of lake trout removed each year. This removal is the largest nonnative fish removal project in the country, and the lake trout presence is considered to be the most serious threat to park ecology. Time will tell if this action will be effective in returning the lake to its native trout.

The third assault on the park cutthroat trout population is whirling disease. The parasite *Myxobolus cerebralis*, which causes this disease, was first found in Yellowstone Lake cutthroat trout in 1998, particularly its north-side tributaries. Because of this infection, Pelican Creek was closed to fishing in 2003. Infection was also observed in cutthroat in Clear Creek, another major spawning tributary near the north side of the lake. As the decade advanced, infected fish were found in the Yellowstone River as far downstream as Hayden Valley.

These three conditions made the preservation of Yellowstone cutthroat the park fisheries managers' most important project. But there were other items of concern within park waters. A Firehole River rainbow was observed hosting whirling disease, and severe infection has been identified in Cougar Creek. In addition, cuttbow trout have been identified in the waters of Slough Creek's meadows above the campground.

Next in priority for park fisheries managers is the restoration of fluvial native cutthroat trout and Montana grayling through the Native Trout Restoration Program. Conceived in 2010, this program also addresses threats and increases biological monitoring and research on the status of Yellowstone fishes, especially the native salmonids. First Goose and Gooseneck Lakes, in the Firehole River drainage, were treated

Grayling Creek, named for its past salmonid inhabitants, is now a location of a native salmonid reintroduction effort. If these salmonids were to reestablish, fly fishers would have a chance to experience what fishing was like here in the early twentieth century. (Bruce Staples collection)

to remove rainbow trout, then westslope cutthroat were reintroduced. Only in Last Chance Creek of the upper Grayling Creek drainage were westslope cutthroat trout confirmed to exist in park waters. In 2013 the Grayling Creek drainage, excluding Last Chance Creek, was treated to remove all exotic species, then westslope cutthroat trout and fluvial grayling were reintroduced.

Whether or not these introductions have succeeded is uncertain because some of these grayling have been caught in Hebgen Lake, but none have been reported as caught in the creek through 2018. It remains as to whether grayling encountered in the Gibbon River were born there or are escapees from the lakes above. Therefore, research was begun to determine their origin.

Rarer now than grayling within park boundaries, pure westslope cutthroat trout were once the only trout to inhabit the Madison and Gallatin drainages below park barrier waterfalls. Thus sites within these drainages are being explored for westslope cutthroat reintroduction. Upper Cougar Creek is considered by park fisheries biologists to be a reintroduction candidate, and fifteen miles of its reach above where it goes subterranean was poisoned in 2018. The electroshocking program begun in 2015 to remove rainbow and cuttbow hybrids from the Slough Creek meadows is making progress.

With enough information gained, the originally salmonid-free waters of the Gibbon River drainage above Virginia Cascades, including Ice, Grebe, and Wolf Lakes, were poisoned to remove exotic species, and in 2018 these three lakes were stocked with grayling. Plans are in place to poison the river from Virginia Cascades down to Little Gibbon Falls in the near future. Goose Lake in the Firehole River drainage has also been treated to remove nonnative salmonids.

Grebe and Wolf were also stocked with westslope cutthroat. Cascade Lake, also hosting grayling (and Yellowstone cutthroat trout) adjacent to these but in the Yellowstone River drainage, was not treated. All three lakes, being above or near eight thousand feet in elevation, should be climate refuges. This move, considering the popularity of the river and Grebe Lake, caused concern for the loss of excellent fishing for exotic salmonids. However, the possible addition of westslope cutthroat and fluvial grayling to the variety of salmonids for the angler to encounter in Yellowstone National Park is exciting.

In 2001 native salmonids in Yellowstone National Park were placed under a catch-and-release fishing regulation, which was extended to Firehole River brown trout. A five-fish possession limit was placed on all nonnative salmonids in park waters by 2007, with the exception that all Yellowstone Lake lake trout caught must be killed. Likewise, a barbless hook regulation was established for all fishing in park waters. More stretches of the Firehole River became closed to protect geothermal features and to minimize injuries to the general public.

Aquatic invasive species (AIS) could have devastating ecological, economic, and recreational impacts on Yellowstone National Park. Because of the urgent need to prevent these destructive species from entering the park, felt-sole and other fibrous-material-sole waders and boots were banned permanently in 2018. How effective this ban will be

Montana grayling and rainbow trout were introduced into Grebe Lake early in the twentieth century. The lake, as with the rest of the upstream Gibbon River drainage, was recently treated to remove all salmonids as part of the native salmonid reintroduction program. (Public domain)

is questionable because other parts of boots (laces, tongues, and the folds of material) with soles of any material are also potential nesting sites for certain aquatic invasive species. Certainly, this ban has made the West Yellowstone fly-fishing industry alter their wading boot inventories. In addition, all watercraft entering the park can only be launched if they are accompanied by a park boating permit. As of 2018 these craft must also have a Yellowstone Park AIS inspection before launching in park waters.

West Yellowstone greeted the twenty-first century with a subzero morning. By the time warm weather arrived, it was obvious that increased fishing pressure was coming to the park and nearby waters as quality coldwater fisheries outside the Greater Yellowstone diminished. Increased visits meant fly-fishing retailers must build inventories accordingly. The number and ownership of fly-fishing shops established in the 1990s in West Yellowstone remained much the same. Brad Richey became the sole owner of Madison River Outfitters in 2001. Rick Welle guided for the business, retaining his record as the third-longest-serving guide in town, Doug Pope being the second behind Bob Jacklin.

John Juracek, no longer a partner but remaining as a participant in Blue Ribbon Flies, expanded his striking outdoor photography skills into a commercial venture while producing thoughtful and elegantly written commentaries on fly fishing, conservation, and other outdoor topics. John still ties for Blue Ribbon Flies and occasionally works in the shop. His thought-provoking blogs grace Blue Ribbon Flies' website on occasion.

Arrick Swanson continued to offer flies of his own creation as well as those of other contracted tiers. For Arrick's Fly Shop, the presence of Paul Stimpson, beginning in the 1990s, would continue Gary LaFontaine's spirit in fly design and presentation strategy authority. Paul would go on to tie flies for many West Yellowstone fly shops. He also swapped tying flies with independent guides for float trips. Beginning in

Eagle's Store as it appears today. It remains active in the angling community and is the longest-standing retailer of fly-fishing merchandise in town. In the past such fly-fishing luminaries as Charles Borberg and Bud Lilly began their shops within Eagle's. (Bruce Staples collection)

Big Sky Anglers now occupies the location that was once Bud Lilly's Trout Shop. A full-service shop, it offers merchandise, information, and guiding services. (Bruce Staples collection)

A "changing of the guard" at Blue Ribbon Flies. Cam Coffin has been part of this business for decades. As the new owner, he extends the shop's reputation for offering the superb products, service, and information provided for decades by Craig and Jackie Mathews and John Juracek. (Bruce Staples collection) ▶

1994, Bud Lilly's Trout Shop went through a series of owners, the current of these changing the Trout Shop's name to Big Sky Anglers.

In 2014 Craig Mathews sold Blue Ribbon Flies to Cam Coffin, a thirty-year employee, head guide, fly tier, and highly experienced fly fisher. As did Bud Lilly, Craig maintained a part-time presence in the shop to attract the fly-fishing public. Throughout the new century, Blue Ribbon Flies flourishes, with its fly tiers offering new patterns every season. One of these tiers, Rowan Nyman, left Blue Ribbon in 2003 to become a featured fly tier and guide at the Firehole Ranch.

Blue Ribbon Flies also continued to provide guide services for the Papoose Creek Ranch on the middle Madison River, for the Sun Ranch, and for the fly-fishing public. Later in the decade Blue Ribbon embraced the tenkara technique and became an enthusiastic factor in promoting it as well as offering products used for it. Efforts to preserve the Greater Yellowstone area's priceless coldwater fisheries were now becoming of major importance, and Blue Ribbon Flies answered the call in a major way.

Accolades continued to arrive for Bud Lilly. Remembrances of his days owning the Trout Shop were in demand on the banquet circuit, and these have been preserved in the Montana State University Trout and Salmonid Collection. Bud's *Guide to Fly-Fishing the New West* combined his two earlier books and offered some new thoughts. Here he identifies the traits that make an excellent fishing guide and adds depth to his thoughts on fishing etiquette. He also offers thoughts on approaching different water types and on achieving successful fishing during all seasons. The fly patterns he discusses and recommends are mostly old and proven traditional patterns. Bud discusses new approaches to conservation, but believes that progress to retain fisheries quality has stalled somewhat. He offers that stocking, perpetuation of kill regulations, lack of access, and insufficient funds for such initiatives as whirling disease research are the reasons.

Bud is not the only Lilly family member to stay in the fly-fishing industry. Greg managed the Healing Waters Lodge into 2004 and then began Tight Lines Management based in Sheridan, Montana.

Several iconic fly-fishing personalities, never residing in West Yellowstone, were instrumental to the town's gaining its reputation as a destination and center of fly-fishing knowledge. But Bob Jacklin and Craig Mathews were now the major fly-fishing personalities in town, both having roots back to Bud Lilly, Pat Barnes, and Jim Danskin. Both Bob and Craig spent major time on the off-season fly-fishing show circuit in order to gauge interest in and sustain the image of local salmonid fishing, and to promote coldwater fisheries conservation, heritage preservation, and fly-fishing education. Both supported Project Healing Waters.

For Bob, the Federation of Fly Fishers, now Fly Fishers International (FFI), became a major outlet for personal contributions. Here he would share his vast knowledge of fly-fishing techniques through destination presentations centered on the opportunities in the Greater Yellowstone region. When, after a thirteen-year hiatus, the Federation returned in 2004 to West Yellowstone with their annual international conclave, Bob was a major player. He lined up the facilities needed for hosting the conclave's various functions, and no one in town did more to promote the show. In the middle of the decade he also served as the president of the federation's Western Rocky Mountain Council. Having gained a reputation as one of the world's finest fly casters, Bob shared technique secrets with anyone interested in improving their technique. It would be a common sight to see Bob take a neophyte customer across the street to the Museum of the Yellowstone's lawn to give on-the-spot instruction on the use of a newly purchased balanced outfit.

But fly-casting instruction and passing on angling knowledge was not the end of Bob's contributions. He had amassed a reputation as a fly tier able to master all forms of the art. Few tiers had his broad scale of knowledge and ability. This was recognized in 2000 when he was that year's recipient of FFI's Buz Buszek Memorial Fly Tying Award bestowed for contributions to the art of fly tying. (The following year's recipient would be Bruce Staples, one of the authors of this work.)

In this new decade, Bob's guide service continued, as did his love for taxidermy. His passion for preserving West Yellowstone's place in the fly-fishing world is expressed publicly in his conception, preparation, and 2018 completion of a detailed display on

The Museum of the Yellowstone features a room presenting the town's historic contributions to fly fishing. Bob Jacklin with Cal and Jan Dunbar provided much of the effort to establish this collection. (Bruce Staples collection)

this subject within the town museum. In this work, Bob captures major events and personalities in the town's fly-fishing history beginning in the nineteenth century to the present day. Added to all of these accomplishments are his financial and time contributions to Trout Unlimited and to efforts by such organizations as the Trust for Public Land, the Henry's Fork Foundation, and the Greater Yellowstone Council.

In the late 1990s, Yellowstone Park superintendent Michael Finley had expressed to regional businesses the inability of the park, due to budgetary shortfalls, to provide many necessary visitor services. In 2001 Craig Mathews, after some years donating a portion of Blue Ribbon Flies' gross income to the park, brought Patagonia's Yvon Chouinard on board to form 1% for the Planet. Through this program, member businesses contribute at least 1 percent of their annual gross sales to grassroots groups approved by the organization for performing environmental actions. Specifically in Yellowstone Park, donations were meant to make up for the budgetary shortfalls Finley had described. Blue Ribbon Flies set the example for regional businesses to become active in 1% for the Planet. Craig and Jackie served on the organization's board for a time.

Before the Trust for Public Land entered efforts to acquire river access from Three Dollar Bridge upstream on the Madison River, Blue Ribbon Flies had begun initial actions to do so. With the Trust for Public land involved, Blue Ribbon was in the forefront of completion in 2006. A few years later the trust, with input from Craig, preserved public access to the river through completion of the Olliffe Ranch project. Now four miles of public access on the Madison River from Three Dollar Bridge upstream to Raynolds Junction Bridge is available for walk-in fishing (fishing from a boat is not allowed here).

Craig and Jackie Mathews remain celebrated personalities after retiring from Blue Ribbon Flies. They remain active in ongoing activities to protect and preserve quality Greater Yellowstone area fisheries. (Courtesy Terry Middleton)

Arrick and Lorie Swanson extend West Yellowstone's tradition of husband-and-wife teams operating a fly-fishing business in town. Arrick's Fly Shop, offering an online business, remains open throughout the year. (Bruce Staples collection)

Distinguished awards rolled in for Craig and Jackie's conservation efforts during the decade. First was the Nature Conservancy's Business Conservation Award for protecting wild trout habitat and wildlife migration corridors. In 2000 the Greater Yellowstone Coalition bestowed on them the GYC Outstanding Business Award for giving the most to protect the Greater Yellowstone Ecosystem. In 2003 Blue Ribbon Flies was the recipient of FFI's Lee Wulff Award for efforts in protecting and preserving wild trout habitat, clean air and water, and wild places for the enjoyment of future generations. Also early in the decade, Craig was named Angler of the Year by *Fly Rod & Reel* magazine. In 2018 Craig was the recipient of FFI's Frank and Jeanne Moore Award for "extraordinary contribution to the conservation of our fisheries resources and a notable contribution to community service."

Craig, however, believes the biggest conservation award he has received or will ever receive is the seldom-bestowed Protector of Yellowstone Park Award. Blue Ribbon

Flies received this award in 1997 for its work and support in sending 1 percent of its West Yellowstone business's gross sales to the park through the Yellowstone Park Foundation to help fund fisheries projects that protect, preserve, and enhance the park for future generations.

Arrick's Fly Shop also developed through the new century. An expanded guide service and more fly tiers came on board. The shop's website developed through the years to feature an online store, newsletter, "how-to" section, guide reservation service, and fishing report. The most important addition to the shop, however, came in the form of a seasonal Yellowstone Park interpretative park ranger stationed at Old Faithful. Her name was Lorie Miller, and she brought to the job a love of the outdoors and wildlife developed during a Michigan childhood, a love of teaching, and an earth sciences degree. She and Arrick met in 2009. They married and now run the shop as a team.

Lorie is learning fly fishing's many facets from a fine teacher, her husband. This husband-and-wife team aspect repeats itself, as we have seen, throughout West Yellowstone's fly-fishing history. Lorie, with fifteen years of public school teaching experience, adds to the number of teachers who grace the ranks of West Yellowstone fly-fishing professionals. The Swansons offer a program for experienced fly fishers wanting to broaden or improve their skills, but of particular interest to the couple is mentoring entry-level fly fishers. They therefore also offer an instructional program designed to develop fly-fishing skills in beginners.

With respect to preserving Montana's fly-fishing heritage, a unique and major effort began in the late 1990s at the Montana State University Library in Bozeman. Bud Lilly and Paul Schullery acted as advisers to the library on this project. Within a few years it would be known as the Trout and Salmonid Collection administrated by the university library and known as the Bud Lilly Trout and Salmonid Bibliography. The collection is now the basis of the world's primary trout and salmon resource center. It's another honor for Bud Lilly and his contributions to fly fishing.

As in past decades, Father Time took his toll on fly-fishing contributors to West Yellowstone's heritage. Many of those who passed away never lived in West Yellowstone but contributed much to enhance the town's image as the center of the best inland trout fishing in the country. Frank Matarelli faded from the scene, selling his home in West Yellowstone. Dave Whitlock's final visit came in 2004 when he conducted fly-fishing classes. While doing so on the Madison River below Lyons Bridge, he marveled at the changes that had occurred since his initial visits in the 1960s. Solitude there, he noted, was a thing of the past.

Gary LaFontaine died of acute lateral sclerosis (Lou Gehrig's disease) in January 2002. From his home in Deer Lodge, Montana, he visited West Yellowstsone on his way to the surrounding quality waters and while there participated in many fly-fishing-related events. Several of his visits to adjacent waters were subjects of his literary efforts.

Scotty Chapman, who lived in West Yellowstone twice during his tenure as a Yellowstone National Park ranger, passed away in 2001. Ernest Schwiebert passed away in January 2006, Ken Swanson in 2007, Jim Danskin in June 2008, and Jack Gartside in December 2009. Sylvester Nemes never lived in West Yellowstone, but was active in many of its fly-fishing events. He passed away in February 2011.

Wally Eagle died in May 2013. Cal Dunbar, having done so much to promote the quality of fly fishing in the West Yellowstone area, passed away in 2017. Nick Nicklas,

Blue Ribbon Flies' long-tenured guide and major fly pattern contributor, passed away in 2014. Lefty Kreh passed in March 2018.

But it was Bud Lilly's death on January 4, 2017, that signaled the end of an era. It is likely no one else realized as much as Bud the economic value of wild salmonids to the state of Montana. He was a most vocal defender of catch-and-release fishing and fought to end stocking fish in Montana's rivers. He championed that fly fishing was more than just catching fish; it provided the opportunity to appreciate the out-of-doors. After retiring, he would guide business, military, and political leaders to prized Montana fly-fishing waters. He lobbied for any actions conserving wild fish and their habitat, and fought any efforts he felt endangered salmonids. He was truly a trout's best friend.

After a string of owners who kept the name "Bud Lilly's Trout Shop," in 2016 Justin Spence, Joe Moore, and Jonathan Heames merged to purchase the shop and form Big Sky Anglers. Joe owned the original version of Big Sky Anglers, Justin had owned the seasonal and tiny West Yellowstone Flies beginning in 2006, and Jonathan had for years guided for West Yellowstone fly shops, including for Bob Jacklin.

Major internet impacts to the West Yellowstone fly-fishing industry came in the first decade of the twenty-first century with the expansion of electronic media demanding that businesses have a website. Any quality fly shop must now have its own site, and for those in West Yellowstone doing so would be almost a necessity considering the popularity of regional fisheries. Many fly fishers, now wise to the ways of computers, would judge the quality of services a shop offered by the content of their website and particularly of their fishing report. Not only would trips be planned based on fishing report content, but shops would be patronized because of

Increasingly women are discovering fly-fishing. Some become guides, business owners, product representatives, or authors. (Courtesy Jim Schollmeyer)

The DeLacey Creek Trail with a three-mile walk is the shortest route to Shoshone Lake from West Yellowstone. More visits take place from the south side of the lake, but West Yellowstone offers a shorter trip from such locations as Jackson, Wyoming, or any other park entrance. (Bruce Staples collection)

the accuracy and timeliness of that report. Walk-in sales always shrank drastically during the off-season, so online stores became almost a requirement to provide income during the off-season and also to reserve guide services for the next season.

Like the fishing reports, the "where to fish," and "how-to" sections of the website had to be maintained and updated at the expense of the owner and ultimately reflected that owner's integrity as a knowledgeable source of local fly-fishing information. Fly shop websites would function as an electronic catalog by offering items for sale, creating an income during the off-season for fly-fishing retailers. Websites could also provide contact information and links to services such as lodging facilities that a visiting angler might require.

Thus all West Yellowstone full-service fly shops featured websites and connection to social media before the end of the first decade. Some also produced "how-to" DVDs on such subjects as fly tying and equipment purchase and care.

CHAPTER 11

THE FUTURE

How long will West Yellowstone remain as the center of our best inland salmonid fishing? The future looks bright. An ominous cloud on the horizon, however, is that fewer young people and entry-level folks in our country are getting into fly fishing. Hopefully this is temporary. Some of this has roots in the increasing cost of transportation and the near addiction to electronic media. But this is not the case worldwide, where fly-fishing in some areas is increasing in popularity, and enthusiasts from faraway places are becoming more numerous in town.

Yellowstone National Park management is on record of supporting fishing not only because of its economic value, but also because so much financial and political support for sustaining its fisheries comes from persons enjoying them. As the human population of the region climbs, there will be increased pressure to designate water for municipal needs. Certainly there will be more schemes to tap into the park's natural resources, especially water, for nothing more than financial gain.

The Henry's Fork in Island Park played an important role in the formation of West Yellowstone. The Harriman family, founders of the Yellowstone Branch Line railroad, owned a large portion of it below the Last Chance area. This springtime river scene from the Railroad Ranch, now Harriman State Park, illustrates why the river in the park attracts fly fishers on an international basis. (John Juracek photo)

Black and grizzly bears are significant inhabitants of the West Yellowstone area and can appear in town. Encounters and sightings near streams and stillwaters are common. Fly-fishing retailers in town offer items such as bear spray and claxon horns meant to counter aggressive behavior and minimize encounters. They also maintain up-to-date information on bear presence and dispense advice with respect to avoiding encounters. Perhaps the most thorough information on how to remain safe in bear country is on Yellowstone Park's website. (John Juracek photo)

Another question, of less impact on the economic future of the regional fly-fishing industry, is that of replacement of the fly-fishing icons. From Eagle, Martinez, and Johnson to Barnes, Brooks, Danskin, and Lilly and on to the present suite of iconic persons, will there be a continuum of recognizable personalities in town?

Significant efforts are ongoing around West Yellowstone to preserve and to reestablish native salmonid species in waters deemed suitable. An interesting question arises: Will the West Yellowstone region also become a refuge for the exotic salmonids first introduced in the late nineteenth century?

Restrictive angling regulations in Idaho, Montana, and Yellowstone National Park certainly will help preserve regional salmonid populations, but they will require continuation of the present broad public support. History shows fishing pressure in the area seems slowed only by war, depression, and increasingly restrictive regulatory changes. But after these occurrences, fishing pressure has bounced back. The economic value of high-quality salmonid fisheries, coupled with the fact that other regions hosting such a presence are diminishing, suggests that further increases in fishing pressure are coming to the Greater Yellowstone area.

Of course, the bulwark for protection is the presence of Yellowstone National Park and Grand Teton National Park, and increasingly public and governmental agencies realize that the immediate surroundings must fall under the same protection umbrella. The high-quality water coming from these parks and their surrounding region is slowly being realized as a most valuable natural resource in the future of the West. Thus protecting this quality, so vital in future economics, helps ensure continuation of a healthy salmonid population. The infrastructure for championing this protection is in place in the form of organizations such as the Greater Yellowstone Coalition, the Henry's Fork Foundation, Friends of Yellowstone, Trout Unlimited, the Nature Conservancy, the Trust for Public Land, the Whirling Disease Foundation, and many others, and, thankfully, strong public support.

Yes, the long-term geologic future of the area is uncertain, but humans can do nothing with respect to shaping it. This may also be the case with respect to climate change, which may be altering living conditions for salmonids in Greater Yellowstone waters. Winters seem less severe and summers warmer. Water temperature measurements indicate that some area stillwaters seem to be warming. Nevertheless, the matchless regional salmonid fishery is here today and for the foreseeable future to enjoy and to treasure.

CHAPTER 12

FAMED WATERS

Nowhere inland in our country is there such a concentration of accessible high-quality salmonid waters as can be found immediately around West Yellowstone, Montana. Several areas have boasted such a reputation in the past, and many have done so for solid reasons, but presently for West Yellowstone there is no competition in this regard. This statement is sure to be disputed, and certainly pretenders abound. But if one looks objectively at what is present in the Greater Yellowstone region and in other locations, the conclusion is inescapable. To begin with, no other area in the country has an equivalent to the protected high-quality coldwater fisheries of Yellowstone National Park. The park's management policies are likely the reason for this, and these policies are at the root of the subculture that has been growing in the region to protect waters, lands, and natural resources. And over the decades this culture has expanded to place what is known as the Greater Yellowstone region under its protective umbrella.

Flowing northwesterly out of Yellowstone Park, the West Gallatin River closely parallels US Highway 191. It can become crowded with fly fishers in season. Where it leaves the highway, the farther one travels upstream, the more solitude is realized. (John Juracek photo)

The Lamar River in peak-stage runoff. After winters of heavy snowfall, runoff season can extend into early July on many streams. (Bruce Staples collection)

In this chapter we offer descriptions and thoughts on forming a fly-fishing strategy for some of the area's major waters. Organization of this chapter is by drainage. Doing so provides continuity in the flow of information. Note the introductory words at the beginning of the Centennial Valley and Graben Lakes waters presentations. Waters of these areas are remoter from West Yellowtone than others discussed; miles of unpaved roads lead to these. Paved highways, with the minor exception of the Taylor Fork of the Gallatin River, are near waters of all other drainages discussed. In addition, fly-fishing literature and media contain so much easily available information on the physical nature and approachability of other drainages discussed here that repetition of such seems redundant. At the beginning of each featured water is an introductory section providing basic information. Note that GPS coordinates for convenient access points are included for each water discussed. In many cases, several coordinates are given. Likewise, in cases where more than one access route to the subject water is available, we give the most direct or most convenient.

With respect to gear, we suggest the most suitable fly-casting systems, but personal preference overrides these. Fly patterns, so dependent on personal preference, are therefore generalized. Facilities recommendations provide the basis for internet searches to determine complete services. Information resources include federal, state, and municipal agencies, visitor centers, and ranger stations from which more detailed information can be obtained. Pertinent United States Geologic Survey (USGS) flow station gage numbers (where available) and USGS 7.5-minute (1:24000) topographic maps are identified to help pinpoint the character of a given water and its immediate surroundings.

Also given in this discussion of famed waters are descriptions of noted resorts that cater to fly fishers. Descriptions of these are given because most have operated for several decades. Including them is appropriate because each has an important role in West Yellowstone's fly-fishing history, and all are currently operating. More information can be found on their websites.

CENTENNIAL VALLEY WATERS

Although forty miles distant from West Yellowstone, Centennial Valley waters play a major role in its fly-fishing history. From Don Martinez and Vint Johnson to the present fly-fishing retailers in town, all either offered guided trips there or provided inquiring fly fishers with detailed strategic thoughts for success on its waters.

Centennial Valley is a small-stream paradise, and presently within its streams reside trophy-size brook and cutthroat trout and Montana grayling. The cutthroat trout are not the westslope subspecies but the Yellowstone variety, likely introduced before distinction between the two was considered important. Up to the recent past, trophy-size rainbow trout were present in Culver Pond, having been introduced early in the twentieth century, and were planted in the now-dry McDonald Pond. Thus there has been ample time for these rainbows to get into the drainage and begin hybridizing with resident cutthroat. However, rainbow trout are nearly eliminated from the drainage above the lakes, resulting in an end of the hybridization process.

There have been other alterations to waters in the valley. The most notable occurred in the early twentieth century when Elk Springs Creek was diverted from Upper Red Rock Lake to Swan Lake to improve its habitat for duck hunting. Recently it has been returned to its natural channel into Upper Red Rock Lake in an attempt to improve its historic grayling spawning run. Odell Creek, about two-thirds the size of Red Rock

The Red Rock Lakes National Wildlife Refuge prohibits fishing from boats on Widgeon Pond. This minimizes disturbances to migratory waterfowl. Large cutthroat trout can be encountered here through limited shoreline fishing. (Bruce Staples collection)

McDonald Pond on Elk Springs Creek, once famed for hosting very large rainbow trout and an occasional grayling, no longer exists. It was a destination for many guided anglers from West Yellowstone until the refuge drained it. (Bruce Staples collection)

Creek, is adjacent to Lakeview. Flowing into Lower Red Rock Lake, it hosts brook trout, cutthroat trout, and grayling. Strategies, salmonid behavior, physical nature, and angling approach to it are much the same as for Red Rock Creek.

McDonald Pond, in the Elk Springs Creek drainage, has been drained. No fishing is allowed on the lakes and the river marsh between in order to protect waterfowl. Fishing from shore would be nearly impractical anyway because of the boggy shorelines. There are other small valley streams on the refuge reputed to host grayling runs, but their runs are not of the quality of Red Rock Creek.

Culver Pond

Access: Elk Lake Road to Culver Road going east to Culver Pond

Equipment: 4- and 5-weight systems with floating and intermediate lines and long delicate leaders; damselfly, dragonfly, and speckled dun life-cycle patterns, and traditional nymph, leech, and streamer patterns

GPS coordinates: Culver Pond 44.625136, -111.624875

Nearest facilities and services: West Yellowstone, MT; Upper Lake Campground on South Valley Road; Elk Lake Resort

Information resources: Red Rock Lakes National Wildlife Refuge Visitor Center, Lakeview, MT; Hidden Lake Bench USGS topographic map

Salmonids present: Brook trout and Montana grayling

Culver Pond, also known as the Widow's Pool, brought numerous fly fishers with and without guides from West Yellowstone to the Centennial Valley. It remains a forty-mile journey from town, the last fifteen on gravel roads. About 1900 Bill and Lillian

Culver dammed Picnic Creek to form a stock watering pond. They stocked it with cutthroat trout and grayling from local streams for subsistence purposes, but soon found the demand for the unusual sportfishing brought a reliable seasonal income, so they added brook and rainbow trout to the pond. It was likely the first pay-and-fish preserve in Montana. Fly-fishing visits to this place of legend began around 1910 and continue to the present. At one time the daily bag limit here was one hundred fish a day! The act of introducing brook and rainbow trout here would have future consequences to other Centennial Valley waters.

After Bill's death, the pond was commonly known as the "Widow's Pool." Some of the first evidence in print about the fishery and its quality is a 1913 photograph of two fishermen with a catch of very large trout, appearing to be rainbows. Over the years famed fly fishers including Howard Back, Pat Barnes, Jack Hemingway, and Bob Jacklin wrote of their appreciation of and successes in fishing the pond.

Springtime road conditions dictate when the pond can be reached, and late October usually signals the end of fishing here. In 1959 the US Fish and Wildlife Service broke open the original earthen dam and built a new dam about half a mile farther down Picnic Creek, thereby connecting the original Widow's Pool with the downstream pond. Thus the current pond is about three-quarters of a mile long and about thirty acres.

Bob Jacklin has fished this pond since 1968. Over the years, he's caught and released many two- to three-pound brook trout, with the largest being five pounds in 2000. His largest fish from the pond, caught in 1973, was a twenty-six-inch cuttbow. Experiences such as these combined with challenge and serenity are reasons why many fly fishers cherish Culver Pond. This pond has been dewatered several times

Although nearly forty miles from town, the Widow's Pool was an enticing place to fish up to a few years ago with large brook and rainbow trout rising in the evenings. Brook trout remain there. Evening fishing meant driving back to town with about twenty-five miles on gravel roads in the dark. (Bob Jacklin collection)

over the years, certainly having a negative impact on the hosted fish. Although its population seems to have rebounded somewhat, the pond produces fewer large trout than in the past.

Currently Red Rock Lakes National Wildlife Refuge management intends to recondition Culver Pond to become suitable to sustain a grayling population. Fishing success here does not come easy. Concentration, timely visits, and observation are required. Fishing from boats or flotation devices is prohibited. Wading should be

Only walk-in fishing is allowed on Culver Pond to protect waterfowl. Also known as the Widow's Pool, the pond is currently populated by brook trout. (Bob Jacklin collection)

Examples of the sizes that brook and rainbow trout once attained in Culver Pond. Recently the pond hosted only brook trout but in the future may host Montana grayling. (Bob Jacklin collection)

Culver Spring as it appears today. All buildings built and occupied by Lillian Hackett Hanson were demolished on acquisition by the Red Rock Lakes National Wildlife Refuge. (Bruce Staples collection)

minimized, and the visiting fly fisher must be willing to walk banks extensively and with stealth in order to locate feeding and rising fish.

Going fishless is common to those not heeding these thoughts. Fishing in the evening and early morning and during low-light conditions brings the best chances for success. Doing so also means traveling for miles to and from West Yellowstone over gravel roads in darkness. Damselfly, midge, and speckled dun life-cycle patterns work well here if the fly fisher is well versed in stealth. Wet flies such as nymphs and small streamers seem to bring the most success at the pond. Bob Jacklin's favorite is a size 10 yellow Muddler Minnow. To date brook trout inhabit Culver Pond, but if refuge management proceeds with reconditioning plans, grayling could be the sole future inhabitants.

Red Rock Creek

Access: Adjacent to South Valley Road and from Elk Lake Road east of Lakeview, MT

Equipment: 4- and 5-weight systems with floating line; BWO, caddisfly, golden stonefly, PMD, and yellow sally life-cycle patterns, and leech, soft-hackle, terrestrial insect, and traditional attractor patterns

Red Rock Creek is in a panoramic setting with the Centennial Range to the south and west. Mountains coupled with the broad expanse of the valley truly places the creek in "Big Sky Country." (Bruce Staples collection)

GPS coordinates: Red Rock Creek 44.616520, -111.656130
Nearest facilities and services: West Yellowstone, MT; Upper Lake Campground on South Valley Road; Elk Lake Resort
Information resources: Red Rock Lakes National Wildlife Refuge Visitor Center, Lakeview, MT; USGS flow station gage 06006000; Mount Jefferson and Upper Red Rock Lake USGS topographic maps
Salmonids present: Brook and cutthroat trout, Montana grayling, Rocky Mountain whitefish

Situated in a best example of "Big Sky Country," Red Rock Creek is perhaps the most fascinating small stream in West Yellowstone's vicinity. It is the trunk stream for all tributaries flowing off the Centennial Range to the south and from the hills to the north and east above Alaska Basin. All of these are the Missouri River's ultimate headwaters, and Red Rock Creek collects them to flow into Upper Red Rock Lake.

Originally westslope cutthroat trout, Rocky Mountain whitefish, and Montana grayling were the native salmonids in Centennial Valley streams, but the arrival of homesteaders would bring major changes. Some impounded creeks to form ponds for watering stock, as cattle husbandry was the only practical way to sustain a living; market hunting and trapping would do so only temporarily. Owners transplanted native salmonids to become a food source. Eventually some owners, Lillian Hanson being one, introduced rainbow and brook trout, some of which would escape to populate connected waters, including Red Rock Creek. It is likely that the rainbows bred with cutthroat trout to produce hybrids. Later, Yellowstone cutthroat trout were also introduced to these waters. The resulting cutthroat trout, which grow to large sizes, that inhabit these waters today have given rise to some controversy because of possible past interbreeding with rainbow trout.

Cold runoff water on reaching Upper Red Rock Lake signals awaiting grayling and the controversial cutthroat to begin their spawning runs to the creek's hospitable gravels. Gravels with an upwelling of water are chosen because eggs deposited there will be exposed to dissolved oxygen in three dimensions, and therefore develop most efficiently. About this time of year the road over Red Rock Pass opens, and travelers can observe spawning activity in the creek, turbidity permitting. The Montana general fishing season begins in mid-May, but within the refuge boundaries it opens in mid-June to minimize human interference with salmonids. Here the angler is encouraged to have utmost care for the grayling and obey the special regulations (catch-and-release for grayling, no bait or lead permitted, and barbless hooks encouraged) for fishing refuge waters.

As runoff water recedes, beavers reconstruct breached dams. These form impoundments that spangle the creek throughout its reach and result in additional overhead cover, but they inhibit fish passage downstream. Thus it is common to encounter dams purposely breached to allow easier autumn passage back to the lake for post-spawning cutthroat and grayling.

As waters drop and warm, a predictable sequence of aquatic insect emergences begins in Red Rock Creek. Yellow sally stoneflies are among the first to emerge, and

An Alaska Basin sunset is a vivid example of a high-country sunset. No doubt it has been enjoyed for at least a century by fly fishers heading to town after enjoying fishing in such places as the Widow's Pool. (Bruce Staples collection)

Beaver dams such as this one constructed on Red Rock Creek may hinder migration but also provide overhead cover for resident salmonids. Beaver ponds of a young age can offer spectacular fishing. (Courtesy LeRoy Cook)

soft-hackle patterns presented downstream to rising brook and cutthroat trout and grayling are effective. PMDs begin emerging for a monthlong session, with a few golden stoneflies emerging during its early days. Afternoon caddis activity spans the entire season, but the most interesting action comes when terrestrial insects begin their activity in the second half of July. Throughout this time a slowly retrieved small leech pattern is sure to bring responses from beaver-pond-dwelling trout and grayling.

Through all these strategies it is possible to encounter cutthroat over twenty

Native grayling have been displaced from all waters in the region except the upper Red Rock River drainage. Measures are being taken to expand their presence in these waters. Catch-and-release fishing is applied on waters in which they are present. (Bruce Staples collection)

inches and both brook trout and grayling exceeding fifteen inches. But encounters with cutthroat of these sizes came close to ending through a regrettable bureaucratic blunder. Somewhere in the chain of bureaucracy outside the refuge, an opinion took hold that cutthroat trout were decimating the grayling population by feeding on their fry. The fact that cutthroat trout and grayling coexisted in so many regional waters up to the mid-twentieth century was not given credit. Thus began a three-year program to remove cutthroat trout from the creek. Beginning in 2014 cutthroat ascending the creek to spawn upstream were trapped just below the Red Rock Creek bridge on the Elk Lake Road. Females were killed and sent to nearby food banks. Males were released into nearby Widgeon Pond. Some of the cutthroat killed or released approached thirty inches in length. Thankfully, this baseless activity ended in 2016.

Much to the relief of regional fisheries scientists, West Yellowstone fly-fishing retailers, and all fly fishers, not all large cutthroat were killed. This became obvious when juvenile cutthroat were increasingly encountered and reports of encounters with very large cutthroat began filtering in by 2017. Now the numbers of large cutthroat are increasing, and the grayling population seems steady. So, what is the real culprit here? Looking into the past, westslope cutthroat and grayling coexisted in many area streams until brook, brown, and rainbow trout were introduced into the Madison and Gallatin River drainages and replaced these natives. Brook trout were introduced into Centennial Valley waters several decades ago. They inhabit Upper and Lower Red Rock Lakes and Odell and Red Rock Creeks. On becoming adults they are notorious for preying on fry and fingerings of other salmonids. This fact makes them the best candidate for negatively impacting any grayling population. Eliminating brook trout from Centennial Valley waters seems one way of helping maintain their grayling population. Thus a brook trout daily bag limit of twenty-five is in effect on refuge waters.

GALLATIN RIVER DRAINAGE

West Gallatin River

Access: US Highway 191

GPS coordinates: Big Horn Pass Trailhead 44.928498, -111.053578; Fan Creek Trailhead 44.953450, -111.060401; Highway 191 pullouts 45.012455, -111.080933

Equipment: 4- and 5-weight systems with floating and sink-tip lines; BWO, caddisfly, golden stone, giant stonefly, PMD, Trico, and yellow sally life-cycle patterns, and terrestrial insect and streamer patterns

Nearest facilities and services: West Yellowstone, MT; Yellowstone National Park; Baker's Hole Campground; Parade Rest Ranch

Information resources: Yellowstone National Park; West Yellowstone Visitor Center; Divide Creek, Joseph Peak, Big Horn Peak, Sunshine Point, and Lone Indian Peak USGS topographic maps

Salmonids present: Brown and rainbow trout and Rocky Mountain whitefish

Gallatin Lake in Yellowstone National Park gives birth to the West Gallatin River. A fishless tarn, it sits just under nine thousand feet in elevation in a cirque on the north side of Three Rivers Peak. From here, as an alpine stream, the West Gallatin River tumbles toward the northwest for miles through an upland valley before sliding into a meadow characteristic of its reach through the park. While traveling north along US Highway 191, the Gallatin comes into view on the right in a sloping meadow near milepost 22. Angling from the southeast, the river parallels the highway, where it will remain in sight for miles.

A trailhead takes you to the top of this meadow after a five-mile walk. Rainbow, a few brown, and Yellowstone cutthroat trout are present here, perhaps the only part of the river where a visitor is nearly guaranteed solitude. Sliding through the meadow, the river maintains some gradient but becomes more hospitable to trout as it deepens and hosts more food forms. Not far below the trailhead, Fan Creek enters the river from the east.

This creek, also approached by a trailhead, is the major tributary within the park, and it holds cutthroat to surprising sizes as well as cutthroat-rainbow hybrids. It runs, however, through country notorious for grizzlies, so one should be cautious when venturing within. Fawn Creek, Fan's major tributary, not quite a half mile above the confluence with the river, also holds cutthroat and the same hybrids. In these streams, cutthroat are Yellowstone rather than the original westslope subspecies. When the westslopes diminished here earlier in the twentieth century, they were replaced with Yellowstone cutthroat because these were so abundant and available at park hatcheries.

About a mile below the Fan Creek confluence, Bacon Rind Creek enters from the west. It too holds cutthroat and cutthroat-rainbow hybrids, but in smaller sizes than hosted by Fan Creek. As autumn approaches, most trout move out of Bacon Rind Creek to the river below to seek sanctuary in deeper water.

Next the Gallatin crosses Highway 191 to flow adjacent on the west. Now, noticeably larger, it becomes a more interesting stream with deeper holes and runs and an undercut in each of its numerous bends. Numerous pullouts along the highway allow for easy access, and a game that Gallatin enthusiasts seem to play is to try the river at these pullouts, systematically working either upstream or down.

About four miles below the Fan Creek confluence, Specimen Creek coming from the east adds its water. Originating in fishless lakes at high altitude, the north and east forks of the creek converge about two miles east of the highway. From here to its confluence with the river, the creek and some water in both forks host cutthroat and cuttbow hybrids. A trail to Sportsman Lake accesses this reach of Specimen Creek, where one can find solitude, wonderful scenery, and beautifully colored and eager small trout.

Not far below, the west bank of the Gallatin forms the boundary of Yellowstone National Park. Land beyond is part of the private Black Butte Ranch, but one can still fish the west bank by remaining within the high-water boundary. Not far below is the Taylor Fork and a bit farther the developing community based on the Big Sky Resort. Our discussion of the Gallatin will end at the Taylor Fork confluence. Solitude found in the days when Bud Lilly fished here as a youth is pretty much gone.

Next the Gallatin drops through its steep-sided canyon, where waters are increasingly shared with rafters and kayakers in season. Few trophy trout reside in the canyon, but the river here is easily approached and waded, and casting to its waters is a breeze. Formerly a domain of westslope cutthroat, grayling, and Rocky Mountain whitefish, angler preferences fostered the introduction of rainbow and brown trout here early in the twentieth century. These gradually took over, leaving Rocky Mountain whitefish the only native to survive in numbers. Most trout in good sizes inhabit the river where it runs adjacent to the highway. The average size of trout here is about a foot in length, with a range from six to eighteen inches.

The season on the river within the park begins on Memorial Day weekend, but in normal-water years the river is usually not fishable until around mid-June. Around the end of the month, numerous large stoneflies mature, fly, mate, and drop eggs. Resident trout respond with gusto. Mayfly emergences are not significant in this reach, and Charlie Brooks declared that he had seen only Baetis and Ephemerella types, both in limited numbers. But when the river becomes fishable and wading easy, no more than hip boots are needed. In fact, on warmer days wading wet here is refreshing. Now the best strategy during the first days when the river is fishable is to present caddis life-cycle patterns and nymph patterns that simulate those of giant and golden stoneflies. With clearing and dropping waters, any drifting caddis pattern becomes not just effective but fun to use. Stonefly nymphs of any pattern will be effective until trout begin keying on adults, then, as with nymphs, pattern is not as important as presentation.

Yellow sally emergers will begin to bring results that can last the season. As time moves into summer, the real enjoyment a fly fisher can have on this reach begins as dry attractors and terrestrials become effective. Presenting traditional classic patterns takes one back to yesteryear when Bud Lilly and Pat Barnes promoted these as the best patterns for good times on the river. You will find that these classic patterns are just as effective, under equal presentation conditions, as those in vogue today. But if one insists on being "in style" with respect to fly patterns, newer patterns in the same size range will work just as well.

Emerging giant stonefly nymphs signal the beginning of the "high fly-fishing season" in the Greater Yellowstone area. Reaching the Gallatin and Madison Rivers near town around the first of July and the Yellowstone River the first of August, all of fly fishing is captured by the emergence's arrival. (Bruce Staples collection)

Fishing the Gallatin, or streams physically similar, provides the best evidence that presentation overwhelms pattern selection. The argument given above on pattern selection also applies to the choice of terrestrial insect patterns. Do not overlook beetle and ant patterns for use here. All terrestrial patterns remain effective until late September frosts reduce the number of terrestrials and their importance in the trout's diet. For presenting these fly types, a rod of 4-weight or less will result in the most enjoyment.

With diminishing aquatic insects as autumn arrives, streamers are the most reliable patterns for encountering the larger trout residing here. The aquatic insect diehard can present caddis and midge life-cycle patterns for achieving success. If one prefers to try nymphs, old classics always produce. The same can be said for any bead-head patterns.

Although grayling are gone from the drainage, the Gallatin River's extreme headwater streams may hold a few westslope cutthroat trout. These waters are therefore candidates for reintroduction of this much-diminished native. Now in the twenty-first century, most fly fishers might applaud their establishment in waters such as Bacon Rind Creek, Fan Creek, and Specimen Creek. Park fisheries managers are now in favor of this reestablishment, but studies must first be performed to gauge chances for success of such an effort. Let's see what the future holds for this effort, as this native cutthroat deserves to be present in greater numbers.

Taylor Fork of the Gallatin River

Access: Taylor Fork Road off US Highway 191
GPS coordinates: West Gallatin River confluence, 45.072140, -111.199426
Equipment: 4- and 5-weight systems; BWO, caddisfly, PMD, golden stone, and yellow sally life-cycle patterns, and terrestrial insect, traditional attractor, and streamer patterns
Nearest facilities and services: West Yellowstone, MT; Swan Creek Campground; Wapiti rental cabin; Nine Quarter Circle Ranch
Information resources: West Yellowstone Visitor Center, Custer-Gallatin National Forest Bozeman Ranger District Office, Lincoln Mountain and Sunshine Point USGS topographic maps
Salmonids present: Brown, cutthroat, and rainbow trout

The Taylor Fork, just outside the northwest corner of Yellowstone Park, is the largest upstream tributary to the West Gallatin River. It is a major runoff stream through draining some of the highest parts of the Madison Range. It also tends to become turbid when summer thundershowers invade its upper reaches. This turbidity can enter the West Gallatin River, making it somewhat discolored for miles downstream. Nevertheless, it offers good fishing, especially when terrestrial insects reach their peak population during midsummer. West Yellowstone fly-fishing retailers would send inquiring visitors there when dry weather conditions prevailed in the area. Since the second half of the twentieth century, the growing fly-fishing industry in the Big Sky community on the West Gallatin River, not far below downstream, has done the same.

The Taylor Fork Road parallels nearly all of this stream, which runs mostly through public land. The major exception is the Nine Quarter Circle Ranch, through which this road proceeds for about half a mile with parking restrictions.

Whether you are camping or just fishing, it is important to remember that this area is bear country. About five miles from the highway, you will come upon the

runs. With more restrictive regulations and better surveillance, larger rainbows are now more frequently encountered, and West Yellowstone fly-fishing retailers are again recommending the lake as a destination for large rainbow trout.

Damselfly emergences can provide wonderful fishing on Antelope Prong and Horn Creek Arm, also known as Neely's Cove, and on the extreme south end known as the West Fork Arm, and to a limited amount at the north end. A particularly effective pattern for damselfly nymphs here and on all the Graben Lakes is Bill Schiess's Light Olive Crystal.

Cliff Lake is accessed from Highway 287. One crosses Three Dollar Bridge, passes through the old Cliff Lake town site, and travels a few miles on the well-maintained gravel road to the fork. Going left takes one to the renowned lodge formerly known as Neely's, now the Wilderness Edge Retreat, on Horn Creek Arm.

Going right at the fork, one climbs Wade Lake bench. At the top of the bench, the north end of Cliff Lake is on the left and Wade Lake is on the right. Continuing on and then soon bearing left takes one to the developed campground on the northwest corner. Fishing can be best right after ice-out where transition water and shallows host food forms. A single-lane public road from the Wilderness Edge Retreat ends at a boat launch site on Horn Creek Arm.

The Wilderness Edge Retreat succeeds what originally was Neely's Resort begun in the 1920s. The retreat has a rich hundred-year history and offers comfortable accommodations and guided fishing outings. (Bruce Staples collection)

Horn Creek Arm and Antelope Prong are good early-season locations. Fish cruise here looking for food. Streamers, Woolly Bugger types, and dragonfly nymph imitations are best fished here with sinking lines such as type 2s and a leader of at least 8-pound test.

As the lake warms with advancing summer, fish migrate to deeper water, but on occasion evening and early morning will produce smaller and midsize fish. By autumn with cooling weather, large fish come back to shallow water to forage before winter sets in. Again, large streamer and Woolly Bugger patterns presented using full-sinking lines are effective.

NEELY'S RANCH

Vern and Ruth Neely began, in 1919, one of southwest Montana's first resorts catering to the sportfishing public. Cliff Lake already had a reputation for producing large and abundant westslope cutthroat trout and was visited mostly by anglers on horseback. Some of these were Hebgen Dam workers. Well-to-do sportsmen coming from nearby retreats also frequented the lake. During the 1920s Vern built new housing for clients near the Horn Creek inlet, placed docks on the lake, and built rowboats to better access the superb fishing. Ruth cooked meals and maintained accommodations for clients. The ranch and resort were nearly self-supporting by the mid-1920s, and son Monta, born in 1915, began taking part in their operation.

The Neelys impacted the trout makeup of Cliff Lake immensely through introducing rainbow trout fry in the 1920s. By the late 1920s Cliff Lake would be famed for producing large rainbows. According to records preserved by Laurie Schmidt, co-owner of Wade Lake Resort, George Elliot, in 1928, caught a twenty-four-and-a-half-pound rainbow from Cliff Lake. It took three hours to land this lunker. He used a bamboo fly rod, silk line, and gut leader, but, alas if you are a fly fisher, a Colorado spinner! Trolling streamers would also be an effective method to encounter trophy rainbows at the time. The Selby Special was among the popular trolling patterns used there.

The Neelys stocked Hidden Lake, Goose Lake, and Otter Lake, about six miles to the southwest, with rainbow fingerlings. They also ran a Cliff Lake guide service with boats and motors for a fee, and outfitted pack trips to Goose, Hidden, and Otter Lakes. Don Martinez, operating out of his West Yellowstone tackle shop beginning in the 1930s, directed people to Neely's Ranch to enjoy the superb fishing for large rainbow trout in all these lakes. Medium-size native cutthroat, he offered, were also present in Cliff Lake.

Vern passed away in 1955, and Monta ran the resort until 1989, when he sold operations and property to Mark and Sheri Stokman, who expanded the resort and added a restaurant. John and Janet Duncan are the present owners of the resort, now called Wilderness Edge Retreat.

The Neely family did much to establish access to the Graben Lakes. This trail sign at the Wilderness Edge Resort indicates that Hidden Lake is six miles to the south and commemorates Monta Neely, who succeeded his parents in operating the original Cliff Lake Resort. (Bruce Staples collection)

Elk Lake

Access: North on Elk Lake Road from South Valley Road junction
GPS coordinates: Elk Lake Resort, 44669525, -111.630763
Equipment: 5- and 6-weight systems with floating, full-sink, and intermediate
   lines; damselfly, dragonfly, and speckled dun life-cycle patterns, and leech,
   scud, and streamer patterns
Nearest facilities and services: West Yellowstone, MT; Elk Lake Resort
Information resources: Beaverhead–Deer Lodge National Forest, Elk Springs
   Creek and Hidden Lake Bench USGS topographic maps
Salmonids present: Cutthroat and lake trout

Elk Lake has produced lake trout to twenty pounds and more. These are native, with Elk one of only four such lakes in Montana having this presence. In Elk Lake these trout are protected by a catch-and-release regulation. Near ice-out time they can be caught in relatively shallow water through the use of sinking lines, stout leaders, and streamer flies, but as the season advances and waters warm, they move to deep water. Late in the season they can be caught when they come to spawn near shorelines having submerged rocks. During these times large, brightly colored streamers presented on full-sinking lines provide the best means for action.

Originally Elk Lake hosted westslope cutthroat trout that reached large sizes, but their numbers diminished as fishing pressure with liberal creel limits increased. To compensate, Montana fisheries personnel introduced Yellowstone cutthroat trout and periodically released more to maintain their population. The turn of the twenty-first century, however, has seen an evaluation of management to restore the westslope cutthroat, and prospects look good for restoration. Both cutthroat subspecies are now present and can be caught in Elk Lake, but the Yellowstone cutthroat, not being supplemented, are diminishing. The lake also hosted grayling, but their current presence is extremely rare. Rainbow trout, introduced decades ago by homesteaders, are also rare.

The north end of the lake forms a large, shallow bay rich in plant life that hosts a huge mass of insect life and baitfish. This bay is a famed area for fishing just after ice-out, and fishing here at that time can be effective through the use of intermediate and sink-tip lines to present small leech and dragonfly nymph imitations. Flotation devices are appropriate here, as shorelines are mostly too soft to wade. The road from Elk Lake Resort accesses the north end of the lake. Because of the possibility of rain making the access road muddy and slippery, a four-wheel-drive vehicle is perhaps the best conveyance. Later in June to early July, this bay hosts an excellent damselfly emergence.

The south end of the lake is a smaller version of the north end, but much more easily accessed. Fishing here is good, but can be more crowded due to the presence of a small, undeveloped campground. Nearby is the Elk Lake Resort, formerly Selby's. Here boat launch facilities are available for a fee.

The forty-mile ride to Elk Lake from West Yellowstone is in itself a worthy venture. From Targhee Pass, one proceeds around the east side of Henry's Lake via US Highway 20 and then west on the Red Rock Road on the south side of the lake to the Red Rock Pass Road. Following this road over Red Rock Pass, then west on the Red Rock Pass Road, brings one into Alaska Basin, the eastern appendage of Centennial

Valley. The striking view to the south and southwest is the abrupt north face of the Centennial Range, the summit of which is the Continental Divide on the Idaho-Montana border. On traveling farther west, the Red Rock Pass road divides into the South Valley Road and Elk Lake Road. Here one bears right onto the Elk Lake Road going to the lake. Much of the area is in the Red Rock Lake National Wildlife Refuge. In its seventy-plus years of operation, this most beautiful and remote of preserves in the federal fish and wildlife system is a great success story. The refuge has rescued the majestic but delicate trumpeter swan from near extinction and provides the high-quality wetlands it requires. For many an angler visiting the area, a trumpeter ascending, descending, or flying overhead becomes a welcomed and awesome distraction.

Another bonus with respect to approaching Elk Lake is the presence of several upper Centennial Valley waters hosting salmonids. McDonald Pond once hosted large rainbow trout but is now drained, though it is being considered to host grayling. Red Rock and Elk Springs Creeks, both flowing westerly to Upper Red Rock Lake, are also easily approached. Both creeks open to fishing annually on June 15 to protect spawning cutthroat and grayling. East of the refuge, waters open to fishing with the Montana general season. Red Rock and Elk Springs Creeks both host grayling to the point of being among the best remnant populations that Montana has to offer. Stealth and the presentation of tiny dry flies is the name of the game for success on these small and beautiful streams. East of the Elk Lake Road, all waters on the refuge have a June 15 to September 30 angling season.

All of these waters, except the upper end of Red Rock Creek, are on the Red Rock Lakes National Wildlife Refuge and thus managed to favor migratory waterfowl. Keep this purpose in mind if you consider venturing here, because, based on the status of the swan, any of these waters, most likely the impoundments, can be closed to human access if deemed necessary to protect the magnificent bird.

ELK LAKE RESORT

Fay and Edna Selby first built cabins on the property in the early twentieth century and lived in one until the lodge was finished. In 1934 the couple and their sons built the original Elk Lake Camp and began hosting guests. The Selbys were fly fishers, and son Harvey's creation, the Selby Special, became a favorite fly for visiting anglers. Many guests trolled it on Elk Lake, while others fished it in area streams. Fay and Harvey guided guests to the area's superb fishing while Edna cooked meals, tended the lodge, and tied flies. Along with the Selby Special, the Royal Coachman, Picket Pin, and black Woolly Worm were popular patterns she tied for guests.

The Selbys built and maintained the road from the lodge to the upper end of Elk Lake and on to within a half mile of Hidden Lake. This became the favored route for travel to those lakes, as the original road built by the US Forest Service was primitive at best. During hard winters they could drive over thick ice on Elk Lake, making this route temporarily easier.

Harvey built a boat dock at the upper end of Elk Lake and another on Hidden Lake not long after the lodge was completed. He also built and placed boats on both lakes and guided anglers to these locations, with horses being the most reliable mode of transportation. He built the camp's new lodge in 1948. Celebrities including Jane Russell and Justice William O. Douglas were among its guests.

Elk Lake Resort with the Centennial Range in the distance to the south. For nearly one hundred years famed personalities have come to the resort to relax and escape life's pressures. (Bruce Staples collection)

Goose and Otter Lakes were also angling destinations from the Elk Lake Resort. Pat Barnes fished these lakes as a youngster with his dad, and after he began his West Yellowstone shop he used Selby facilities to bring fly fishers from West Yellowstone. The Selbys knew nearby Culver Pond (Widow's Pool) as "Granny's Pond," and it along with McDonald Pond and Elk, Hidden, Goose, and Otter Lakes made this corner of the Centennial Valley a storied destination for fly fishers.

Ownership has changed hands several times, but the Elk Lake Resort is still in the midst of fabled fishing for brook, cutthroat, rainbow, and lake trout and Montana grayling. Now outdoor-oriented persons visit the resort on a year-round basis.

Hidden Lake

Access: North end of Elk Lake Road and quarter-mile trail to lake

GPS coordinates: Trailhead 44.714134, -111607689

Equipment: 5- and 6-weight systems with floating, intermediate, and full-sink lines; damselfly, dragonfly, and speckled dun life-cycle patterns, and leech, scud, and streamer patterns

Nearest facilities and services: West Yellowstone, MT; Upper Lake Campground on South Valley Road; Elk Lake Resort (offers rental boats on lake)

Information resources: Deerlodge-Gallatin National Forest, Cliff Lake USGS topographic map

Salmonids present: Rainbow trout

Hidden Lake is the most remote of the four major Graben Lakes. Nearly pristine and strikingly beautiful, its angling season opens each year on June 15 to protect shoreline spawning and some migratory bird usage. Its waters go subterranean to emerge as springs that form a creek flowing north into the south end of Cliff Lake. The four-wheel-drive road heading north along the west shore of Elk Lake goes to within a quarter mile of the lake to a trailhead.

From here the right-hand fork of a well-maintained trail descends to the private Elk Lake Resort boat dock, where boats owned by the lodge are docked. The left-hand fork of the trail skirts the west side of the lake, goes on to pass Goose and Otter Lakes, and then heads along the southeast side of Cliff Lake and on to the Wilderness Edge Resort. For decades going back to the Neely family presence, this trail conveyed anglers to all these wonderful lakes.

Hidden Lake requires about a quarter-mile walk from the end of Elk Lake Road to the Elk Lake Resort boat livery. Many anglers opt to carry floatation devices to the lake, but livery boats can be rented from the resort. It is practical to carry float tubes down the trail to the boat dock or along the trail skirting the west shore of the lake to reach lightly fished areas.

Formerly a domain of westslope cutthroat, rainbows released by homesteaders have taken over here and they range to large sizes. Fishing early in the season and from mid-September through October with full-sink and intermediate lines, streamers, and leech and Woolly Bugger patterns seem to bring the best results. Bays along the west side and the south end are best for late-June damselfly emergences, and

Hidden Lake has been a backcountry fly-fishing destination for at least a century. Elk Lake Resort's boat livery is at the lake's southwest corner. Originally Hidden Lake hosted westslope cutthroat trout. The Neely family are likely the ones who introduced rainbow trout here about a hundred years ago. (Courtesy Bruce Staples)

Stillwater tranquility is a reward for fishing Hidden Lake, host of vigorous rainbow trout. It is the only major Graben Lake free of motorized recreationists. The nearest road ends about a quarter mile from the southwest corner, thus discouraging portaging any boat other than a small flotation device. Elk Lake Resort has a rental boat livery at the southwest corner of the lake. (Bruce Staples collection)

later for gulpers going after midges and speckled duns. Some pale morning duns can emerge in these bays during summer, but they are not a major event attracting feeding fish.

Wade Lake

Access: US Highway 287 to Cliff Lake Road and Wade Lake Road
GPS coordinates: Campground and boat dock 44.808347, -111.565115
Equipment: 6- and 7-weight systems with floating and full-sinking lines; damselfly, dragonfly, and speckled dun life-cycle patterns, and leech, scud, and streamer patterns
Nearest facilities and services: West Yellowstone, MT; USFS Wade Lake Campground; Wade Lake Resort
Information resources: West Yellowstone Visitor Center, Custer-Gallatin National Forest, Cliff Lake and Hidden Lake Bench USGS topographic maps
Salmonids present: Brown and rainbow trout

This is the only Graben Lake that hosts brown trout. It also has a healthy population of rainbow trout introduced decades ago by homesteaders. A westslope cutthroat population preceded the current brown and rainbow trout residents. Wade Lake is probably the most heavily fished of these lakes, likely because of its reputation for producing large brown trout. It produced the current Montana state record brown trout in 1966, a twenty-nine-pound behemoth. Late in the next decade, as if to prove the record fish was no fluke, Wade produced another mammoth brown only a few ounces lighter. It has also produced, like Cliff Lake, rainbow trout exceeding twenty pounds.

Such behemoths can be out of range for the fly fisher due to the depths at which they reside, up to one hundred feet. It is, in fact, the deepest of the Graben Lakes. Nevertheless, fly fishing can be successful here for brown trout achieving double-figure poundage. One strategy for encountering the large fish residing at depth in Wade Lake is to fish at night. Guaranteed to find an acceptable amount of solitude, those fishing at this time use lead-core line below a fast-sinking line. Combined with a stout leader and a brightly colored, weighted streamer or Woolly Bugger pattern, this technique can be effective down to depths of forty feet from July through September. Simply trolling streamer and Woolly Bugger patterns from a flotation device paralleling drop-offs can be effective almost any time if one uses a full-sinking line.

Wade Lake is the easiest of the Graben Lakes to reach. From Highway 287 one crosses Three Dollar Bridge, passes through the old Cliff Lake town site, travels a few miles on the well-maintained gravel road to a fork, and bears right. At the top of the Wade Lake bench, the north end of Cliff Lake is on the left and Wade Lake is on the right. Bearing right takes one past the Wade Lake Resort, formerly Elliot's, on the west side of the lake.

Just beyond the resort is the popular developed campground that serves as a base for those coming to troll the depths and waterborne fly fishers. As summer warms,

Wade Lake originally hosted westslope cutthroat trout, but by the mid-twentieth century they were replaced by browns and rainbows. Famed California fly tier Doug Prince gained experience on Wade Lake in the 1940s that resulted in his Prince Nymph. (Bruce Staples collection)

Wade Lake is the farthest north of the Graben Lakes. Springtime and autumn are the best times to fish here. The lake becomes popular with waterborne recreationists during summer. (Bruce Staples collection)

however, it also serves as a base for Jet-Skiers, water-skiers, and other motorized aquatic activity, making another reason why night fishing is attractive here. Parts of the west shoreline are available to fly fishers attempting to wade shallows. Speckled dun emergences take place in these shallows during the summer, and trout residing there respond. If not interfered with by motorized recreation on the lake, the resulting gulper activity can be enjoyable. Drop-offs near the campground and its vicinity are precipitous and most of the shoreline is timbered, thus use of a flotation device is ideal. For those seeking more range, motoring to distant parts of the lake to launch flotation devices is practical.

Like Elk and Cliff Lakes, Wade Lake is open to ice fishing. The main spawning area for browns in the fall and rainbows in springtime are springs at the south end. This area is off-limits to fishing to protect not only the fish but also the delicate habitat that hosts them.

ELLIOT'S RESORT

As with resorts on Cliff and Elk Lakes, West Yellowstone fly-fishing retailers sent visitors to Elliot's Resort after Wade Lake became known as a superb westslope cut-throat trout fishery. George Elliot opened this resort on the southwest side of Wade Lake in the early 1930s after homesteading its land in 1918. He was a contemporary of the Neelys, likewise Missouri homesteaders, and as with the Neelys on Cliff Lake, introduced rainbow trout into Wade Lake. While fishing nearby Cliff Lake in the late 1920s, Elliot caught a twenty-four-and-a-half-pound rainbow trout after a three-hour battle. His gear consisted of a bamboo rod, silk line, and gut leader. Alas, if you are a fly fisher, his terminal gear was a Colorado spinner. This fish stood as a Montana state record rainbow trout for decades.

Elliot's wife's grandson, Forrest Hill, eventually took over the resort and changed the name to Hill's Resort. The Montana Fish and Game Commission planted brown trout in Wade Lake during the 1950s, although area residents believe they were in the lake earlier. The 1959 earthquake destroyed the original resort, but it was soon rebuilt. The full-service, year-round Wade Lake Resort is currently owned by Dave and Laurie Schmidt and offers boat rentals and fishing guides for guests.

Henry's Fork Drainage

Henry's Fork

Access: US Highway 20

GPS coordinates: Flat Ranch Preserve 44.581412, -111.336690; Mack's Inn upstream 44.490535, -111.285785; Coffee Pot area 44.491715, -111.364471; Box Canyon 44.416540, -111.394270; Last Chance–Harriman State Park 44.355787, -111.414079

Equipment: 5- and 6-weight systems with floating line; BWO, PMD, Trico, flav, speckled dun, mahogany dun, golden stone, caddisfly, and yellow sally life-cycle patterns, and terrestrial insect and traditional attractor patterns

Nearest facilities and services: Island Park, ID; USFS Buffalo River, Box Canyon, and Riverside Campgrounds; Pond's Lodge; Henry's Fork Anglers; Three Rivers Ranch Outfitters; Trouthunter; Angler's Inn; Mack's Inn

Information resources: Caribou-Targhee National Forest, Island Park Ranger Station; USGS flow station gages 13039500 and 13042500; Island Park, Big Springs, Island Park, Island Park Dam, and Last Chance USGS topographic maps

Salmonids present: Brook, cutthroat, and rainbow trout

The Henry's Fork's ties to the West Yellowstone fly-fishing community are historic and rich. Because the United States Geological Survey adheres to Henry's Lake as the Henry's Fork's source, we will do the same. We will end our discussion of the river just above the Pinehaven summer home area because from that location downstream the Henry's Fork is more easily approached from Ashton, Idaho. It is worth noting here that in the vicinity of that town, the river's salmonid fishery is of at least equivalent quality as the reach we will address.

In its entirety the Henry's Fork is considered by many in the fly-fishing community to be the finest trout stream in America. It came into extraordinary popularity in the 1970s. Before that decade its reach in Island Park was much a domain of the wealthy

Henry's Lake in the distance through a summertime haze. The foreground features its outlet running through the Nature Conservancy's Flat Ranch Preserve, a popular fly-fishing destination from town. (Bruce Staples collection)

and a few local anglers. Closest to West Yellowstone is the reach immediately below Henry's Lake known commonly as Henry's Lake Outlet.

Here the river flows about ten miles, much of which is through vast and beautiful Henry's Lake Flat, where it courses through riffles, a few deep holes, and willows, and gains volume from groundwater and tributaries originating in the Henry's Lake Mountains. Until recently the meadow below the crossing was mainly private land used only for raising livestock. The Nature Conservancy's Flat Ranch Preserve now protects most of the river in the meadow below the US Highway 20 crossing.

Until the Nature Conservancy acquisition, the river and its surroundings were devastated through more than a century of overgrazing, bank erosion, willow removal, and diversion. Now within the Flat Ranch Preserve, the conservancy is having success in returning quality to the meadow. Scientific planning rotates livestock use in a manner that minimizes impact. Resident flora and fauna enhancement is of equal importance to the application of educated livestock usage. The growing success of enlightened management on the Flat Ranch Preserve can be observed through the return of an early-summer wildflower bloom so intense that people passing by on the adjacent highway stop and observe in admiration.

During times of continuous abundant water flow, the river here hosts a fine trout population. This population is dominated, in terms of large fish, by escapees from the lake above, with brook, cutthroat, and cutbow hybrids continually introduced. In extended times of good water flows, the river holds a superb continuum of emerging aquatic insects. Included are many of the major mayfly genera found in the famed Last Chance–Harriman State Park reach below. Caddisfly and midge emergences go on through the season, and in season damsel and dragonflies emerge and become important food forms. As the season progresses, terrestrial insects in major abundance become important food forms for resident trout, but as the waters warm, fishing success can be elusive. Throughout the season this reach also features much less angling pressure than downstream reaches, thus it has a small, intense group of advocates during good water years.

Dewatering of this reach presents a continuous problem. Unlike in the river below Island Park Dam, efforts to establish a minimum flow have been fruitless. Arcane water management of Henry's Lake is the reason, and only acceptance of the larger economic value of a minimum flow concept by those managing use of the lake waters will allow this to happen. During times of drought, flow out of the lake has been turned off entirely when it is deemed that water for agricultural purposes is threatened. This can happen for an entire season, or can take place anytime from spring to autumn. Fortunately such management practices are on the wane in the region, and studies have revealed that there is room for a minimum flow through this reach. Perhaps in time such will be established. Certainly, the Henry's Lake fishery should not be compromised by releases, and agriculture must have a fair share of this water, but establishing at least a maintenance flow in the reach would add to the economic base of the region.

Below the Flat Ranch Preserve, the Henry's Fork flows again through private land for a few miles before meeting the Big Springs outlet. Impacts from livestock grazing

Moose are common inhabitants of riparian areas along streams and lake shorelines. Give them as wide a berth as should be given to any large wildlife. You are the intruder. (Bruce Staples collection)

and relocation of the river from its natural channel on the upper end decrease its quality here, but on the lower end it courses through a swampy, but protective, willow thicket in Targhee National Forest. Soon this reach, still known as Henry's Lake Outlet, meets the larger and purer flow from Big Springs. When it does, the river is truly large and holds a continuous flow.

Everything natural is present in the reach to make it an outstanding salmonid fishery, but as we will see, incursion by humans has compromised this ability. The first feature of note here is the series of huge holes known as "The Bathtubs," or simply "The Tubs." Formerly these hosted huge but difficult trout. Trout this size are occasional nowadays, but the sturdy Rocky Mountain whitefish remains present here in sizes ranging to over three pounds. From this confluence downstream for a few miles, access to the river is public, then private property flanks the river to above Mack's Inn. The river here appears as a large meadow stream with a silted, sandy bottom holding occasional gravel lenses and large weed beds. Summer recreational boating is common here.

This reach from the confluence of Big Springs Outlet and Henry's Lake Outlet to Mack's Inn is really where the legendary Henry's Fork begins. In *Trout*, Ray Bergman relates fishing the Tubs with Scotty Chapman. Charlie Brooks also fished them. Wally Welch hosted Joe Brooks here, among other locations on the river. In season during the 1930s, Don Martinez sent clients here to enjoy cutthroat trout below Mack's Inn adjacent to the highway crossing.

The gradient increases almost continuously as the river flows for about four miles over bedrock covered with a thin layer of gravel. The Henry's Fork now alters to a riffle-and-run stream, and hillsides and benches begin to confine it. Soon the top of the quarter-mile-long Coffee Pot Rapids thunders a warning to leave the river. Below the rapids, the river runs to Island Park Reservoir through a brief, but beautiful, section of riffles punctuated by a few deep runs. All of the reach from the Big Springs–Henry's Lake Outlet confluence to Island Park Reservoir is fishable, with a salmonid population eager to respond to dry flies.

Mack's Inn, established nearly a century ago, remains the recreation center on the river above Island Park Reservoir. The lower end of this reach was part of the Trude story. Several fishing clubs established their retreats here, mainly above Coffee Pot Rapids. But all this was in the past, and much of it before the formation of Island Park Reservoir. Since then conditions on the reach have changed, and not for the benefit of the wild trout population.

Periodic introduction of silt coming from a century of livestock grazing along Henry's Lake Outlet remains. Until recently motorized boating impacted riverbanks and in-stream structure. Hand-propelled boating remains throughout the reach, and although interruptive to angling, is a legitimate activity for the many recreationists in the area. Sewage inflow from adjacent subdivisions has always been suspected of altering water quality. The former practice of releasing hatchery rainbow trout has decreased the number of resident wild trout. Harvest of salmonids is allowed throughout the reach, and careless persons leave offal along its banks. And it is now realized that the presence of Island Park Reservoir has interrupted the late-season rainbow trout migration into the reach.

Thus this reach from the Big Springs–Henry's Lake Outlet to Island Park Reservoir, naturally beautiful and made up of several different water types, is presently the most altered by mankind in the upper river. Yes, there are efforts to improve the quality of the river and its surroundings here, as the local business community and landowners now realize its economic value. Recently the Idaho Department of Fish and Game has turned to releasing Yellowstone cutthroat trout into the river rather than hatchery-reared rainbow trout. They were once native to the entire river, and are now present in good numbers. Hopefully they can reestablish in the much-altered river here, but doing so will be an uphill fight.

Island Park Reservoir interrupts the natural state of the Henry's Fork. Thus we will not discuss it other than to say that as a quality fishery it is intermittent because of frequent and major draw-downs for agricultural purposes. This contrasts with what Hebgen Lake adds to the Madison River fishery. Below Island Park Dam the Henry's Fork continues in legendary status. Restrictive angling regulations (catch-and-release fly fishing only using barbless hooks, no fishing from boats) protect the fishery here, and for a vast number of fly fishers, it remains a primary destination.

Box Canyon is at the top of this most renowned reach. For three miles below Island Park Dam, the river courses through the narrow canyon. Here is why so many consider the river in Box Canyon a destination. Its rocky bottom is the most productive type for producing aquatic insects as well as for holding trout. Rocks varying in size from pebbles to small automobiles make good cover for both. So do the depth and the presence of good holding water. From spring to autumn, the temperature of the water coming from the reservoir above is ideal for salmonid and aquatic insect growth. Food, based on the nutrient-rich water, is tremendously abundant, most notably in the form of giant stonefly nymphs. But caddis, mayflies, and other insects also abound, along with baitfish and crayfish. Add terrestrial insects in season, and the canyon offers for trout what amounts to a never-ending buffet of round-the-clock available food. No wonder trout here can grow to such large sizes. Now blessed with a minimum flow through the winter months, it appears that Box Canyon may hold its reputation indefinitely.

The abundance of giant stonefly nymphs here dictates a most effective fly-fishing strategy. Any form of giant or golden stonefly nymph pattern is a must throughout the season. Presentation dominates pattern selection, and Mike Lawson is on record as saying that a spark plug fixed with a hook would probably work. His point is that any giant stonefly nymph pattern used must be placed near the bottom of the river for success. In season, other strategies work well, including presentation of caddis life-cycle patterns, terrestrial patterns, and, particularly in the late season, streamers.

Access to the Box Canyon reach is relatively easy. Original Highway 191 parallels the lower half of the canyon, and a foot trail winds upstream from this road to the Buffalo River confluence. From these, several trails go through the canyon wall to the river. The west side of the canyon offers more challenging access from the parking area on the west side of Island Park Dam. Floating (although fishing from a boat is not allowed) is the most effective means to access the canyon from the launch site below the dam to the canyon mouth.

Box Canyon village marks the mouth of the canyon. As if resting after its jaunt through the canyon, the river slows to a jog here. Exiting a run famed for holding trout ranging to over twenty pounds, it widens and curves to the east to approach Last Chance. Now the river is in sight of US Highway 20 and literally a stone's throw from the road. For a half mile it courses the highway closely, and in season hordes of fly fishers can be testing the waters. This reach continuing through Harriman State

Will Godfrey went from guiding for Bud Lilly to establishing his own shop, the first full-service fly-fishing shop in Island Park, Idaho. Will participated in FFF Conclaves as a sought-after auctioneer. As shown here, he also introduced youths to fly tying and all other aspects of fly fishing. (Courtesy Gerry Randolph)

Park is the basis for the elegant House of Harrop fly patterns and Mike Lawson's progression of mayfly, caddisfly, and terrestrial patterns. Had it not been preserved by persons of foresight, fly-fishing lore would have been much poorer and the personalities associated with it would likely not have current stature.

At Last Chance the river bottom is ideal for hosting insects. Rubble provides overhead cover, weeds and porous rocks host clinging types, sandy gravel supports burrowers, and the gentle current allows the presence of swimming types. This bottom type and gradient continues well into Harriman State Park. In the park below, the river widens and shallows and an even gentler current takes over in what some call "Bonefish Flats." All this marks the site of "Green Drake Madness" come the latter part of June each year.

About halfway through the reach down to the US Highway 20 bridge (Osborne Bridge), the river narrows at a stock bridge to rush through a short chute, then widens again. Now it is more complex than above, having deep areas and numerous channels and islands. Large trout and the food forms that allow them to grow abound here.

On gliding past the array of historic ranch buildings marking the park center, the river begins to change once more. After going around a large island and part of the pine forest, it picks up gradient then goes through the conspicuous riffle just above Osborne Bridge. The reach just below the bridge is of gradient similar to that at Last Chance, but the river is weedier and the bottom not as rocky. As the gradient slows downstream, sand and silt interspersed with gravel make up most of the bottom. It's ideal brown drake habitat, and it is also easily waded although not easily crossed. Springs enter, keeping the water quality high through this section of the park. Wood Road 16 accesses the lower end of the park, and for many anglers this is the choicest location of the reach.

The Last Chance rest stop on the upstream boundary of Harriman State Park is a place of legend in fly-fishing lore. Beginning in the 1970s, crowds of fly fishers assembled here to enjoy the waters in the park below or to prospect along the Last Chance reach. Noting these crowds, enterprising folks set up informal fly shops out of campers, trailers, and station wagons at the rest stop parking lot, particularly during the latter half of June when Green Drake Madness prevails. Flies, tying materials, leaders, lines, and various gear, all with tales credible and incredible, were the fare.

As the crowds grew, René Harrop and Mike Lawson commiserated over the loss of solitude on the reach, but saw their businesses benefiting. Bing Lempke held court here, dispensing information on trout behavior and insect characteristics. From time to time he offered examples of his elegant fly patterns tied on the spot within his camp trailer or perhaps the night before in a Last Chance motel. From here Andy Puyans savored the Last Chance reach of the river. Scott Sanchez speaks of tying flies on the dashboard of his car in a frenzied effort to provide patterns to simulate what trout where keying on during his visit. Syl Nemes staged here to begin his soft-hackled forays into the Harriman reach. Here Bud Lilly began his first float trip through what was then the Railroad Ranch in the 1960s. He remembers marveling at the lack of anglers, only to find at the end of the trip that his presence was before the traditional June 15 opening! The rest stop remains a jump-off point for visiting fly fishers as well as the site for events that celebrate the river's history and quality.

Perhaps the most complex emergence of aquatic insects known in the fly-fishing world takes place on the Last Chance–Harriman State Park reach of the Henry's Fork. The progression of insect emergences in this reach is repeatedly documented in fly-fishing literature, so there is no need to present another version here. Several different insects can emerge simultaneously at peak times, thus fly-fishing success can elude even the most experienced angler visiting the reach. The two best descriptions of this progression and how to approach it can be found in Charlie Brooks's *The Henry's Fork* and Mike Lawson's *Fly-Fishing Guide to the Henry's Fork*. Lawson's book in particular offers strategy gems based on his decades of intense fly-fishing experience on this reach, and not all of what he offers is based on the famed water's mayfly emergences. René and exceptional Bonnie Harrop's *Learning from the Water* also provides a wealth of information on fly-fishing this reach unmatched anywhere in fly-fishing literature.

The best advice to offer is that the visiting fly fisher should stop at a local shop to obtain current information on the progression of insect emergences and which ones are attracting trout at a given time. These shops are literally right on the river, a situation that does not often exist on the waters we discuss in this work. The advantage to the fly fisher of having shops on the river's edge is that information received there on angling conditions is almost instantaneous. Thus the angler can literally exit the shop and walk to the river to apply the knowledge just received.

Henry's Lake

Access: US Highway 20, State Highway 87, Henry's Lake Road

GPS coordinates: Bill Frome RV Park 44.650186, -111437234; Henry's Lake State Park 44.617695, -111369794; Henry's Lake Hatchery 44.665233, -111386922

Equipment: 6- and 7-weight systems with floating, intermediate, and sink-tip lines; speckled dun and midge life-cycle patterns; and leech, streamer, and attractor patterns

Nearest facilities and services: Island Park, ID; Henry's Lake State Park Campground; Bill Frome RV Park; Mack's Inn; Wild Rose Ranch

Information resources: Island Park Ranger Station; Sawtell Peak, Targhee Pass, and Targhee Peak USGS topographic maps

Salmonids present: Brook, cutthroat, and rainbow trout

Henry's Lake is an example of what good a dam can do for a fishery. Before the dam was built in 1923, the lake was much smaller and shallower at no more than seven feet deep. Its shores were mostly muddy and weedy, making it difficult to approach, except in winter. Islands formed of dense weed mats interwoven on trapped logs floated on the lake, their courses governed by the usual winds. Some of these islands were strong enough to support camping. From late spring to autumn, weed growth on the lake bottom was copious enough to raise the water level and also host enormous amounts of aquatic life-forms. But numerous submerged springs were present in the lake to keep its water hospitable for trout throughout the year: cooler in the summer and warmer in the winter.

Historically Yellowstone cutthroat were the only resident salmonids, and they were the basis for a subsistence fishery used at times by Native Americans. Tributary streams, in these early times unaltered from their natural state, hosted immense springtime spawning runs, and the Native peoples congregated around them to remove enough fish to satisfy their immediate needs. The trout population was enormous, and when the first European Americans arrived just after the mid-nineteenth century, some saw a commercial use for this abundance.

Gilman Sawtell, after establishing his ranch in 1868 on the north shore, was the first commercial fisherman on the lake. Markets were in the Montana mining towns to the north and the growing Mormon communities to the south. As much as ninety tons of trout per year were removed from the lake. Near the turn of the century, the State of Idaho stepped in to make commercial fishing illegal, and sportfishing began to give Henry's Lake its lasting fame. Sportfishing begun in the late nineteenth century was practiced by mostly a few well-to-do anglers, having the means to reach the relatively isolated lake, and a few local practitioners.

During the early twentieth century stocks of fish diminished, and the establishment of a state hatchery in 1924 on the north shore was the next major public effort established to reverse this trend. But it was increasing demand for irrigation water that brought about the dam that would eventually make Henry's Lake one of the finest trout fisheries anywhere. When the North Fork Reservoir Company completed the dam on the outlet for private agricultural interests, the resulting impoundment deepened and cooled the lake to optimal conditions for producing enormous numbers of large trout. As the regional highway net was completed and sportfishing became available to the general public over the next few decades, the lake's reputation as a premier fishery began to grow to what it is today.

Angling on Henry's Lake begins with the opening of the Idaho general angling season on Memorial Day weekend. Winter does not completely leave the area, situated well above six thousand feet, for weeks after the opening. In fact, there have been opening weekends when the lake is not ice-free. Thus any visitor during springtime should be prepared for the lake's famed snow squalls, icy waters, and frequent whistling gales. Such conditions can last well into June, but the challenging weather should not deter the fly fisher from trying the lake, because time-tested strategies can result in some fabulous angling.

Perhaps the best strategy designed to keep the fly fisher the least wet is wading shorelines. The north shore is the best location to practice this approach, and public access is easily available at the state fish hatchery. Extensive wading to the east or west can be done from the hatchery as long as one remains within the high-water shoreline due to private land along the lakeshore. Leech patterns in small and medium sizes presented on sink-tip, intermediate, or floating lines and long leaders can be effective. Experience shows that proper presentation (a slow, undulating retrieve with frequent stops along the bottom) is more important than reliance on a specific pattern. One also should remember that leech patterns moved slowly along the bottom also simulate dragonfly nymphs, another preferred early-season food form.

The north shore is also relatively safe for early-season tubing and pontoon boating, as prevailing winds are from the southwest and will thus tend to blow back toward shore. Sink-tip and type 2 sinking lines are best for float tubers and pontoon boaters presenting leech and streamer patterns adjacent to the shoreline. Some shoreline wade fishing, float tubing, and pontoon boating using the same tactics is also available at the outlet, along the west shoreline, and along the southwest-side cliffs in the early season, but fish populations in these areas may not be as dense as along the north shore.

In the early season, large midge emergences can occur almost anywhere on the lake. The best time to present midge patterns is soon after the emergence has begun. This can happen anytime, so the visiting angler should be prepared with patterns and lines suitable for presenting midge emerger patterns at various depths when either wading or fishing from a boat or flotation device. When fish taking emerging midges are encountered, techniques such as using a strike indicator on the surface above a drifting emerger pattern placed at an effective depth can be deadly. Any emerger pattern in sizes 16 through 20 will produce when presented in this manner with a very slow retrieve or when allowed to drift with the wind. Bloodworm patterns are popular during these times, and presentation of parasol patterns and variations are becoming popular during midge emergences on the lake.

The most reliable locations from which to launch powerboats into the lake are from Henry's Lake State Park on the southeast side and the Fremont County (Bill Fromm RV Park) boat dock on the west side. For a small fee some private landowners on the lake, including Staley Springs Resort and Wild Rose Ranch, allow trespass to the lakeshore. For safety reasons, boats without power are not recommended on the lake because the sudden and strong winds that commonly occur from mid-morning to twilight produce capsizing danger or make it difficult to return to a point of origin.

With a powerboat, one can experience good early-season fishing by motoring to areas around inlets where spawning fish are returning to the lake. Nearly all of these inlets are on private land, making it necessary to approach from the lake. Some of the better locations are near the mouths of Targhee, Howard, Hope, and Duck Creeks and along springs emptying into the lake. Leech and streamer fishing with sinking lines is best here, unless fish are taking midge emergers. Sculpins inhabit Henry's Lake, and because they are a preferred forage item, presenting patterns to them should be considered, as trout returning from spawning seek large food forms.

Drift fishing and trolling can be productive in the early season. Drift fishing is performed from keeled boats drifting with the wind, and trolling is done at speeds of less than two miles an hour. Because weed growth is just beginning, most of the lake can be fished using either of these tactics. Leech and streamer patterns on sinking lines ranging from type 4 to lead core, depending on depth of presentation, can be effective. The absence of extensive weeds means snails and shrimp are not yet present in great numbers, and thus fish will likely not key on their imitations.

As the end of June approaches, warming water and the growth of weeds dictate that tactics must change on the lake for angling success. Fishing now becomes more complicated than in the early season because more food forms are available. Not only does the lake bottom become channeled because of weed growth, but the food forms now available to fish disperse to various parts of the lake. Thus as the season progresses from late June to autumn, the fly fisher has the best chance of success by changing strategies to meet the availability of food forms and the resulting changing location of fish.

Some constants can be found for successful fly fishing on Henry's Lake. Wet-fly patterns in shades of medium olive or green will be effective throughout the season because these colors predominate in many of the major food forms present: damselfly nymphs, leeches, shrimp, and caddis pupae. Leech patterns will be effective throughout the season on Henry's Lake, particularly for larger trout. The most useful lines here are full-sink types that allow presentation at depths where fish activity occurs at any given time.

Here's another constant: Brook trout tend to concentrate in shallower waters, except when temperatures there exceed seventy degrees. Gammarus and Hyallela shrimp populations expand in the weed growth to make up a major part of the trout's diet over the season. Fishing shrimp patterns in open water can lead to consistent success, but success improves if one concentrates efforts around the edges of weed beds, where fish will congregate to feed. Water fleas (Daphnia) are one of the most numerous food forms in the lake, but their small size makes them primarily sought after by fingerlings and fry. Water beetles, water boatmen, and backswimmers now populate the shallows and are fair game for cruising fish.

By the end of June and peaking in early July, the emergence for which Henry's Lake is best known begins. This is the damselfly emergence, which has diminished somewhat in recent years. During this event damselflies make up nearly all of a trout's diet. Although damselfly nymphs are present in the lake throughout the season, their activity during these times makes them most available. The strategy is to first find channels among the weed beds through boating, then align casting along the main axis of the channel and retrieve the fly with slow strips and occasional pauses from the depth at which the nymphs are emerging after crawling up submerged vegetation. Atmospheric and water temperatures govern the time of day when most activity occurs, with mornings and evenings usually being best.

Most of Henry's Lake damselfly nymphs are about an inch long and colored medium olive-green. Pattern choice within these requirements is not as important as presentation strategy. As the bulk of emerging damselflies work toward the surface, feeding trout will key on this direction. Thus the angler must go to lines that allow presentations closer to the surface. With time nymphs migrate toward surface features such as exposed portions of submerged logs, brush, weeds, and stumps. They also swim to shallow areas along the lakeshore, and when doing so wade fishing can be effective. One must remember that stealth is required when fish move to shallow water and near the surface in pursuit of emerging damselflies, whether wading or fishing from a boat. Prime fishing spots during the damselfly emergence are the shallow areas between Duck Creek on the south to the Fremont County Boat Dock.

As the damselfly emergence fades past mid-July, strategies for fly-fishing success change again. Evening caddis emergences begin by July, and fish key on them best after the damselfly emergence wanes. The best places to encounter fish feeding on this emergence is around submerged springs. Dry-fly fishing during caddis emergences can be enjoyed in these areas, but the requirement for such is the absence of wind, thus chances for success are best early and late in the day.

By the middle of July, waters are warm enough that trout, particularly larger individuals, are moving toward submerged springs where the water is cooler and thus has a higher dissolved oxygen content. Now fishing close to shore with float tubes and pontoon boats becomes less effective unless done around the submerged springs and mouths of creeks that introduce cooler water into the lake. The mouth of Targhee Creek is one of the best such places at this time.

The stories of large fish being taken at Staley Springs also begin as June turns to July. But as the large fish move in, so do crowds of anglers presenting all types of terminal offerings. With respect to flies, small patterns simulating shrimp, caddis pupae, and damselfly nymphs seem to work best here. The cable below the spring marks where legal fishing begins and the start of the channel going through submerged weeds from the spring into the lake. Intermediate and slower-sinking lines such as type 1 are best in the shallowest water in front of the spring, while progressively faster-sinking lines should be used as one proceeds out the channel into the lake. Leaders about nine feet in length and 3X tippet are most useful throughout the waters below the spring.

When August arrives, and continuing through the first days of September, strategies for success change again. Early August is the warmest time of year in the Henry's Lake area. Lake water usually reaches its highest temperature by early August, and the resulting weed growth expands to fill in many submerged channels. Few areas free of weeds remain out in the lake, thus trolling and drift fishing become much less effective for larger fish than earlier in the season. Boats on the lake diminish, and in general fewer anglers visit the lake during this time. Nevertheless, good fishing can be experienced if one presents leech patterns mainly in shallow waters, near springs, and around creek mouths.

In general, Callibaetis mayflies species emerge from the lake around midday. Staley Springs remains good fishing through August, as trout congregate there because of cool water. Fewer anglers will be present at the spring unless some active fishing begins. Then, as word of success spreads like that of a developing gold rush, anglers seem to emerge from nowhere to descend upon the spring. But when crowding takes place here, other angling attractions can be found on Henry's Lake.

Historically, the best time for encountering brook trout begins as the season moves toward September. Water temperature greatly affects the rate at which brook trout stage in advance of spawning runs. Brook trout population varies over the years and depends primarily on Idaho Department of Fish and Game management policies for them.

In preparation for spawning runs, brook trout begin staging in front of creeks emptying into the lake. Duck, Howard, Targhee, and Hope Creek inlet areas experience this migration, as do springs and creeks along the north shore. The areas around the confluence can be easily accessed for wading and launching float tubes and pontoon boats through public land at the hatchery. Hope Creek can also easily be reached for early-morning and evening fishing from tubes and pontoons. A parking area on the lakeshore at the end of the county road from Red Rock Pass Road provides access to the west end of the cliffs and for a relatively short float to the Hope Creek and Kenny Creek areas.

Within twenty miles of West Yellowstone, Henry's Lake is a popular destination for fly fishers. Wading the north shoreline during autumn to present streamer and leech patterns can be productive, but pleasant weather, as in the above photo, is not always present. (Bruce Staples collection)

Presenting leech patterns remains effective in all these areas, particularly early in the day before mayfly emergences begin. At all times erratic retrieves are best for presenting shrimp patterns, and the angler must remember that in times of stronger light, such as midday, shrimp tend to descend to deeper water. Thus sinking rates of lines should be changed accordingly. Gradually toward the end of the period successful fishing moves continuously to shallow water, and for the fly fisher this trend continues to the end of the season.

For the fly fisher, late-season success on Henry's Lake is more often than not near shore. Thus these times can be the best part of the lake's season for those without boats. To begin, it is appropriate to discuss preparations because shoreline fishing attracts so many anglers in the autumn, when weather can become increasingly uncertain. Indian summer days here can change to blizzard conditions overnight. Warm, windproof clothing, raincoats, and insulated waders should therefore be close by. Hot beverages and a change of clothing should be kept in a convenient location because an accidental dunking without items for recovery can be serious or even fatal. Icing of guides and reels is common, thus this time of the season can also be tough on equipment.

Strong winds and low temperatures keep the wise person from venturing out into the lake in these times of oncoming foul weather. In the past, foolhardy or inexperienced individuals have perished on the lake during foul autumn (and spring-time) weather. With the weather deteriorating, one must also be aware that roads can become treacherous due to blizzards, icing, and blowing snow. There have been times when Henry's Lake ices over before the close of the season.

This weather governs autumn fishing on Henry's Lake. Many fly fishers claim the best fishing is during foul weather. At this time winds roughen the lake surface with waves up to three feet tall. This action stirs up the bottom in the shallows, and fish preparing for winter forage for food forms released from the bottom and from the dying and receding weeds. Thus shoreline anglers look forward to stormy days. Of course, being out on the lake during autumn storms can be disagreeable, so anglers using boats tend to favor fair weather.

Brook trout migrations help attract numerous cutthroat and hybrids, so there is an overall concentration of fish along shorelines. Leech patterns in large and medium sizes produce well along shorelines throughout the autumn season. They also simulate annelids stirred up from wave action and drifting along bottoms. Shrimp and snail patterns are also effective when presented in the shallows to simulate those released from dying weeds agitated by wave action. Sink-tip and intermediate lines can present these patterns effectively, and some fly fishers use floating lines to present these with good effect. Fish around shorelines tend not to be leader-shy when waters are discolored, thus regardless of line choice the use of stout leaders is the rule due to the good potential to encounter very large trout.

Anglers now concentrate along shorelines such as the southwest cliffs, in front of creeks, and the north side. The area around the hatchery again becomes popular and can get crowded except during the worst of weather. From here much of the north shoreline can be waded. Past problems with crowding in front of Hatchery Creek, which interfered with spawning trout returning to the hatchery and hatchery personnel operations conducted to increase their spawning efficiency, led to the establishment of a no-fishing area marked by buoys in front of the hatchery.

Bill Schiess is the dean of Henry's Lake fly fishers. Having fished the lake since his youth as much as one hundred days a season, he has gained a matchless wealth of experience and knowledge of the lake's fishery. Bill shares this knowledge in his book *Fishing Henry's Lake*. Few books devoted to a single fishery contain as much strategy detail as this book. It can be found in all fly shops in the Greater Yellowstone area.

MADISON RIVER DRAINAGE

Duck Creek and Cougar Creek

Access: Duck Creek Road off US Highway 191 and USFS Road 287D off US Highway 287, both north of West Yellowstone, MT

GPS coordinates: Yellowstone Park 44.779146, -111.097379; below Highway 191 crossing 44.775256, -111.132854

Equipment: 5- and 6-weight systems; brown and green drake, caddisfly, damselfly, dragonfly, and speckled dun life-cycle patterns, and leech, streamer, terrestrial insect, and annelid cluster patterns

Nearest facilities and services: West Yellowstone, MT; USFS Baker's Hole Campground; Parade Rest Ranch

Information resources: Yellowstone
   National Park, Richards Creek USGS
   topographic map
Salmonids present: Brook, brown, and
   rainbow trout

Duck Creek begins in Yellowstone
National Park at the junction of Richards and Gneiss Creeks. Although about
two miles from a major highway and less
then ten miles from town, this beginning
has a remote and tranquil atmosphere,
though subdivisions above Hebgen Lake
are visible to the northwest. Westslope
cutthroat and grayling were pushed
out of the creek by brown and rainbow
trout from Hebgen Lake before the mid-
twentieth century.

Duck Creek has two meadow reaches
separated by a short riffle-and-run
stretch that begins just above the Highway 191 crossing. Like the South Fork
of the Madison, it is a meadow stream
above and below this riffle-and-run
stretch at the crossing. Unlike the South
Fork, however, its upper meadow is public land in Yellowstone Park and easily
approached. Above Koelzer's Pond, an
aged private impoundment newer than

Richards Spring in the
Duck Creek drainage
was the realm of trophy
brook trout into the
1980s. Once considered
a secret location,
it is now closed to
all human entrance
because of grizzly bear
activity. (Bruce Staples
collection)

A springtime evening on Duck Creek offers tranquility as well as the possibility of encountering large brown and rainbow trout. This is bear country, so precautions including spray and a claxon horn are sensible additions to gear. (Bruce Staples collection)

Hebgen Lake and just outside the park boundary, to its formation at the Richards-Gneiss confluence the creek flows westerly. It is a perfect example of a meadow stream as it meanders through willow patches and grasses.

Within this large meadow wildlife is usually in view. Bison, elk, deer, beaver, moose, and on occasion bear are among these. Waterfowl are abundant. Just the sight of this near-pristine meadow, bordered by the Burnt Hole forest on the south and sagebrush slopes on the north, inspires photography and quickens a desire to test its waters. Richards Spring, at the head of the so-named creek, formerly hosted brook trout ranging upward to five pounds. Due to concentrated grizzly bear usage, the spring and creek were closed to visitation in 1990s.

A few of the Richards Spring brook trout descendants remain in Duck Creek. Throughout the season any fly fisher visiting the upper meadow must apply utmost stealth and offer perfect presentations for any chance of fooling the wary brown and

Duck and Cougar Creeks combine below the US Highway 191 crossing and offer tranquil fishing during springtime rainbow trout runs and autumn brown and rainbow trout runs from Hebgen Lake. Thick willows hide moose and bears can pass through the area, thus cautious entry is required. (Bruce Staples collection)

Privately owned Koelzer's Pond was formed decades ago by damming Duck Creek. The Yellowstone Park west boundary crosses at the creek inlet. Above the pond, Duck Creek meanders through its large meadow and is enhanced there by numerous springs. (Bruce Staples collection)

rainbow trout residents. As with Duck Creek in its meadow in the park, brown and rainbow trout rival in size those in the adjacent Gallatin and Madison Rivers. Peculiarly, no Rocky Mountain whitefish inhabit the creek.

In its meadow reach below the highway, Duck Creek enters Cougar Creek, which flows into Hebgen Lake's Grayling Arm. Here silt defines more of the stream bottom, willow patches thicken, beaver holes increase, and so does the chance of encountering moose. Cougar Creek here is less remote and not as scenic as Duck Creek in the meadow above. A subdivision is within a few hundred yards to the north, and highway noise is more pronounced. Large brown and rainbow trout are present. Because of the thicker willow background, the creek is less easily approached than in the upstream meadow. Nevertheless, stealth must be applied.

Throughout, both creeks have an insect structure consisting of dragonflies and damselflies, relatively sparse mayflies, and caddisflies. Some brown and a few green drakes emerge around the first of July and some speckled duns a bit later. As the days advance after mid-June, Duck Creek and lower Cougar Creek offer good dry-fly fishing as terrestrial insects increase, but stealth remains necessary due to dropping flows.

Earthquake (Quake) Lake

Access: US Highway 287

Equipment: 6- and 7-weight systems; damselfly, dragonfly, and speckled dun life-cycle patterns, and leech, streamer, and terrestrial insect patterns

GPS coordinates: Beaver Creek Campground 44.854161, -111.369773; public boat launch 44.854757, -111.387571

Nearest facilities and services: West Yellowstone, MT; USFS Beaver Creek and Cabin Creek Campgrounds; Campfire Lodge; Slide Inn

Information resources: Earthquake Lake USGS topographic map

Salmonids present: Brown and rainbow trout, Rocky Mountain whitefish

Charlie Brooks writes in *The Living River* that the lake formed by the August 17, 1959, earthquake inundated perhaps the best reach of the Madison River in terms of producing large trout. He described the stream before being submerged as "beautiful and majestic." Pat Barnes also lamented the loss of this reach of the river that was among his favorites.

Here the river was Charlie's ideal, and his love of presenting heavily weighted stonefly nymphs proved consistently effective. In his wonderfully readable style, he describes how the dam formed by the landslide was at first highly unstable, while ultimately creating a lake almost 250 feet deep and larger in surface area than when *The Living River* was released (1979). A larger volume of material moved as a result of the earthquake, he claims, than went into the construction of Hoover Dam. After formation of the lake, there was fear that if water backed up to the base of Hebgen Dam, failure could result from its base being undermined. Had either or both dams failed, the consequence would have been a certain disaster for the river below.

Interestingly, one has to wonder how many salmonids were killed by the slide. Charlie relates that the US Army Corps of Engineers took heed from what happened to the town of Kelly, Wyoming, in 1927 when the two-year-old Slide Lake Dam resulting from the Gros Ventre landslide partially failed. The Corps, according to his

Quake Lake Dam, caused by the August 1959 earthquake, established the youngest natural lake in the Greater Yellowstone area. Earthquake Lake is now a major destination fishery, hosting brown and rainbow trout ranging to trophy sizes. (Bruce Staples collection)

description, came immediately to stabilize the dam, cutting fifty feet of rubble off its top and easing the gradient of its face to achieve stabilization. The result behind the Slide Lake Dam was the present somewhat-sinuous lake, up to 180 feet deep, no more than a half-mile wide, and a bit over four miles long.

In addition to lamenting the loss of the river in the canyon, Charlie points out that because waters come off the top of the lake to the river below, its entire reach down to Ennis Lake, about sixty miles, would be warmed during the summer above the former optimal temperatures for trout habitation. Spring creek inflows on the lower half of the reach, however, help return the waters nearer to optimal temperatures. Charlie also laments the loss of spawning water, now inundated by the lake, as well as a huge population of aquatic insects, including his favorites, the nymph stage of golden and giant stoneflies.

We tend to think of lakes as requiring geologic time to be formed. But Earthquake Lake, which we will discuss by its common name, "Quake Lake," was formed almost in an instant. It is the only natural lake on the Madison River. In fact, it is the youngest natural lake in the Greater Yellowstone region, beating Slide Lake on Wyoming's Gros Ventre River by a bit more than three decades. What makes this lake even more unusual is that it was formed within the memory of many people. As we have noted previously, this is the case with only a few lakes in the American

West, and West Yellowstone holds many earthquake stories, including those on the formation of Quake Lake.

In elevation, Quake Lake is about 160 feet lower than the full-pool elevation of Hebgen Lake. Quake Lake has the unusual feature of an inundated pine forest along both its shorelines. This forest is most dense below the Beaver Creek confluence. Looking down into the depths during periods of calm winds, the forest is an eerie presence of treetops and limbs holding moss stringers that wave in an invisible current. Both a hazard to boaters and a hindrance to anglers, the underwater forest has a positive benefit in providing abundant cover for trout and in being an extensive host of food forms. It is rotting away, but in gradually reducing form it will probably be a permanent feature of the lake.

Presently Quake Lake hosts trout ranging to larger sizes than the reach of river it consumed, particularly in respect to resident brown trout. They now range to double-figure poundage in the rich and sheltered waters of the lake. Bob Jacklin can testify to this, having almost unexpectedly caught on June 16, 2006, a ten-pound brown trout in the river just above the lake. Almost certainly this behemoth was a lake fish foraging in the high-quality river waters. Browns confirmed to be up to thirteen pounds have been taken from the lake. Those of even larger sizes are claimed to been encountered but not landed due to their diving into the submerged forest. Rainbow trout also flourish in the lake, rich with overhead cover and impenetrable sanctuaries formed by the groves of sunken pine trees. Rainbows ranging to five pounds are fairly common here and certainly grow larger. All this makes for a rich local folklore on the size of trout that

How long will Earthquake Lake's drowned forest stand? Its only equivalent is the drowned forest at the upper end of Wyoming's Lower Slide Lake. Both represent a hazard to flotation devices but offer fine overhead cover for hosted salmonids. (Bruce Staples collection)

Looking west from the Earthquake Lake Visitor Center on US Highway 287. From here the Madison River flows into its upper valley, with the benches holding Cliff and Wade Lakes farther to the west. Below the dam begins the reach where fishing from a boat or flotation device is not allowed downstream to Lyons Bridge. (Bruce Staples collection)

Quake Lake hosts and how to encounter them. As is the case with so many regional waters, only Rocky Mountain whitefish remain of the original native salmonids.

In some ways, Quake Lake suffers the fate of lesser-famed waters situated between waters of greater literary renown. When the Madison River is discussed, Quake Lake is usually skipped or barely mentioned. On each side of the lake are reaches of the Madison River that are frequently featured in the fly-fishing media. Upstream is Hebgen Lake, and on the other side of the mountains sits Henry's Lake. These waters have been heralded in fly-fishing literature from before the middle of the twentieth century, whereas Quake Lake was not born until nearly a decade later.

In addition, it took another decade to build Quake Lake's fishery to quality status. Indeed, Charlie Brooks's description of the lake in *The Living River* and his predictions for its fishery remain the most detailed in print. Charlie wrote this book nearly thirty years ago. Even "guidebooks," which are becoming increasingly popular, barely mention its presence. Thus you will find little in fly-fishing literature on strategies for fishing its large trout population holding more than its share of trophy individuals. But to those in the know, Quake Lake in the proper season is a destination. All this, with due respect to Charlie's lamentations on the loss of a superb Madison River reach, makes Quake Lake the region's newest high-quality coldwater fishery.

Ice-out on Quake Lake normally occurs in the middle of May around the time that the Montana general angling season opens, traditionally on the third Saturday of May. At this time an effective method of fishing is to present streamers and nymphs at the edges of ice remaining on the lake. Many fly fishers place their flies on an ice shelf over a drop-off, pull the fly into the water to sink a few feet, and then retrieve it. The amount of time to do this is limited to only a few days and requires communicating with local fly-fishing shops to determine when ice is leaving the lake. Rainbows, having recently spawned in the river above, will be passing through the upper part of the lake, looking for food items including forage fish.

Not long after ice is off the lake, runoff loads in Beaver Creek do much to determine the start of the continuous fly-fishing season on Quake Lake. This creek, entering near the top of the lake, drains high country on the southeast slope of the Madison Range that rises to over eleven thousand feet. In abundant-water years, it can bring cold, turbid meltwaters to the lake almost as late as the first of July. It is also the major source of silt coming into the lake because Hebgen Lake above acts as a settling basin. This creek, incidentally, hosts a good population of cutthroat trout that are protected by a late angling season opening.

To a lesser extent, silt associated with runoff from Cabin Creek also enters Quake Lake through the river above. At times springtime flows out of Hebgen Dam can be changed depending on power and irrigation demands downstream in Montana. These too can compromise Quake Lake angling early in the season. But as spring merges into summer, inflows usually stabilize, and the lake becomes a wonderful destination for fly fishing.

Access to the best fishing is at the top end of the lake. The Campfire Lodge is situated on Highway 287 near the river about a mile above the lake, and provides a full

The Campfire Lodge has a century-long history of serving fly fishers. Its location on the Madison River between Hebgen and Quake Lakes ensures popularity. The lodge offers all angling services to its clients. (Bruce Staples collection)

complement of services from meals and lodging to space for recreational vehicles and tents. Across Highway 287 from the lodge, Cabin Creek flows through a campground bearing its name. Not far down the highway from the lodge, Beaver Creek Campground offers the best access on the lake. Situated on a bench above the lake, there is an access near its west side where the original highway goes into the lake. This spot is used to launch craft ranging from motorized boats to flotation devices. The lodge and the two campgrounds are all suitable bases for fishing the best waters of Quake Lake.

From the Campfire Lodge, a well-maintained gravel road parallels the Madison River on the north side. It ends a few hundred yards from where the river enters Quake Lake. Thus for the fly fisher a choice is presented here as to whether it is more practical to wade the shallows at the top of the lake or launch a personal watercraft.

Beaver Creek enters the lake about a half a mile downstream. Beaver Creek Campground, not far from the site of the now-submerged Halford Camp, is a bit farther down the lake on the same side, and occupants frequently walk to the creek confluence to fish in the limited space available. Situated on a bench overlooking the lake, it is adjacent to some of the best areas for fishing. Shallows abound in front of the campground and across the lake that here is only several hundred yards wide. Just as with the shallows at the inlet, these provide some of the best fly-fishing locations that Quake Lake offers. There are shallows farther down the lake, but the submerged forest makes their approach by powerboat quite hazardous. Personal watercraft and good physical condition are the safest and most practical requirements to approach these areas. Some deepwater fishing is easily available from the backside of Quake Lake's dam. A primitive road allows access here, but launching larger craft is difficult.

Almost daily all lakes in the Greater Yellowstone region experience midday to late-afternoon winds, Quake Lake included. But winds here can howl up and down the lake to almost alarming proportions, as the canyon above is a natural Venturi tube. For those presenting dry flies when this wind begins, the only way to do so is with its direction. This famous wind can also be hazardous to boaters not aware of its onset and their location relative to the submerged forests. The wind disrupts the joys of fishing for Quake Lake gulpers, but typically is absent during the early hours of the day and usually dies down in the evening, allowing dry-fly and other kinds of fishing to resume.

Buck and Ben Goodrich and LeRoy Cook are among the most knowledgeable of the Quake Lake fly fishers. Their experience runs decades and spans the entire season on the lake, usually beginning in June and extending into November. They both offer that having a strategy is necessary for achieving fully enjoyable fly fishing on Quake Lake. They agree that location must be considered when forming this strategy. Angling is possible at the dam, but this is mainly a deep-water area, making fly fishing difficult.

Certainly, shallow areas around the lake offer better angling where easily approached and relatively free of obstructions, but the submerged forest also hosts a large population of fish due to the abundant food forms. Obviously, it is harder to fish this forest because of the submerged trees and the possibility during a backcast of snagging treetops extending out of the water. Shallows exist in many locations, but other than at the upper end of the lake, one must approach from out in the lake because much of the shoreline is not accessible by roads or requires maneuvering through or around the submerged forest. In fact, the entire south shoreline has no roads.

At the end of runoff season, an effective strategy is to fish the drop-off areas around the shallows with streamer and leech patterns on sink-tip, intermediate, or full-sink lines. Evenings and early mornings are the best times for this strategy, but stormy daytimes can alter results. Throughout the shallows, caddis, mayfly, and stonefly life-cycle patterns can be effective, particularly for smaller fish that congregate here waiting for insect emergences. Near the end of June a few damselflies will emerge in this area but seem not to be a major food form for trout. A bit later, stoneflies are present, having been wind-blown from the river above the lake, and create exciting dry-fly fishing. By mid-July terrestrial patterns become increasingly effective, particularly near banks, and once more the fly fisher can experience the exhilarating experience of having very large trout take floating patterns. Trout continue to cruise the shorelines in good numbers here much of the season, looking for prey whether forage minnows, insects, or even small mammals.

By midsummer, the gulper phenomenon here is as intense as that on Hebgen Lake upstream, albeit in a smaller setting. But fly fishers in the know forsake it for a chance of a fish of a lifetime that may respond to well-placed streamers, hoppers, or even a hair mouse along shorelines. This strategy seems most effective when these patterns are presented toward the shoreline from out in the lake. Thus advantage comes from using a flotation device or wading the abundant shallows. The use of powerboats along the shorelines startles fish into deeper water. Noise and vibration from these boats are enough to do so, but the higher profile of powerboats and drift boats decreases success. Nevertheless, the strategy of concentrating efforts on the shorelines and drop-offs can hold well into the autumn season.

When autumn frosts descend on the region, a return to presenting streamer patterns across drop-offs and in the estuary brings many encounters with trophy-size brown trout. Browns of spawning ilk will stage in these areas to later move into the river above. As November approaches, chances increase for encountering these large fish, but so does foul weather and bad driving conditions. So this is the season when caution and keeping warm becomes almost as important as angling strategy.

Veteran Quake Lake fly fishers believe that the next Montana state record brown trout resides within the water-bound trees. Is it reasonable to predict the same for rainbows? Who knows, but the problem of getting that big one out of the sunken forest remains. This, of course, adds to legends of the size of Quake Lake trout, and to the increasing number of stories of "how I lost that big one down in the trees!" When and if that record brown or rainbow comes out of Quake Lake, it will gain the angling status it deserves.

Firehole River

Access: Grand Loop Road south of Madison Junction

GPS coordinates: Pullout and picnic areas between Firehole Falls and Nez Perce Creek 44.592634, -110.830670; Nez Perce Creek Picnic Area 44.5786323, -110.831156; Fountain Flats Drive 44.568442, -110.834656; Little Firehole River 44.483151, -110.853801

Equipment: 4- and 5-weight systems with floating and sink-tip lines; BWO, caddisfly, golden stone, midge, PMD, Trico, and yellow sally life-cycle patterns, and terrestrial insect and streamer patterns

Nearest facilities and services: West Yellowstone, MT; Madison Junction
   Campground
Information resources: Yellowstone National Park; West Yellowstone Visitor Center; Old Faithful Inn; Old Faithful Lodge; USGS flow station gages 06036805
   and 06036905; Madison Junction, Lower Geyser Basin, and Old Faithful USGS
   topographic maps
Salmonids present: Brook, brown, and rainbow trout

About twenty-five miles southeast of West Yellowstone, the Madison and Pitchstone
plateaus come together in an isolated and beautiful area traversed by the Continental Divide. In about twenty-five square miles are the Bechler, Firehole, and Lewis
River headwaters. Madison Lake, little more than a marshy pond, and a few small
streams give birth to the Firehole River flowing north. It is almost unbelievable for
many visiting fly fishers to accept that about 120 years ago the Firehole was devoid
of salmonids. To believe this, consider the changes that have taken place in the
Firehole River since the August 1959 earthquake, then apparently accelerated by the
earthquakes of the early 1970s.

In *Remembrances of Rivers Past*, Ernie Schwiebert's sixth section is on the Firehole. He also labels it a "brown trout stream" and observes that resident trout here
"seldom see (aquatic) insects larger than size sixteen flies." This dates from his first
experience fishing the river in 1965. By then the brown drake emergence of huge
proportions that occurred during early summers before the 1959 earthquake was
disappearing.

Charlie Brooks also tells of this emergence, but judging from his writings, he
is more interested in the effectiveness of dragonfly nymphs, such as his Assam
Dragon, in fooling large Firehole River trout. Their populations, he proclaims, were
not impacted by the thermal effects of earthquakes. Conversely, he observes that
populations of giant stoneflies have been impacted. And he is right, because they
are now rare except for small numbers existing in the more-oxygenated waters of the
canyon just above Madison Junction. From the late 1940s through the 1970s, perhaps
no one fished the Firehole River as much as Charlie, and no one kept track of its
characteristics like he. Although opinionated, he certainly was honest: We therefore
must consider his observations and experiences here as carrying much weight and
consider their importance in predicting the loss of large trout from the river.

Scientists and fly fishers alike observe that Baetis mayfly species emerge year-round
from the river. Considering this fact and that the river is at optimal temperatures
for trout habitation in winter, the Firehole could offer its best fishing at this time.
Schwiebert recommended mainly eastern patterns for presentation during mayfly
emergences. Charlie did the same with respect to dry flies. So did Bud Lilly and Pat
Barnes, because early in their business experience so many clients were easterners.
But in the five decades since Ernie made his visit and Charlie plied its waters, western
patterns have taken over in popularity on the Firehole.

The Firehole has the lengthiest official stocking record of waters in Yellowstone
National Park. All planting in the river ceased in 1955. Fortunately, some bizarre
attempts at introduction failed, including a 1920s Yellowstone Lake cutthroat trout
introduction. Would westslope cutthroat have been a better introduction considering their recent history in the downstream waters of the Madison River? Because of

The Firehole River–Nez Perce Creek confluence holds a picnic area popular for gearing up to fish and for taking time off for lunch or to exchange on-the-stream stories. (Bruce Staples collection)

successful introductions, the Firehole may be the best example of turning a barren stream of considerable size into a great salmonid fishery.

Yellowstone Park abounds in what appears to be the epitome of beautiful trout streams. Here are the Bechler River in its vast, pristine meadow and view of the Grand Teton Range; the Fall River with its willowy, stair-step meadows and somber pine forests; the Heart River in primitive beauty between Heart Lake and its canyon; and the breathtaking beauty of Slough Creek in the park's upper reach. So why is the Firehole, from Old Faithful downstream, considered by so many fly fishers to be the classic trout stream and the most beautiful river in the park? Given that the beauty of the Firehole in the reach below Old Faithful is beyond dispute, the answer to this question is simple: Only the Firehole among these streams has a road paralleling most of its hospitable length for trout. Thus for an outdoor writer with a deadline, it is prudent to travel a well-maintained road to view an obviously beautiful stream teeming with trout to large sizes rather than hike miles into the backcountry to view the same.

This has been the case, beginning with Hewitt's visits, for much of the twentieth century. In the 1930s, it was Ray Bergman's turn to visit then promote the Firehole River. Since these early accolades, it has been featured in outdoor magazines and books as much as any stream in the region. Ernie Schwiebert labeled the river below

Old Faithful as "perfect dry-fly water." Charlie Brooks considered the Firehole to be "the finest dry fly stream in the nation." From statements such as these, and from being easily accessed, it is visited by fly fishers more than those beautiful streams mentioned above combined.

Above the reach of major thermal water input beginning around Old Faithful, the Firehole River is chemically typical of a high-elevation stream. Its waters are slightly acidic and nearly barren of dissolved nutrients. Caddisflies are by far the major aquatic insect. In these waters, any small-stream strategy will be successful. This part of the Firehole, nearly a third of its entire length, is roadless and isolated. It is also relatively inhospitable, being of higher gradient and of short growing season. It hosts only smaller brook trout and a few browns. If one must fish the Firehole during midsummer, this is perhaps the best place to do so without impacting thermally stressed trout.

From where massive amounts of thermal water enter beginning around Old Faithful, Firehole River waters become slightly alkaline and richer in nutrients. Here the river does not host a wide diversity of aquatic insects, but as is common in such waters, the total number of hosted insects is large. From the highway bridge above Old Faithful down to the top of Biscuit Basin the river is closed to fishing to preserve water quality for culinary purposes and to protect thermal features.

Our discussion treats the Firehole as having two seasons each year. The first opens on the Saturday morning of Memorial Day weekend and runs through June. This is followed by a "recess" running through July and August. Then, as the atmosphere cools to frosty September nights, comes the second annual season that runs to the early-November closure. We address the river from Biscuit Basin on downstream, but

Old Faithful, more than any other natural feature, is the reason for human development in the Madison River drainage. The best fishing on the Firehole River begins below Old Faithful. (Bruce Staples collection)

Nez Perce Creek, a major Firehole River tributary, offers uncrowded conditions for those fly fishers willing to walk upstream for a mile or so. Brown and rainbow trout ranging to moderate size inhabit the creek. If you choose to fish here, be "bear aware." (Bruce Staples collection)

first a few words on strategy may help in approaching this river. Lightweight systems with long, fine leaders are the rule. The dry-fly patterns discussed should be mostly in smaller sizes, 16 through 20 being the norm. Almost anywhere, stalking from the bank is a better approach to active fish than wading. Wade only when necessary, and strive to do so over solid substrate in the shallowest water available.

The most heavily fished reaches of the river are from Biscuit Basin through Muleshoe Bend, named by Charlie Brooks, and from around the Nez Perce Creek confluence through the "Firehole Broads," also named by Charlie, and the portion along the highway to the cascades below. These sections hold good numbers of trout. Early in the season the waters of the canyon below Firehole Falls can also be heavily fished. Formerly, Fountain Freight Road was open to traffic from its junction at Nez Perce Creek upstream to the Lower Iron Bridge. Now it is closed to all but foot and bicycle traffic. Speaking of Nez Perce Creek, if one is willing to walk upstream a bit over a mile to get above the bulk of thermal features, it offers good fishing for small brown and rainbow trout.

The Fountain Freight Road closure has significantly reduced fishing pressure along the river in the upper part of what is called Fountain Flats. Thus walking up to the bridge, a distance of about a mile and a half, then fishing back down can be rewarding. Just below the bridge one passes the Ojo Caliente Bend that Charlie Brooks proclaimed to host the largest trout in the river as well as abundant insects before thermal warming took place in the early 1970s.

Scuds are all but gone, caddis are diminished but still plentiful, and small snails abound. Below the bend is the long reach through Fountain Flats that holds undercut

Fountain Freight Road and the Firehole River above the Nez Perce Creek confluence. One must walk from the Nez Perce Creek picnic area to fish the river adjacent to Fountain Freight Road and above the bridge. (Bruce Staples collection)

Legendary Muleshoe Bend on the Firehole River is now off-limits to fishing. The National Park Service elects to close any place in the park where natural features or wildlife can be physically threatened or where passage is dangerous. (Bruce Staples collection)

banks, potholes, and weed beds. Throughout the season expect your best fishing to take place during cloudy or stormy days. Pack a raincoat and windproof jacket. Regardless of when you visit the Firehole River and where you fish it, traverse thermal areas with caution, and remain on established trails. Park management may close areas at any time around thermal features that are in danger of man-made damage. The river at Muleshoe Bend, for example, is now closed to human access.

The early season on this catch-and-release, fly-fishing-only stream begins at the season opener near the end of May. Water is coldest at this time because of runoff, but the stream quickly clears of snowmelt from headwater country, none of which reaches nine thousand feet in elevation. By early June the river is in prime condition for fly fishing, with an array of blue-winged olive and pale morning dun mayflies, and more numerous small caddisflies and midges. Experienced anglers recommend emerger, soft-hackle patterns and nymphs near the surface for fish keying on either mayflies or caddisflies. They also concentrate their fishing in the early morning and in the evening. Generally, presenting small caddis imitations may be the most effective strategy this time of year. For the Brachycentrus and Hydropsyche caddisflies, pupal patterns and low-profile dry patterns are most reliable.

Around early June giant stoneflies emerge from waters in the Firehole Canyon just above Madison Junction. Fleeting at best, this emergence is not consequential every year, but in the waters immediately above the canyon, within it, and in the Madison River immediately below, fish can be caught for a few days on large dry imitations.

Firehole Falls is a barrier to upstream migration of brown and rainbow trout originating from Hebgen Lake. The swift water below the falls produces a brief early-summer giant and golden stonefly emergence which is seldom fished. Adult stoneflies are wind-blown into the river above and catch the attention of resident trout. (Public domain)

The Little Firehole River and Iron Spring Creek hold little thermal water. They therefore serve as a cooler summer refuge for trout escaping from the much warmer Firehole River. (Bruce Staples collection)

Western green drakes (flavs) appear by mid-June, when the water is beginning to warm. For the Isoperla stoneflies that emerge throughout the season, any small yellow sally patterns work well. Midge pupa patterns produce now, as well as in the late season. Small Woolly Bugger patterns are effective this time of year. Two life-forms fly fishers tend to overlook when fishing the Firehole River are damselflies and dragonflies. Their numbers here appear not to be impacted by the warming of waters. Thus both are abundant, and in the early season nymph patterns for them can be very effective.

As July begins waters warm and can reach into the eighties. Trout have difficulty staying active due to reduced dissolved oxygen, and their growth rates halt. Aquatic insect emergences diminish. Those trout staying in the river feed less, particularly during daylight hours. Advocates for sanctuary now have a reasonable issue that should not be argued: For the most part, larger trout in the river seek sanctuary in the cooler waters of Fairy Creek, Sentinel Creek, the Little Firehole River, and Iron Spring Creek. These streams are thus refuges from the warming river, and for purposes of preserving trout, should be honored as such during times of thermal stress.

The late season on the Firehole begins about the time summer wanes in the region. September brings frosty evenings, fewer daylight hours, and more variable weather to the river and surroundings. Mature brown trout and also rainbow trout move upstream to colder reaches of the river to spawn. The cooling waters become more hospitable to trout and many of their aquatic food forms. Diminishing terrestrial insects including hoppers, ants, and beetles remain, and their imitations will bring strikes from fish foraging near banks and from undercuts. Rhyacophila caddis again emerge in good numbers. White miller caddis patterns are particularly effective in the afternoons and evenings. The same is true for blue-winged olive mayflies, but they are smaller than those of the early season. Midges are always present and so are the tiny black caddis known to some as black dancers. Streamers are never very effective because no bait-fish inhabit the river. The exception to this is that the Hebgen Lake fish that run into the river below Firehole Falls can be taken on properly presented streamer patterns.

At this time of year the number of anglers is down from the late-spring-to-late-summer peak. Nevertheless, there is a fly-fishing migration to the river to fish early-morning responses to Trico activity. The Firehole River comes alive from the summer doldrums, with fish responding to blue-winged olive and late-season caddis activity. An increasing number of fly fishers are responding to the October caddis activity, but nothing attracts them as much as the late-season run of Hebgen Reservoir brown and rainbow trout to upstream spawning areas in Yellowstone Park, of which the Firehole River below its falls hosts a minor portion. But as time advances through October, the threat of winter weather increases.

Though much is known about this beautiful river, it remains the subject of many legends. A modern one begun by outdoor writers, persisting to this day, is that the Firehole is a "limestone stream." It may look like the epitome of such, but when one looks at its chemical makeup and geologic surroundings, it fails the test. Limestone streams are rich in dissolved calcium bicarbonates, introduced from the country rock through which they flow. The Firehole flows through country mainly under-lain by volcanic rock, rich in soluble forms of sodium, that influences the chemical makeup of the geothermal waters that massively enter it. Therefore the river is rich in dissolved sodium bicarbonates (though enough dissolved calcium bicarbonate is present to ensure a good population of aquatic insects). The thermal character of the river also impacts its aquatic insect makeup. From the viewpoint of enjoyment, it is beyond debate that the Firehole River is among the most beautiful of trout streams and an absolute delight to visit.

Gibbon River

Access: West Entrance Road to Madison Junction
GPS coordinates: Madison Junction 44.645323, -110.857899; Gibbon Meadows 44.695190, -110.743650
Equipment: 4- and 5-weight systems with floating and sink-tip lines; BWO, cad-disfly, golden stone, PMD, Trico, and yellow sally life-cycle patterns, and terres-trial insect and streamer patterns
Nearest facilities and services: West Yellowstone, MT; Madison Junction Campground
Information resources: Yellowstone National Park, West Yellowstone Visitor Cen-ter, USGS flow station gage 06037500, Madison Junction and Norris Junction USGS topographic maps
Salmonids present: Brown and rainbow trout, grayling, Rocky Mountain whitefish

Sources of the Gibbon River are above eight thousand feet on the Solfatara Plateau, where winter snowfalls can accumulate to tens of feet. Thus the source waters remain exceptionally cold until moderated by geothermal inflows below. They combine at Grebe Lake, where the drainage first hosts salmonids introduced by humans, and from there the Gibbon flows into Wolf Lake. Grebe, Wolf, and nearby Cascade Lake in the Yellowstone River drainage east of the Continental Divide are commonly referred to as the Grayling Lakes. Notice that our discussion on the upper river and lakes is in past tense. This is due to the poisoning the river above Virginia Cascades and below, an action undertaken by park fisheries management to eradicate all salmonids in preparation to reintroduce westslope cutthroat and fluvial grayling.

After leaving Wolf Lake, the river meanders a bit on the edge of the plateau, then after rushing through it slows and winds through Virginia Meadows. Here small brook trout, a few small rainbow trout, and grayling resided. All of these were a delight to fish with the lightest of rods, floating lines, and small dry attractor and caddis patterns of size 14 or less or bead-head nymphs in the same sizes. A certain amount of stealth was required for success here because the open meadow makes a human form conspicuous.

On leaving the meadow, the river tumbles down Virginia Cascade; runs through a lodgepole pine forest south of Ice Lake, historically barren but once stocked with brook, cutthroat, and rainbow trout and grayling; and then runs into the meadows at Norris Junction. Here, as it winds its way, the Gibbon is joined by Solfatara Creek, formerly a delightful small stream to fish, which increases its size before leaving for Norris Geyser Basin below. The trout here, more rainbows than brook trout, were larger but the numbers of grayling diminished significantly. The entire reach

Here is an example of using stealth to present a fly. It is a necessary strategy for meadow reaches of the Madison, Gibbon, Gallatin, and South Fork of Madison Rivers as well as on Duck Creek. After a day of using this posture and the "Henry's Fork hunchback" stance, a hot bath or shower is a must. (Bob Jacklin collection)

is alongside roads, is easily visible, and holds an attractive and popular picnic area. Consequently, the river here was heavily fished.

Like the Firehole, the Gibbon has an important input of geothermal water. For the Gibbon this begins in volume as it winds around the north and west sides of Norris Geyser Basin, a reach not particularly attractive for fishing and somewhat dangerous because of thin-crusted thermal features. Geothermal inflow at its largest amount enters the Gibbon here but continues as the river descends, adding about one-fifth of its flow. This addition complicated resident salmonid behavior and aquatic life in general in the Gibbon, but it also made for a long growing season.

A slight drop in elevation to Elk Park, then more cascades and Gibbon Meadows are next. Very large brown trout are hosted here. Next, as the river falls from the plateau, comes Gibbon Canyon hosting magnificent Gibbon Falls. Mostly small trout reside in the rushing waters below, but an occasional trophy can be encountered in a deep run or hole.

The river through this canyon has been paralleled for decades by a segment of the Grand Loop Road. Proving detrimental to the river because of toxic runoff components, much of the road below Gibbon Meadows is now rerouted onto the plateau to the east. From this location the road descends to the river about half a mile below Gibbon Falls and continues to accompanying the river to its confluence with the Firehole. A one-way loop hosting reduced traffic to view the falls remains.

The gradient below the falls flattens as the canyon widens. Resident salmonids, mostly brown and rainbow trout but with a smattering of brook trout and a few Rocky Mountain whitefish, increase in size and numbers. Then about a mile or so above Madison Junction it is out onto National Park Meadows. In effect, then, the Gibbon descends from plateau to plateau as if descending a staircase. Risers are the canyons and cascades. Each tread is where the river slows down in a meadow, and each land increases in size from Virginia Meadows to National Park Meadows.

Now in National Park Meadows, the Gibbon meanders beautifully for nearly two miles, rich in holding water, more abundant in food forms, and with plentiful large trout. Its journey ends just south of Madison Junction in confluence with the Firehole River to produce the Madison River.

As we have seen, the Gibbon was barren of salmonids above Gibbon Falls. In all, nearly one and a half million rainbows would be released throughout the river before their stocking ceased. Laughably, 250 smallmouth bass were released in the Gibbon in 1893 but failed to establish. Grayling are caught from time to time in the river, but their presence raises the question as to whether they have come from the lakes above or are members of a remnant river population. Reports of grayling being caught throughout the river in recent decades raise hopes that they may be repopulating its waters.

Brown and rainbow trout moved in below the falls from the original 1890 stocking in the Firehole drainage, and rainbows also descended from above the falls. Along with brown trout, they replaced the native westslope cutthroat trout and grayling. Grayling stocked in Grebe and Wolf Lakes, beginning in the 1930s and ending in the 1940s, were sometimes encountered, particularly above the falls.

The Gibbon River is the Rodney Dangerfield of the Madison drainage in the park, as it gets the least respect of its major streams. It is about one-third the size of the Firehole, the river most like it in the park. Outdoor writers have perpetuated this evaluation. Charles Waterman, for example, in *Mist on the River* offers that the Gibbon

The lower Gibbon River meanders its way to its confluence with the Firehole River, thus forming the Madison. This easily approached meadow reach receives much fly-fishing pressure during the fall run-up season. (Bruce Staples collection)

River is overshadowed (as a fishery) by other area streams. He considers the river to be a "consolation prize" after going on an unsuccessful grayling outing elsewhere. All this seems unfair, and here's why: The largest confirmed brown trout caught in the park came from the Gibbon and it was not a Hebgen Lake run-up fish. This fish, nearly ten pounds, was caught near Norris Geyser Basin, miles above Gibbon Falls.

The waters in Gibbon Meadows and Elk Park have also produced browns of several pounds, events that no longer happen on the Firehole above its falls, and only rarely in the Madison except when Hebgen Lake fish are present. Large rainbows reside throughout the Gibbon below its falls, but like their fellow resident large browns, they are wary almost beyond belief.

Another point that anglers tend to overlook that makes the Gibbon worthy of greater respect is that most of the Hebgen run-up browns spawn each autumn in its waters, as do spring and autumn rainbows. Thus as the twentieth century advanced past its midpoint, the Gibbon hosted more large trout than the Firehole. This wonderful little river therefore deserves respect because it is so vital in maintaining the fine reputation Hebgen Lake owns as an outstanding fishery. And there is another reason that should increase the Gibbon's claim for equality: Its brown drake emergence has no equal on either the Firehole or Madison within the park. One must go to Slough Creek, the Henry's Fork, or the Fall River basin streams to find one that exceeds it.

The Gibbon, having slightly acidic waters, has a wide array of aquatic insects, but as is common in such waters, the total number of hosted insects is not exceedingly large. In its upper reaches the river hosts mostly caddis species. Stonefly species are never abundant throughout the river, due in part to its acidic nature, but in all its low-gradient reaches damselflies and dragonflies are important food forms. Mayfly species and numbers increase as the river descends, but such mayflies as blue-winged olives, pale morning duns, and slate cream duns never reach the importance of caddis as a food form.

The Gibbon below its falls has been restricted to fly fishing only since 1968, and two fish over sixteen inches are allowed creeled each day. Fortunately fly fishers overwhelmingly release all fish, so fishing on the Gibbon has improved substantially in the last four decades.

Like the Firehole and Lewis Rivers, the Gibbon is one of the first streams in the park to become fishable when the season opens. Waters may be high and clear, with Wolf and Grebe Lakes acting as moderators for runoff flows, and in-stream temperatures are moderated by geothermal waters.

In all high-gradient reaches, traditional dry attractor and caddis patterns in sizes ranging from 12 down to 18 will bring up fish throughout the season. Small bead-head nymph patterns are also effective in these water types. All one really needs for presenting these flies is a floating line and leader of medium strength. In the early season, streamer and dragonfly nymph patterns presented deep in the National Park Meadows reach provide the best chance to encounter run-up Hebgen Lake rainbows and a few resident lunker browns. But this strategy quickly becomes less effective as the season advances into June and when the run-up fish return to the lake.

Gibbon Falls is a barrier to trout moving upstream from below. The river above was once devoid of salmonids, but early-twentieth-century US Fish and Wildlife actions introduced them to populate the river and its upstream drainage. (Courtesy Supercarwaar)

The brown drake emergence in late June to early July is the next attractive time to fish the Gibbon. Doing so is strictly an evening affair. Dinner in West Yellowstone between five and six in the evening and being on the river in Gibbon Meadows around seven with emerger and dun patterns and resolve to be stealthy is the norm. Minimized wading is vital, as is presenting patterns downstream with stout leaders. In the nearly three hours of fishing, there is a good chance of encountering a large fish in the fading light. Don't overlook the lower Gibbon as the season advances through the summer, as a well-placed ant, beetle, or hopper pattern can bring up a lunker in the river below the falls. Rae Servatius was one who knew this fact well and therefore frequented the river during summer.

In the late season the angling attraction is the run of large brown and rainbow trout from Hebgen Lake. These trout have made a journey of nearly thirty river miles, so they too deserve respect. Presenting streamer patterns deep is the name of the game, and presentation skill, not pattern type, is most important. Autumn conditions make fishing most attractive here. The atmosphere is cool and bracing, and gone are the insect pests of warmer months. The river is low and easy to wade, although such an action should be minimized, particularly in its meadow reaches. Crowds have thinned, and wildlife presence increases. Stalking the large brown and rainbow trout with nearby bull elk bugling challenges, coyotes yipping their presence, and migrating geese honking overhead conveys one back to the nineteenth century when the park was young.

Hebgen Lake

Access: US Highway 287 and Lonesomehurst, Madison Arm, and Madison Rim (Horse Butte) Roads

Equipment: 6- and 7-weight systems; damselfly, dragonfly, midge, speckled dun, and Trico life-cycle patterns, and leech, streamer, and terrestrial insect patterns

GPS coordinates: Cherry Creek Campground 44.750895, -111.264076; Spring Creek Campground 44.784389, -111. 275484; Lonesomehurst Campground and boat dock 44.730376, -111.231959; Rainbow Point Campground and boat dock 44.780763, -111.179265; Madison Rim Road 44.747921, -111199347

Nearest facilities and services: West Yellowstone, MT; USFS Baker's Hole, Beaver Creek, Cabin Creek, Lonesomehurst, and Rainbow Point Campgrounds; USFS Basin Station rental cabin; Campfire Lodge; Yellowstone Holiday Lodge; Firehole Ranch; Kirkwood Marina

Information resources: Hebgen Dam, Madison Arm, and Mount Hebgen USGS topographic maps

Salmonids present: Brown and rainbow trout, Rocky Mountain whitefish

Hebgen Lake's formation caused the biggest change in the makeup of the region's salmonid population. Without it, brook, brown, and rainbow trout released in the Gibbon and Firehole Rivers upstream would have eventually populated the river below, but not as quickly.

Of the original salmonid natives, only the sturdy Rocky Mountain whitefish remains in the reservoir and the waters above in abundance, including individuals up to four pounds. Utah chubs, introduced by careless bait fishermen, also thrive in Hebgen Lake. When they rise to take food forms on the surface, they can confound fly fishers. But their young make good forage for large rainbow and brown trout.

Bison can be found at many fly-fishing locations around town. They are commonly seen in large meadow reaches of streams and around lakes. They should not be approached by anyone. (Courtesy LeRoy Cook)

Hebgen Lake's South Fork Arm offers a refuge from winds that usually roughen the surface of the lake proper. Popular Lonesomehurst Campground is at the center. The intersection of the South Fork Arm and the Madison River Arm (middle right) begins a favored location for fly fishers during the August gulper season. (Bruce Staples collection)

Hebgen Lake has nearly sixty miles of shoreline, is sixteen miles long, and is up to three miles wide. With numerous shallow bays and inlets, especially along the north-west shoreline, it hosts a variety of aqueous habitats. During low water, mudflats on its upper end can be treacherous, unattractive, and unproductive. Quake Lake is not far below, giving the unusual setting of a man-made lake that is older than a natural lake on the same river. Before the reservoir was formed, the Madison River gathered tributaries, Cougar and Grayling Creeks and the South Fork of the Madison being the major ones, in the broad flat basin. Now the reservoir shoreline is peppered with summer homes and resorts. Motorized boat traffic and recreation on the lake becomes rampant in the summer months because of relatively warm summertime waters.

Hebgen is fished year-round, with ice fishing being popular after the usual November ice-up. Ice-off typically occurs by the second week of May. Almost daily, wind across the reservoir strengthens after mid-morning and lasts until evening. Prevailing southwesterly winds, those coming downslope from the Gallatin Range to the east, and those coming up the remains of the Madison Canyon below fan out across the lake with intensity, sometimes making subsurface fishing difficult and surface fishing impossible. At these times it is best to seek one of the many west-side bays, of which the South Fork Arm can be the most productive.

Of the three major arms (or estuaries) on this reservoir, the South Fork Arm, by far the smallest, can be the easiest to fish. Not particularly attractive during low-water times, it has, however, the advantage of being shielded from the windiest conditions on the reservoir. There is a public boat ramp at Lonesomehurst Campground located a few miles north of US Highway 20, and nearly its entire shoreline can be fished by wading. Primitive roads access the arm's entire eastern shoreline, from which, at many locations, personal watercraft can be launched. The South Fork Arm is productive year-round, with large trout migrating through it early and late in the season.

The Grayling Arm on the northeast side of the lake is expansive, but shallow. Summer homes dot its northeastern end. During summer blue-green algae often form during low-water conditions, depleting dissolved oxygen and imparting toxic conditions to mammals. Thus mid-season fishing here is usually not as productive as on the rest of the reservoir, but as the season moves toward autumn and waters cool, brown trout will migrate through the arm to travel into Grayling, Cougar, and Duck Creeks to spawn. At this time, presenting streamers in these creeks above their estuaries can be productive. Fishing in the estuaries, however, can be fruitless and even difficult if low waters prevail late in the season, exposing deep mudflats.

The Madison Arm is a major feature of the reservoir. Extending southeasterly for about six miles and narrowing from an initial width of about a mile, it holds the Madison River channel and is a major destination during the middle of the angling season. Roads access much of its shoreline, and public access is abundant except on the south side near its mouth where private property is abundant. By late summer brown and rainbow trout accumulate in the upper reach of this arm to begin their spawning migration into the Madison River above. In the early season the Madison Arm holds rainbow trout that have spawned in the river above and are returning to disperse around the reservoir. These rainbows provide good early-season action for

Rainbow trout prosper in the waters around West Yellowstone. This Hebgen Lake inhabitant, taken and released during the gulper season, is a good example. Fly fishers from around the globe descend on Hebgen Lake in August to enjoy this event. (Bruce Staples collection)

those presenting streamer patterns from either shorelines or boats. This strategy is, in fact, a good one along all of the reservoir shorelines throughout the angling season.

Through effects of the 1959 earthquake, the reservoir does not inundate as much of the river above. A United States Geological Survey quadrangle of the area printed before 1959 shows Hebgen Lake within a few hundred yards of the Highway 191 bridge three miles north of West Yellowstone. Now the high-water mark is more than a mile below this bridge.

In the early season, regional anglers flock to Hebgen to fish around its shorelines and troll its waters. At this time it is usually the first of the region's major stillwaters to open, as Henry's Lake opens on Memorial Day and Yellowstone Lake on June 15, and Quake Lake may have poor fishing conditions due to discolored runoff waters entering its upper reaches. Personal watercraft dot the reservoir shorelines at ice-out, with occupants using sinking lines to present streamers and Woolly Bugger patterns to foraging fish. Midge emergences, prolific throughout the season, can result in some good early-season fishing through presenting life-cycle patterns. Localized damselfly emergences occur, particularly along the northwest shoreline in the bays beyond the South Fork of the Madison estuary and in scattered weedy areas of the Madison and Grayling Arms.

As the middle of July approaches, the event for which Hebgen is famed begins. Speckled duns (Callibaetis genus) are the most common mayflies to inhabit western stillwaters. All western stillwaters having submerged vegetation host speckled dun nymphs. They emerge throughout the season, with peak times in midsummer. When the number of nymphs emerging peaks, trout feed greedily on them near the surface as well as on floating duns. Their takes, often accompanied by a gulping sound, gave rise to the term "gulper," and at any given time many fish can be observed participating. Because the gulper phenomenon is so extensive here, Hebgen has received major fame.

Certainly, Hebgen is not the only stillwater where this emergence causes major trout activity. Beginning in the 1970s, the gulper event also had much to do with the rapid growth in popularity of float tubes for fishing western stillwaters for trout. The low profile of an angler sitting in a flotation device allows a much closer approach to wary fish near the surface than can be achieved while sitting or standing in a boat. Soon works heralding the advantages and joys of float tubing for trout spangled the media, and another way to fish for trout developed.

With speckled dun emergences beginning as early as the first week of July on Hebgen, enthusiasts flock to the lake. Activity begins between nine and ten in the morning during the peak of gulper action, normally around the first week of August. Madison Arm shorelines are a favored location for those seeking gulper activity, but bays along the west-side road also offer good activity. Fish will concentrate on taking nymphs and duns first, then as midday approaches switch to taking spinners, but all this terminates when the wind arrives. If it dies in the evening, a return to the water means enjoyment of gulpers taking spinners until dark.

At times speckled duns are joined in emergence by Tricos, and their spinner falls also attract gulpers. Trico emergences usually peak a bit later in the year than those of speckled duns, and they are tougher to imitate and present because of their tiny size. Long, fine leaders and accurate casting are the keys to success during gulper activity.

One of the most interesting approaches to trout fishing can be enjoyed at this time: judging the path that a gulper takes and the interval at which it takes its prey.

The Madison River is likely the most popular destination for fly fishers visiting waters around West Yellowstone. Fly fishing can continue year-round. (Courtesy Patrick Daigle)

area waters. Bob Jacklin spent his first nights in the area here until moving to the Alpine Motel in town.

"My Part of the River" proclaims Charlie Brooks in the title for chapter 12 of *The Living River*. He is referring to its reach within the park. As we have seen earlier, this book is the most comprehensive work yet on the Madison River offered from an angler's point of view, so one should study it on considering the best path to fishing success anywhere on it. To begin, Charlie laments that the river near the Madison Junction Campground experiences too much angling pressure, but offers that on moving a half mile downstream, this pressure is reduced significantly. Charlie made his observation on crowding in the late 1970s. He should see the crowds on "his part of the river" today! And for good reason: Fly-fishing literature and media is spangled with praises for and tales of the river here. And it is only a few minutes from all the facilities West Yellowstone has to offer.

The river along the West Entrance Road is among the park's most beautiful. See it in the early season when wildflowers add a mosaic of color, and you are likely to agree. In *The Living River* Charlie points out why it is not the classic meadow stream, but to most observers it appears here to be such. Elk, moose, bison, and deer inhabit the meadows. Waterfowl and birds of prey are numerous. Coyotes and possibly a wolf can be seen looking for prey. This is, after all, home for these creatures, and we are intruders. Thus shouldn't we be the ones to give due passage and to respect position here? Not all of those eager-eyed fly fishers you see in pullouts struggling to don waders, string up rods, apply sunscreen and insect repellent, and select flies do so.

True, the meadows seem to dominate, but gradient is present within the water, and the reach offers riffles and runs. The first going downstream is the area adjacent to the highway above Nine Mile Hole. To this point the river has dropped less than forty feet in elevation. The next, Long Riffle, begins downstream of the gliding run below Seven Mile Bridge. The river stays within sight of the highway for about three miles then disappears from view, turning northwesterly to Cable Car Run. Below, and out of sight of the highway, is a succession of deep runs known collectively as the Barns Holes, all with faster-moving water, and then the Beaver Meadows.

Speaking of named river features such as the Barns Holes, Long Riffle, Nine Mile Hole, Big Bend, and others, it would be repetitious to speak in detail of them when Charlie has done so with such eloquence. Read *The Living River* to become oriented with these and other named places to find what lies within them. You will enjoy doing so.

With respect to presentation strategy in "My Part of the River," much also has been written. Suffice it to say here that in the early season blue-winged olives and pale morning duns are the first mayflies to be effective in getting attention from trout. The blue-winged olives can emerge into the late season, and the pale morning dun emergence lasts into July. The trick is to be present when fish are keying on these. Overcast or mostly so may offer the best times for this. For those seeking more action from mayfly emergences, the Trico emergence beginning in August is a mayfly activity extension. Humid mornings are usually best to enjoy a Trico spinner fall.

Just inside the park's west entrance, the Barns Holes area is a place of legend. With such renown, being within a few miles of West Yellowstone and easily approached, it attracts numerous fly fishers throughout the season. (Bruce Staples collection)

The Beaver Meadows, so named by Charlie Brooks, offers miles of water between the Barns Holes and Baker's Hole. It is a prime location for enjoying autumn brown and rainbow trout running up from Hebgen Lake to spawn in upstream waters. (Courtesy Bruce Staples)

Caddis are numerous in the river, and presenting patterns for their life cycle is effective almost any time. But the best time to have success with them would be during early-summer evenings when trout respond to their emerging and egg-laying swarms. A few golden stoneflies are also present in swifter waters, and from time to time patterns for their nymphs and adults can also bring action.

Presenting likenesses for all of these food forms requires careful wading, fine tippets, and natural drifts for success. Some allowance for heavier tippets and delicate casting may be made if one presents damselfly and dragonfly nymphs into deeper water. Both are numerous in the deeper slow waters throughout the reach, and until summer begins in earnest, presenting these patterns offers the best chance for encountering a large brown or rainbow trout.

Many of the large rainbows present at this time are moving back to Hebgen Lake after spawning in the lower Firehole River and in the Gibbon. At times, a large streamer plied deep through these waters will entice one of these travelers, or even a resident. Charlie's favorite for this strategy was a Dark Spruce Streamer. No doubt, though out of style with today's adherents to all things artificial, it is still effective.

The Madison River along the West Entrance Road at Seven Mile Bridge. Note the traffic on the road. Traffic such as this slows travel to many fishing locations. Fly fishers must take traveling time into consideration when planning to visit any water in the park. The earlier in the day one can begin traveling to such a location, the better. (Bruce Staples collection)

In late June, particularly around Seven Mile Bridge, green drakes can emerge during years of abundant water. Here aquatic plant beds wave beautifully in the current and host these famed mayflies. Concentrate your efforts on presenting imitations of these big mayflies below the bridge, as the river immediately above can be treacherous to wade and approach.

The middle of July ushers in the terrestrial season throughout the reach. The famed Grasshopper Bank, not far below the bridge and named by Dave Whitlock, speaks for itself. Terrestrial patterns can be effective anywhere along the river, including deeper channels in the Long Riffle and Cable Car Run, during summer and into the first frosts of autumn.

Every terrestrial pattern available in local shops or described in fly-fishing literature comes with a story attached that promotes its effectiveness. Do not take these tales too seriously: All will attract fish if presented with a natural drift.

Beginning with the Long Riffle and down into the Beaver Meadows, giant stoneflies become numerous, adding another item to be simulated early in the season. When they emerge the window for success is just a few days.

The Barns Holes are out of sight from the highway. A bit less than a mile inside the West Entrance, a turn-off to the left accesses them. Fishing here can be even more crowded than along the West Entrance Road, particularly when browns and rainbows migrating upstream from Hebgen Lake make their first appearance. The downstream parts of the Barns Holes are the last section of river accessed by road until it leaves the park at Baker's Hole.

Within these two landmarks the river flows about four miles through the Beaver Meadows, so named for those residents than have dammed tributaries within, built conspicuous lodges, and created holes that have caught numerous anglers. Within this reach, the river moves down a moderate gradient. Thus though surrounded by a meadow, it cannot be labeled a true meadow stream as it drops nearly one hundred feet in elevation. Attraction to fishing here begins for most anglers with the terrestrial season, but it really becomes a destination when brown and rainbow trout begin their spawning migration near the end of August.

But getting into the best that the Beaver Meadows has to offer requires effort, whether coming upstream from Baker's Hole, across from Highway 191, or downstream from the Barns Holes, and successful fishing may mean walking several miles in a day. Thus solitude can be experienced here, but not as much as during a few decades ago, relative to the hordes fishing along the West Entrance Road. The prize will be a chance to encounter migrating trout ranging to several pounds. These make up the bulk of large fish in the river until the season closes the first weekend of November.

A few miles below, where the river exits the park, is Baker's Hole. Here the river twists and turns about the Montana–Yellowstone Park boundary, requiring licenses from both entities in order to be fished uninterrupted. Baker's Hole Campground is also hallowed ground in the minds of fly fishers. It is another location where Charlie Brooks held court, and Don Martinez speaks of his fishing experiences here. It was a destination of a youthful Wally Eagle, who rode his bicycle from town with

Autumn brings fewer tourists but concentrates fly fishers on the Madison River. Brown and rainbow trout migrating from Hebgen Lake to spawn in upstream waters are numerous and aggressive. Park and walk-in locations are numerous along the West Entrance Road. (Bruce Staples collection)

Run-up brown and rainbow trout from Hebgen Lake provide fly fishers the opportunity to encounter trophy-size individuals in prime health. (Bruce Staples collection)

◀ Bruce Staples landing a Madison River rainbow trout. Hebgen Lake rainbow trout begin their spawning migration into the river by late August. Early in their migration the river just above the lake is the best location for encountering them as well as brown trout doing the same. (Bruce Staples collection)

Stuffy Martinez to enjoy some fishing. Jack Gartside used it as a home base from which to experience the river and nearby waters, and to tie flies. Bob Jacklin had used it in a similar manner. Just outside the park, adjacent to Baker's Hole, cabins were built during the 1920s along the Madison River by Wallace Brown. These cabins, later known as "Thornton's Camps," would become famed through hosting celebrity anglers.

So it seems fitting that this celebrated reach of river within the park is marked at the beginning (Barns Holes) and exit (Baker's Hole) by locations held in high esteem by fly fishers. Below the park boundary the Madison crosses US Highway 191 and its surroundings lose quality rather quickly just above Hebgen Lake due to periodic inundation by the reservoir.

Much of the reach downstream of the Highway 191 crossing was inundated by Hebgen Lake until the 1959 earthquake. The earthquake tilted the Madison Valley such that nearly two miles of river are now present below the highway before entering the Madison Arm of Hebgen Lake. A series of deep holes and runs are present, but as the river approaches the lake, silt increasingly covers its bed. During times when waters are low in the reservoir, the confluence is not attractive and mudflats can make it difficult to traverse. By August there is an excellent Trico emergence above the confluence, and good fishing can be experienced during the terrestrial season. But the major attraction here is the run of brown and rainbow trout from Hebgen Lake below.

The brown trout here run the gauntlet as, curiously, they have not yet been placed under a catch-and-release regulation by Montana fisheries management. Currently five brown trout are allowed in daily possession. Youngsters under the age of fourteen years are also allowed to creel one rainbow per day here. Thus one will encounter late-season anglers flaunting dead fish and entrails rotting in the shallows and along banks.

Between Hebgen Lake Dam and the Quake Lake backwaters lies a unique reach of the Madison. Here the river is a remnant of what was present up to the mid-twentieth century. Hebgen Dam inundates the mouth of the Madison Canyon, and the landslide resulting from the 1959 earthquake forms Earthquake Lake, inundating most of the canyon downstream. This reach is only a mile and a half in length, and it is all

The Hebgen Lake–Madison River confluence is targeted by anglers mostly during the autumn when brown and rainbow trout run up the river into drainage spawning areas within Yellowstone National Park. (Bruce Staples collection)

much the same in character except for a slight lessening in gradient as Quake Lake is approached. Particularly in the section just below Hebgen Dam, it seems reminiscent of Charlie Brooks's description of the canyon water now under Quake Lake.

A road, which was part of the original highway, leaves Highway 287, goes past the Campfire Lodge, parallels the lower half of the reach, then ends in a turnaround a few hundred yards above the confluence with Quake Lake. This reach is open year-round and coupled with accessibility ensures that it receives considerable angling pressure. Cabin Creek Campground and the lodge can be convenient bases from which to fish here.

Short as this reach may be, it holds the largest trout in the river, at least above Ennis Lake. During late winter and early spring, presenting large nymph and streamer patterns brings responses from rainbows migrating upstream to spawn. With spring-time runoff coming from Cabin Creek, much of the reach can be unfishable at times. But with clearing and warming waters, success comes by presenting the large wet flies.

As the days warm further, a significant caddis emergence begins, and this is the time when Bob Jacklin encountered and landed the largest brown trout of his life. He fooled this ten-pound fish through using his Green Caddis Rockworm. His encounter, filled with the excitement of the moment, is captured on a DVD, as the purpose of Bob's trip was to record a fly-casting session. Records show that this is not the only exceptionally large trout to be encountered in the reach. These are likely lake fish that leave Quake Lake to forage on food forms in the well-oxygenated river above. Bob believes that his fish was certainly one of these.

The time to encounter large fish here begins in earnest by the first week of July when giant stoneflies emerge in the reach. Large fish will congregate above the lake at this time, and only increased angling pressure interferes with encountering them. Anglers flock here, but as in the reach below Quake Lake to Lyons Bridge, they are not allowed to fish from boats. As the effects of the stonefly emergence fades from the reach, terrestrials begin to become important in the diet of resident trout. This extends the chance to encounter a large fish. But it is during late autumn when the presence of very large brown trout increases the reach's renown. For those willing to bear late autumn's frigid and often stormy weather, ice in the guides, and frozen fingers, the reward can be a fish of the year, let alone a lifetime. The estuary is a prime location for intercepting these fish, and early and late in the day are the best times to be there. Any large streamer or Woolly Bugger type will do.

Loss in gradient now submerged under Quake Lake has to be accounted for, so as if from the joy of release from confinement, the Madison River tumbles from the lake to enter the valley below. Its raucous character continues for about a mile to the vicinity of the Slide Inn, then begins to ease. All of this is intimidating water to many wading fly fishers, but on taking time to observe, one can see placid spots relative to the raging water. Concentrating on these pieces of water can bring responses for those presenting large stonefly nymphs on fast-sinking sink-tip lines. This is high-quality stonefly water, and wading is the only way to approach it. In one respect this no-boating regulation is certainly wise, because if allowed on the first mile or so of the reach, the number of boating accidents and even fatalities could be higher than socially acceptable.

When the stonefly emergence moves through this fast water, the dry-fly strategy is obvious: drift patterns around cover, past vegetated banks, and into those quiet

The Madison River between Hebgen and Quake Lakes is a popular angling destination throughout the season, but when stoneflies emerge in early summer and when brown trout migrate there in autumn, it can become crowded. (Bruce Staples collection)

lays. Later in the season, presenting terrestrial patterns will be successful. During evenings and early mornings, streamer patterns can always be effective.

Access is easy off the two major highways coming through Raynolds Junction, and the reach is saved from full runoff effects because of the two upstream impoundments. Thus the entire reach receives considerable wade-in pressure, as it is open throughout the year. During the winter season, presenting midge life-cycle patterns brings the most success. With early springtime, presenting wet-fly and nymph patterns predominates throughout the reach. The most effective strategy is to present stonefly nymph patterns, but at times small bead-head nymphs will be effective.

Kelly Galloup brings to the angler's attention that annelids, those aquatic worms, populate the river here in large numbers, thus patterns to imitate them drifting in the current are effective throughout the season, but especially early when the river may be a bit high and eroding its banks. He also adds that even when early-season waters are discolored, trout will respond to blue-winged olive patterns in emerger and dun forms. Caddisflies, craneflies, and midges are always present, allowing for further opportunities, and streamers and egg patterns can be effective for large foraging fish, particularly under low-light conditions.

The parking area just below Reynolds Bridge over the Madison River and just south of the Highway 87–Highway 287 junction is a landmark jump-off location for fishing the river. Fishing here is restricted to walk-in wading downstream to Lyons Bridge. Three Dollar Bridge over the Madison is another popular location for fly fishers to enjoy fishing the non-boating section of the river. The bridge holds a road that provides access to Cliff and Wade Lakes. (Bruce Staples collection)

As the season progresses toward summer, mayfly and caddisfly emergences increase, with pale morning duns, western green drakes (flavs), slate cream duns, and red quills making major appearances. But now comes the time for which the entire reach of the river from the Quake Lake Dam to Ennis is famed and longed for by so many anglers: the giant stonefly emergence. Working its way up from the Ennis area, it attracts fly fishers by the thousands. Telephone lines are full of calls asking for information on the progress of "The Hatch." Fly-fishing websites throughout the regional fly-fishing retail industry are updated almost daily to show its progress. Fly-fishing shops pull out their stock of adult stonefly patterns, and owners hope they have enough to last the season. The same applies for their stock of wading gear and rods, lines, and reels. From all parts of the country—yes, even the world—come the inquiries on the hatch's progress and how to make subsequent plans to intercept this event. Accommodations and rental cars are reserved. Campgrounds along the river fill. So do guide services when the time has come when being a fishing guide means almost round-the-clock work to satisfy and ferry clients up and down the river, to place them where the dry-fly action is, then prepare for the next day.

It's a crazy time that lasts for a few weeks, but in it a season can be made for a retailer, exhaustion is reached for fishing guides, and unforgettable memories or deep frustration can be had for the fly fisher. In the reach from Quake Lake to Lyons Bridge, the activity is muted by the "no fishing from boats" regulation, but crowds of walk-in anglers form as the adult stoneflies become prey for trout. The lodges and campground near the old Hutchins Bridge have no vacancies at this time. Below Lyons Bridge, where fishing from boats is permitted, chaos reigns supreme as anglers scramble to realize action from the stoneflies.

At times, up to one hundred boats can be seen at the bridge launch site waiting to begin efforts to pursue fish chasing the stoneflies. In all this seeming madness, the fact that fish will take other food form imitations is almost overlooked. But conditions return to sanity as "The Hatch" moves upstream and out of the reach. Waters drop to base flows and terrestrial insect and attractor patterns become important. Thus from the end of July through September, fly fishers can enjoy this reach of the river where through the efforts of conservation and public-minded organizations so much access is present.

From October and into November, presenting large wet flies or midge life-cycle patterns is the most effective way to achieve success on the reach. Large, aggressive brown trout are migrating and rainbow trout are stocking up for the nearing winter, thus streamers work well. Midges make up the best of what is left of emerging insects. A major attraction now is that few fly fishers will be on the reach.

And thus the season has come full circle on this eight-mile piece of river. Yes, it is a special reach deserving all bestowed attention. It seems like so much time has passed since the entire reach from the dam resulting from the 1959 earthquake and landslide was dewatered to near dryness for days down to the West Fork of the Madison River confluence. Fish and insect loss was severe, but as a credit to the river's richness and

For years Craig Mathews has promoted winter fishing. Here he braves winter on the Madison River. Craig suggests that presenting midge life-cycle patterns is a good strategy when doing so. (Courtesy Patrick Daigle)

ability to reestablish these life-forms, it regained its population of these well within a decade. This speaks admirably for this most renowned of trout streams and serves as a signal to all that it is special in the world of salmonid angling. And it certainly justifies the protection under which its salmonid population has been placed. Let's hope that such protection and esteem remain.

CAMPFIRE LODGE

Founded in 1921, the Campfire Lodge began business operations the following year. Since then this resort on the Madison River has had several owners. It is situated in one of the best locations for such a resort catering to fly fishers in the region around West Yellowstone. Hebgen Lake is just to the east, and Earthquake Lake is just to the southwest. The entire river between the two lakes is accessible. Below the lodge its gradient eases, and bountiful access is present off an old Highway 287 remnant, also known as the Ghost Village Road.

Fishing from boats essentially occurs only in the lower section just above Earthquake Lake. During the annual July giant and golden stonefly emergences, the lodge occupies one of the best places for productive fishing on the Madison River. The 1959 earthquake did only minor damage. For the Christensen family, owners at the time, the main concern was inundation of lodge buildings from the rising water. This never happened, however, because the Army Corps of Engineers dropped and stabilized the dam resulting from the slide before flooding could take place.

Jim Slattery, a nationally recognized fly tier, and his wife Wendie bought the lodge in 2008. Their property now includes a full-service fly shop, restaurant, RV park, and campground in addition to cabins having a historic nature. Accolades for the lodge, its services, and particularly fine eating are numerous. The lodge closes annually on September 30.

SLIDE INN

The Slide Inn is in Cameron, Montana, not West Yellowstone, but its history and function are so interrelated with the West Yellowstone fly-fishing industry that it must be given some discussion in this work. Its history in fly fishing did not begin until around 1974, when the Niess family bought it from the Strouds, who had bought it in 1963 from original owner Morris Stagger. Before that time it was known as the Stagger Ranch and had a shady reputation with gambling, a makeshift zoo, and other activities, but little to do with fly fishing. The Strouds renamed it Slide Inn after the 1959 earthquake, which had inflicted major damage to their new property. They catered to anglers of all persuasions, bait and artificial (lures and flies) means alike. They also operated a profitable night crawler business and protested vigorously when Montana Fish, Wildlife & Parks banned bait fishing in the Madison River above Ennis Lake.

Jane and Bud Niess bought the Slide Inn in 1974 and ran it for years, continuing to cater to anglers, then turned it over to daughter Nancy and her husband Kevin Conlan. During these years it became the major resort on the reach below Earthquake Lake, with more than three hundred yards of river frontage. Kelly Galloup bought the Slide Inn in 2002 and has fashioned it into a major full-service resort with an emphasis on serving fly fishers worldwide. He brings to it vast fly-fishing and fly-tying experience from his earlier days in Michigan.

South Fork of the Madison River

Access: US Highway 20 to Denny Creek (Lonesomehurst) and Madison Arm Roads

GPS coordinates: Madison Arm Road 44.6769954, -111.186382; South Fork (Mosquito Gulch Road) Road 44.618297, -111.158309

Equipment: 5- and 6-weight systems with floating, intermediate, and sink-tip lines; BWO, caddisfly, golden stone, western green drake, PMD, and yellow sally life-cycle patterns, and terrestrial insect and streamer patterns

Nearest facilities and services: West Yellowstone, MT; USFS Lonesomehurst Campground; USFS Basin Station rental cabin; Madison Arm Resort

Information resources: Custer-Gallatin National Forest, Hebgen Lake Ranger District Office; West Yellowstone Visitor Center; Madison Arm USGS topographic map

Salmonids present: Brook, brown, and rainbow trout, Rocky Mountain whitefish

As with several streams near West Yellowstone, the South Fork of the Madison River is mainly a meadow stream, having two tiers separated by a riffle-and-run section. This section, which crosses US Highway 20 about four miles west of West Yellowstone, is deceptive because it is all that is in view.

Not far above the crossing, much of the stream winds through willow thickets and private land but has an interesting history. Gilman Sawtell's primitive nineteenth-century road from Henry's Lake to Yellowstone National Park crossed here. Harry Dwelle's Grayling Inn hosted anglers seeking encounters with the robust cutthroat trout and grayling population, tourists, and hunters arriving by stagecoach and

The South Fork of the Madison River winds its way through meadows in its lower reach. Up to nearly a century ago, it was reputed to be the best stream in the West for encountering Montana grayling, until brown and rainbow trout replaced them along with cutthroat trout. Rocky Mountain whitefish remain in good numbers. (Courtesy Bruce Staples)

Guiding, teaching, and learning, whether through a walk-in wade trip or float trip, has always been a major part of the West Yellowstone fly-fishing experience. Here a guide advises a client on presentation. The location is a hallowed spot: the Denny Creek confluence with the South Fork of the Madison River. (Bruce Staples collection)

horseback. The railroad put an end to stagecoach travel, so Dwelle sold his property. In a few years brown and rainbow trout from Hebgen Lake began replacing the native salmonids.

Dwelle's original property has had a series of owners for more than a century. The Madison Fork Ranch is the current owner, and the river flows for about a mile through its property. Above this property at the old railroad grade crossing the river is on public land and had a reputation in the past as an excellent stream for brook and brown trout. When rainbow trout fingerlings were introduced, they became fodder for the resident brook and brown trout.

Farther upstream the South Fork flows off the Henry's Lake Range on the Continental Divide and can be accessed by Mosquito Gulch Road. Here it hosts small brook, brown, and rainbow trout and holds some spawning habitat. Solitude here is reliable, and with a lightweight outfit to present small attractor and wet patterns, a day of good fishing can be realized.

Not far below the US Highway 20 bridge, the stream changes in character, now offering about four miles of public access to a beautiful meadow setting somewhat paralleling the Madison Arm Road just to the east. This road leaves the highway just a few hundred yards east of its crossing and heads in a northerly direction. Pullouts along this road provide ample access to the stream made up of oxbow bends hosting deep pools, occasional willows, and beaver lodges. West-side access from the Denny

Creek Road is mostly blocked by private land, some of which is within the Bar N Ranch resort. West-side access can also be obtained by walking upstream within the high-water mark from Lonesomehurst Campground.

With crystal-clear water after run-off, an easing gradient, and water temperatures rarely exceeding the mid-fifties, even in midsummer, this stream at first appears to be an ideal host for salmonids. However, the aquatic insect population is relatively sparse. Nevertheless, it is easy to see why grayling and cutthroat trout once inhabited these waters. Now it is mostly a spawning stream for Hebgen Lake salmonids, with a run of rainbow trout in the spring and brown trout in the fall. A good population of large Rocky Mountain whitefish remains, and they eagerly hit a deeply fished wet pattern. There are some trophy-size resident trout in the stream; however, fishing for them is generally difficult, and success requires patience and stealth to the utmost.

As the river flows downstream through its lower meadow reach to Hebgen Lake, the number of pools diminish and the water widens out with a smooth and even flow to a last section above the estuary. Here the gradient increases to the Denny Creek confluence, where it enters the estuary. This lower meadow section offers some dry-fly fishing. Western green drakes, blue-winged olives, and pale morning duns emerge with Callibaetis mayflies, some caddis, and terrestrial insects providing fishing during the summer season.

The estuary area of the South Fork Arm is skirted by undeveloped roads, making for easy access. Wading is easy here, flotation devices can be conveniently launched, and boats can be launched at the Lonesomehurst Campground boat dock. Presenting streamer patterns in the early season can be extremely effective in attracting post-spawning rainbow trout coming back to the reservoir, some of which attain very large sizes. During autumn months the use of flotation devices and boats in the estuary to present streamer patterns can intercept brown trout moving to the South Fork to spawn. With stealth and good timing, these browns can also be encountered in the stream itself.

YELLOWSTONE RIVER DRAINAGE

Pelican Creek

Access: US Highway 26, service road to trailhead
Pelican Creek Trailhead GPS Coordinates: 44 506307, -110.523459
Equipment: 4- and 5-weight systems with floating and sink-tip lines; BWO, caddisfly, PMD, and yellow sally life-cycle patterns, and terrestrial insect, traditional attractor, wet fly, and streamer patterns
Nearest facilities and services: West Yellowstone, MT; Lake Yellowstone Hotel; Lake Lodge cabins; Bridge Bay Campground; Fishing Bridge RV Campground
Information resources: Yellowstone National Park, Lake Butte USGS topographic map
Salmonids present: Cutthroat trout

Pelican Creek is the second-largest tributary to Yellowstone Lake, the Yellowstone River being the largest. As with the river, fishing season here begins annually on July 15. For two miles above its Yellowstone Lake confluence, Pelican Creek is closed to fishing to protect vital waterfowl habitat. Here and above, the creek meanders

Although somewhat distant from town, fly-fishing retailers sent anglers to Pelican Creek after its mid-July opening to fish for large post-spawning cutthroat trout returning to Yellowstone Lake. Closed for years in the early twenty-first century, it is now open to fly fishing, as its spawning cutthroat trout population appears to be in recovery. (Bruce Staples collection)

Bison were here before human intrusion and thus require respect. Many anglers have experienced their presence when on the waters. Do not approach or disturb them. (Courtesy Dwight Atkinson)

through a vast meadow, larger than that hosting Duck Creek but smaller than that hosting the Bechler River. A danger within Pelican Creek's meadow is a grizzly bear population, but the biggest danger is from the large bison population.

A two-mile walk from the trailhead through the meadow and an occasional pine grove takes one to where the creek is open to fishing. This is high country, being a few hundred feet below eight thousand. This means a short growing season, but Pelican Creek and its major tributary, Raven Creek, host spawning areas with quality water flowing over and percolating through beautiful gravel substrates. Fish from the lake enter the creek to spawn, nearly all of which is completed before the July 15 opening. On returning to the lake these fish are ravenous and will strike at any fly, wet or dry.

It's a smaller-scale situation of what happens in the river above the lake, with only juveniles remaining. So the Pelican Creek drainage is the second-most-important spawning contributor to the lake.

Before the negative impacts of the 1990s struck the Yellowstone Lake drainage above the falls, I would advise and/or take folks seeking a certain encounter with Yellowstone cutthroat trout to Pelican Creek. Such encounters would be numerous in a day of fishing. Wet-fly presentation seemed more effective than that for dry flies, but either way catching and releasing forty or more fish in a day was common. True, the fish were somewhat jaded because of spawning rigors, but the experience of encountering so many fish ranging upward to twenty inches was unforgettable.

Soon after discovering the collapse in the number of fish returning to the creek and drainage to spawn, fishing here was closed. With an increase in returning spawning fish, due to success in reducing the lake trout population in Yellowstone Lake and the resultant increase in the cutthroat trout population, Pelican Creek and its drainage is now open for fishing. The number of returnees is increasing but is nowhere near as many as back in the 1980s. The future of fishing on this creek depends on continued success in removing lake trout from Yellowstone Lake and the elimination of whirling disease from the upper Yellowstone drainage.

Upper Yellowstone River

Access: Grand Loop portion of US Highway 89

GPS coordinates: Otter Creek area 44.698562, -110.503244; Alum Creek area 44.646674, -110.456951; Nez Perce Ford area 44.621973,-110.418623; estuary area 44.599222, -110.387076

Equipment: 5- and 6-weight systems with floating, intermediate, and sink-tip lines; BWO, caddisfly, damselfly, giant stone, golden stone, gray drake, green drake, PMD, red quill, Trico, and yellow sally life-cycle patterns, and terrestrial insect, traditional attractor, and streamer patterns

Nearest facilities and services: West Yellowstone, MT; Lake Yellowstone Hotel; Lake Lodge cabins; Bridge Bay Campground; Fishing Bridge RV Campground

Information resources: Yellowstone National Park, USGS Flow Station Gage 06186500, Canyon Village and Lake Butte USGS topographic maps

Salmonids present: Yellowstone cutthroat trout

The Yellowstone River drains about half of the Greater Yellowstone region, and about 65 percent of the land area is within Yellowstone National Park. The reach between Yellowstone Lake and the Upper Falls will be the center of our discussion. The river below the Lower Falls is more often and easily visited by anglers staging in Gardiner, Montana. The part of the river we discuss has been the second-most-popular angling destination in Yellowstone Park (Yellowstone Lake has been the most popular), and this section formerly hosted about 80 percent of the angling on the river. It is also more conveniently reached from West Yellowstone than from other towns.

One other thought is appropriate, especially for those who have never ventured to this beautiful section of the park: You will be fishing in country within two hundred feet of eight thousand feet in elevation. Changes in weather therefore can be more rapid and violent than other angling destinations we have discussed, so be prepared for such changes even more than on the Madison, Henry's Fork, Gallatin, or Red Rock drainages, which are mostly just over six thousand feet in elevation. We will briefly look at the river below its Grand Canyon, realizing that it is more easily reached from Gardiner and Cooke City, both in Montana.

Above Yellowstone Lake the river is arguably the most isolated of its size in the lower forty-eight states. Regardless of how one chooses to reach this beautiful area, considerable effort is required. Its source is a basin off the west side of Younts Peak southeast of Yellowstone National Park. Below, it flows through the isolated Thorofare Plateau. Due to holding cold and often silt-laden runoff waters until midsummer, it is relatively inhospitable for continuous trout habitation. It does, however, hold a large amount of high-quality spawning habitat. Spawning trout from the lake remain here temporarily, and fishing for them used to be spectacular. Soon after spawning, these fish descend back to the more-habitable lake. By the end of August all that remains are mainly fingerling fish that also soon descend to the lake. So fishing on the river above the lake is quite seasonal, being worth the effort only from the June 15 opening into July.

Yellowstone Lake dominates the nature of the trout population in the river above and below. It acts as a settling, warming, and enriching basin. Although not rich in nutrients compared to other lakes, Yellowstone Lake makes significant improvements to incoming waters. Many streams, in sizes ranging from the river above and Pelican Creek to the smallest rill, feed into it. It also receives huge amounts of geothermal water from adjacent and submerged springs, seeps, and geysers. As a result, the nutrient base available to the river below is greatly improved.

Planktons flourish in the lake, and large amounts of them are carried out into the river below. The carotene pigment of one of these, *Diaptomus shoshone*, imparts the reddish color to the flesh of cutthroat that feed on them in the lake and the river below. The result of all the lake gives is that the river leaving it is larger than above and much more hospitable for trout in terms of food base and physical conditions. Gone is the erosive silt load that would otherwise scour banks, drop in-stream temperatures, and inhibit aquatic insect and plant life. Thus, emerging from Yellowstone Lake, the river begins its fame as an exceptional fishery.

Here it is the river of legend, inhabited by no other salmonids than the Yellowstone cutthroat trout. Charlie Brooks writes in *Fishing Yellowstone Waters*: "Here it emerges as one of the largest trout streams in the nation and one of the best." Thankfully, all attempts in the past to introduce exotic species here have failed. In any case, the river between the lake and the Upper Falls contains perhaps the best solely Yellowstone cutthroat trout population left in any river and most likely the best remaining large-scale stream habitat for them. Sadly, this population is depleted for reasons related to the lake above, which we will soon discuss.

Although exceedingly beautiful, the river here has not been treasured for beauty as much as the Firehole River. Again, most early- and mid-century angling writers visiting the park held brook, brown, and rainbow trout in highest esteem. The upper Yellowstone hosts none of these, thus unconscious prejudice could have been held against it. In these times of diminishing salmonid populations, these prejudices have all but disappeared, as cutthroat trout are now among the most protected salmonids in the country.

A portion of the Grand Loop Highway parallels all of the reach from the lake to the Upper Falls. Downstream of and including the Fishing Bridge closure, large-scale

Fickle weather can vary Yellowstone Lake's surface from glassy to six-foot breakers. Insulated waders are a requirement for all walk-in anglers regardless of weather. Man-made abuses have shrunk the lake's cutthroat trout population drastically, but current fisheries management practices are bringing it back to levels that attract anglers. (Courtesy Dwight Atkinson)

overfishing dominated the river in much of the past. Now, in order to protect the bulk of spawning cutthroat, the river here opens to fishing annually on July 15.

The river immediately below the Fishing Bridge closure is commonly known among fly fishers as "The Estuary." Here it moves very slowly over sandy gravel and weed beds that provide overhead cover and host abundant aquatic insects. In *Fly Fishing the Yellowstone in the Park*, which Bob Jacklin coauthored with Gary LaFontaine, Bob states: "I'd put the Estuary, at the outlet of Yellowstone Lake, near the top of any list of great dry-fly waters." Access and angling here is by wading only, and banks are easily traversed. Fishing is superb throughout the season if one pays attention to presentation.

Water surfaces in the Estuary are mostly smooth and depths are clear, but there is a current, born of waters pushing into the lake above, that can be felt. Thus improper drifts alarm trout foraging close to or at the surface. Dry patterns must simulate closely the life-forms on which the fish feed. Fine, long leaders are vital for achieving a proper and drag-free drift, and knowledge of the prevailing currents helps immensely. So does wading into the best position from which to make a presentation.

In season, gray drakes, pale morning duns, speckled duns, red quills, and Tricos are the mayfly species found here, and this sequence defines the order in which they emerge through the season. Gray drakes, the first to come off in important numbers, do so for about two weeks, and during that time evening spinner falls make for the best success. Blue-winged olives will emerge throughout the season, and the appearance of red quills and Tricos signal that the season is moving on. Midges and caddis are also plentiful most of the season. Thus one must determine at a given time on which of these the fish are feeding. If rise forms are not present, a large attractor pattern can bring fish to the surface. It's a strategy overlooked by many fly fishers.

Downstream is a short reach of fast water inhabited by giant and golden stoneflies. After these emerge and when the wind blows them onto the Estuary, fish pay attention. Thus if you visit this reach of the river in late July or early August and some adult stoneflies are present, try dead-drifting one. But be sure to keep that drift drag-free! If all else fails, a small bead-head Hare's Ear Nymph or midge pupa presented drag-free under a strike indicator can bring results. In fact, presenting nymph patterns this way is one of the best strategies for success later in the season.

Below the Estuary, the Yellowstone River picks up speed and flows through a short canyon. LeHardy Rapids, near the upper end, is closed to fishing because of the relatively dangerous waters present, fragile landscape, and the numbers of fish concentrating there after spawning. The concentration of trout here also makes the area adjacent to the rapids one of the best locations on the river for conducting fisheries research. These activities are usually conducted before the July 15 season opener to minimize interference with visitors.

The base of the rapids remains one of the best fish-watching locations in the park because fish on the way upstream to the lake rest and feed here after spawning in waters below. In fact, John Varley and Paul Schullery point out in *Yellowstone Fishes* that by the mid-1990s more people were fish-watching here than at Fishing Bridge. But above and below the rapids good fishing can still be experienced using different techniques and careful wading. On viewing the water here, the experienced fly fisher will observe it to be ideal habitat for large stoneflies. The best time for success is the first few weeks of the season, but the reach can still be crowded. Thus just after the season opens, large stonefly nymphs drifted on the bottom can be effective, and when these stoneflies emerge near the end of July into August, adult imitations can bring exciting surface fishing. However, caddisflies, particularly *Brachycentrus* forms, and smaller stonefly species are always available to trout here.

After mid-August many fish have passed through this area to the lake above, water levels have dropped, and in-stream temperatures are higher. Nevertheless, a well-placed dry attractor pattern remains effective. So will caddis life-cycle patterns, and as the autumn comes on, blue-winged olive life-cycle patterns presented in the calmer waters can also be effective.

Below, this reach the river, now near the road, slows and deepens with little room on the banks for casting. Not far below, the river widens and slows again, and the gravelly bottom is again conducive to wading. Soon it comes into one of its most famous spots and most heavily fished locations. This is Nez Perce Ford, formerly named Buffalo Ford.

This is where material for such famed works as Sid Gordon's *How to Fish from Top to Bottom*, Swisher and Richards's *Selective Trout*, and Charlie Brooks's *Fishing Yellowstone Waters* and a host of magazine articles originates. It is also the site of a famed bison crossing, thus its original European-American name. But this is also the site where

Formerly known as Buffalo Ford for an obvious reason, this popular Yellowstone location is now named to honor of the Nez Perce Nation's nineteenth-century trek across Yellowstone Park. During the summer season, fly fishers flock to this location. (Bruce Staples collection)

Joan Wulff plays a large Yellowstone River cutthroat trout. She visited West Yellowstone during many of the FFF Conclaves, but also other times to seek a fly-fishing tranquility not available on other waters. (Bob Jacklin collection)

it is believed the Nez Perce tribe under Chief Joseph crossed the river on their way east out of the park to escape hopefully to Canada. Thus the name was changed to express respect for this effort to retain freedom.

A good number of bison frequent the area, so caution should accompany your angling gear. Here most of the river swings east around an island that is in view of the picnic area. The channel west of the island is a sanctuary sent aside for viewing trout in their native state. To the east, the river is shallow and picks up speed. Access is easy, the bottom gravelly, and the water extremely clear.

One must, however, take care not to wade too deep here, as the river is powerful and can drag one downstream. Nevertheless, the river east of the island was one of the premier dry-fly locations in the region and can still become very crowded. Fish here respond to most insect emergences, so one must find feeding lanes by observing rise forms. Feeding lanes are mainly in shallower water, thus deep wading is not required to encounter them. Success comes to those who give fish time to adjust to their presence, then present flies with a natural drift.

An interesting phenomenon can also be experienced here. Tiring of feeding in the current and because wading anglers stir the bottom, releasing nymphs, trout can come to one's feet, hold in the wake, and pick off drifting nymphs. When the fish are not feeding, they reside in the deeper channels around the ford. The most effective way to fish these are with a sink-tip line; a short, stout leader; and a Woolly Bugger type of fly to get to the bottom of the channel where the fish hold. But throughout the season, there are always at least some fish feeding on nymphs, emerging insects, or duns.

The Yellowstone River does not host as many cutthroat trout now as it had in the twentieth century due to the recent arrival of whirling disease and the impact of lake trout on the upper drainage. The cutthroat population is in a comeback mode, however, with individuals averaging larger sizes than in the past. (Bob Jacklin collection)

Fishing is not permitted on the Yellowstone River within most of the Hayden Valley. Thus the river and its surroundings here serve as a refuge not only for cutthroat trout but for all forms of wildlife. (Bruce Staples collection)

In the early season if water levels are high, the wide, slow reach below Nez Perce Ford is, like the lower part of the Estuary, a good location for success. On downstream, the river swings west toward the road, and anyone passing through notes the aroma of rotten eggs from hydrogen sulfide gas emanating from the Sulphur Cauldron, and for some it is overwhelming enough to make fishing uncomfortable. But for those fly fishers of stronger conviction, the river nearby can still be a wonderful location to fish. Bob Jacklin made a point of introducing novice fly fishers to feeding trout here during his days as a Fenwick Fly-Fishing School instructor.

Because wading is certainly more difficult here, crowds are less than at Nez Perce Ford. But the prospecting fly fisher can stand in the pullout from the highway and scan the river to locate feeding fish. One will also note that the feeding fish are in the cool river water away from the runoff entering from thermal springs in the Sulphur Cauldron area. From the Estuary down to the end of this reach has been a very popular moving water location for angling in the park. As many as five thousand anglers per mile of stream have been counted in a season, and yet the reach retains its angling quality. This ability alone certainly makes the river a treasure.

Below the Sulphur Cauldron reach, the river is closed to fishing for about six miles as it courses through the Hayden Valley. Here the river slows and widens in the beautiful valley. Many a fly fisher has eyed it with longing and desire, but the river and its environs are a sanctuary for all wildlife including Yellowstone cutthroat trout, and only viewing that wildlife is permitted. This closure enhances cutthroat populations in adjacent reaches of the Yellowstone River.

Below the Hayden Valley closure, the river widens and deepens from above the Otter Creek confluence to just above Chittenden Bridge. Likewise, the crowds fishing above dwindle. Because of the silty bottom and thick weed beds, green drakes are present in abundance. As the first week in August ends, these insects emerge in great numbers from the reach, and trout feed on them voraciously mid-morning to early afternoon. As the emergence tapers to an end several days later, a good tactic for success is to use a sink-tip line to drift a small Woolly Bugger variation in darker colors just over the top of the weed beds. As one nears Chittenden Bridge, working near the banks becomes the best way to have success. But the brink of the falls nears just below the bridge. Depth and the strengthening current make wading perilous at best, and it's not worth chancing a certain death ride down the falls and into the canyon.

For thirty-six miles the river now flows through one of the most spectacular reaches of canyon in the country. First is the Grand Canyon of the Yellowstone, with its multicolored rock formations, spires, slides, and hot springs. There is no special attraction in the fish hosted here below the falls, but the canyon scenery is certainly beyond spectacular. If anything, because of the continuous fight to maintain position in the swift waters, trout here run smaller than in the river above. Cutthroat-rainbow hybrids are present because no barrier exists to prevent their passage from below, where they thrive in the river. Access to the canyon is only at a few points such as the Seven Mile Hole Trail at Canyon Village.

Wading the swift river here is again perilous at best, thus fishing is pretty much limited to trying the large holes or along the banks. But during times such as the large stonefly emergence in late July, all one needs to do is drift a pattern on the surface of the large deep holes or along the banks, and responding trout will be a certainty. Presentation of large nymphs and streamer patterns near banks is also effective, and the fact that trout feed mainly nearby has probably saved many anglers from a watery death.

As one leaves Canyon Village and drives north over Dunraven Pass, the river flows farther away from the road, making access increasingly difficult. But as one

The Barns Holes, One and Two (Two pictured above with Bob Jacklin casting), are storied destinations on the Madison River. Since the days when Sam Eagle fished here on horseback to the present, fly fishers come in season to encounter large brown and rainbow trout. (Courtesy Kyle Rodriques)

approaches the Tower Falls area, the river returns close to the road, and from the store an easy walk of several hundred yards is all that's required to reach it.

The second part of the Yellowstone River's canyon reach begins not far below Tower Falls, and for twenty miles the river is contained within. Other than around the bridge just east of Roosevelt Lodge, access to the river requires hiking into the canyon near Hellroaring or Blacktail Deer Creeks, where solitude usually reigns. Here the river is most easily reached if one begins in either Gardiner or Cooke City, both in Montana. Thus these towns on the northwest and northeast corners of the park, respectively, are the best jump-off points for fishing the river as it exits the park. Our discussion will end here on what is certainly Yellowstone Park's most important river in terms of hosting a wild cutthroat trout population and visitation by anglers.

For the fly fisher, we will briefly touch on Yellowstone Lake. It is most safely fished by wading shorelines. In doing so the best global strategy is to locate cruising cutthroat trout and present leech and nymph patterns across their direction of travel. Intermediate fly lines are ideal for presentations in this manner. All cutthroat caught in the lake must be released, and many areas on it vital to their survival have been closed to fishing.

We did not discuss Yellowstone Lake in detail, mainly because of the recent unfortunate events that have impacted its Yellowstone cutthroat trout population. Expect, however, that angling restrictions on the lake and the river above and to the downstream falls might be implemented in the future if more declines in their Yellowstone cutthroat trout populations occur. For now the cutthroat trout population in the lake and river above and below to the falls seems to be improving, with fewer fish but individuals up to two feet in length being fairly common.

Protection is not the case here for lake trout that come to the shallows to spawn during autumn. Park officials insist, for good reason, that all lake trout caught from any area in the lake open to fishing must be reduced to possession. (They make excellent table fare.) In fact, in the early season juvenile lake trout will be close enough to the lakeshore that they can be encountered by the fly fisher using a flotation device and a full-sink line to present streamer and leech patterns. But if you use this approach, beware of the near-certain fierce winds and frigid water temperatures.

Certainly, these are not the only quality waters close to West Yellowstone. Discussing all of these waters in detail along with those described in this chapter would certainly fill a book. Suffice it to say that such streams as Gneiss Creek, Grayling, Elk Springs, Odell and Teepee Creeks, and Whitt's Lakes would be considered destination waters if located in other parts of the country. Certainly, there are fly fishers coming to West Yellowstone who consider them as such. Each of these waters hold wild trout ranging to large sizes, and they are of high-quality habitat surrounded by scenic settings. All of these, along with the waters featured in this chapter, are good locations for the hunter of large salmonids, whether cutthroat, brook, brown, lake, or rainbow trout, grayling, or Rocky Mountain whitefish. Being in the shadow of the more fabled waters, they offer solitude not commonly found elsewhere.

For the light-tackle enthusiast, the West Fork of the Madison River, Beaver Creek, Goose and Otter Lakes, Tepee Creek, Nez Perce Creek, Solfatara Creek, Smith Lake, Whitt's Lakes, Tom's Creek, and Cascade Creek are good destinations. The above mentioned creeks are also good candidates for using the Tenkara technique.

Naming these waters only scratches the surface of fly-fishing locations in the area surrounding West Yellowstone. Without a doubt a fly fisher could spend an angling lifetime fishing the region comprehensively.

CHAPTER 13

RENOWNED FLY PATTERNS

For over one hundred years the waters surrounding West Yellowstone have inspired creation of effective fly patterns or the use of certain traditional patterns. Initially most of these patterns were simple and simulated only a few of the life-forms available to salmonids. As knowledge of the relationship between trout and their food forms progressed and as an increased variety of materials became available, no life-form was left out of simulation by West Yellowstone fly tiers.

Fewer thread and hook manufacturers as well as materials and tool providers were present in the fly-tying industry before the mid-twentieth century. Emphasis was on the use of natural materials in those days. Such materials as macaw and argus pheasant quills, jungle cock nails and butts, polar bear hair, and "Swiss straw," not commonly used in trout fly patterns today, were in higher demand then. Use of materials such as these decreased as sources diminished, were outlawed, or could not supply enough to meet the demand coming from the increasing number of middle-class fly fishers. In the latter half of the twentieth century, synthetic materials became increasingly popular in fly tying. Much of the credit for this introduction into the fly-fishing industry, including that in West Yellowstone, goes to research performed by tiers employed at Blue Ribbon Flies.

Collecting all of the fly patterns created for waters in the West Yellowstone area would be close to impossible, and even approaching this would result in enough material to fill a book. The patterns described in the following pages are among the most renowned that have been created or used in the area. Some have not made it into media before this book. Many have gained enough popularity to be subjected to numerous variations but are described here, as much as possible, with original dressings and materials.

Up to around the mid-twentieth century, fly-tying standards were not as stringent as those of today. Thus we have tied older patterns as they appeared when created in order to preserve originality. Substitute materials are offered for certain patterns where original materials are no longer available or difficult to obtain. Likewise, some of the hook models given are discontinued or difficult to find. However, reference guides for equivalent hook models are currently available online or through hard copy.

Many patterns discussed commemorate a famed tier or person, or are inspired by one of the famed regional waters or a landform. Many of these no longer enjoy broadscale popularity, but others endure. Nevertheless, the patterns created and used in decades past remain as effective as newer ones when presented in the same manner and under equivalent natural conditions.

DRY FLIES
Attractor Patterns

Bivisible (Martinez variation)

Hook: #8-16 Mustad 94840
Thread: Black 6/0
Body: Silver tinsel wrapped to cover
  hook shank
Hackle: Silver badger

Edward Ringwood Hewitt originated the Bivisible concept early in the twentieth century. The pattern consists of a lighter hackle such as ginger, dyed light blue grizzly, or silver badger wrapped in front of a darker hackle, such as brown or black. Don Martinez had the utmost regard for it with respect to properties attractive to trout rising to the surface to feed. Martinez's variation consisted of adding a tinsel body before the hackle was wrapped. The above example is tied exclusively with silver badger. His purpose for this variation was to simulate the air bubbles on the insect's body as it drifted on the surface.

Danskin Trude

Hook: #10-16 Mustad 94840
Thread: Red 6/0
Body: Red floss
Wing: White calf tail
Hackle: Brown

The Trude's influence shows up in many fly patterns created in the Greater Yellowstone region. Jim Danskin created this variation to be an easily tied and durable dry attractor pattern. Its high visibility made it a favorite on rough-water reaches of such streams as the Madison and West Gallatin Rivers. He offered it from his shop, a premier West Yellowstone fly-fishing retail operation from 1961 to 1982.

Golden Professor

Hook: #6-10 Mustad 3399A
Thread: Black 6/0
Tail: Sparse red hackle fibers
Rib: Clipped brown hackle
Body: Gold floss or chenille
Hackle: Brown
Wing: Deer body hair

This fly was featured in the Weber Company catalogs of the 1940s, which proclaimed, "It flutters on the water as if alive." The Eagle family offered it to fly fishers from their store, and it was in popular use around West Yellowstone for years around mid-century. Depending on size, it could be used to simulate an adult caddisfly or an adult stonefly. Wally Eagle gifted Bob Jacklin several examples of this pattern. They survived Bob's shop fire of 1990.

Goofus Bug

Hook: #4-14 Mustad 94840
Thread: Yellow 6/0
Tail: Deer body hair
Body: Deer body hair over yellow tying thread
Wing: Upright and divided tips of hair used to form shellback
Hackle: Blue dun

In the spring 1990 edition of *American Angler* magazine, Pat Barnes credits Keith Kenyon for creating this fly during the 1940s. Pat offered that it was originally a secret meant for the Firehole River, but its effectiveness leaked out, and Pat's shop was bombarded with requests for that "goofy deer hair fly." Thus the name "Goofus Bug." This pattern, known in Wyoming as the Humpy, has become one of the most popular of dry-fly attractor patterns ever created.

H&L Variant

Hook: # 8-14 Mustad 7957B
Thread: Black 6/0
Tail: White calf tail
Wing: White calf tail, upright and divided
Body: Rear half of stripped peacock quill, front half of peacock herl
Hackle: Dry-fly-quality furnace saddle

Although not originating in the Greater Yellowstone region, this pattern came into popular use there beginning in the 1950s. Of the West Yellowstone fly-fishing retailers, Pat Barnes promoted it most effectively as an all-around dry attractor. In particular, he recommended it for use for fast-water drift boating, of which the region had an abundance of choices. H&L stand for House and Lot.

Hopkins Variant

Hook: #8-12 Mustad 94840
Thread: Black 6/0
Wing: Slate-colored mallard quill
   sections, trimmed
Tail: Reddish-brown hackle fibers
Body: Blue and yellow macaw quill fiber
Hackle: Reddish-brown with light blue
   hackle facing

Pat Barnes, Wally Eagle, and Bud Lilly remember Don Hopkins as a gentleman and fly-fishing conservationist. Through this pattern Don reveals excellent fly-tying skills. Bud and Pat offered this pattern for sale in their shops, and it had a popularity run of several years. Ray Bergman discussed this pattern in later editions of *Trout*, and J. Edson Leonard did the same in *Flies*.

Horner Deer Hair

Hook: #6-14 Mustad 94840
Thread: Black 6/0
Tail: Deer hair
Underbody: Black tying thread
Body: Deer hair tied in at bend and
   behind head
Wing: Tips of hair used to form body,
   upright and divided

Hackle: Grizzly

This is the forerunner of the Goofus Bug described by Pat Barnes in his spring 1990 *American Angler* article, "Goofus Bug Evolution." From it came the Goofus Bug, with its variety of body colors and versions that remain so popular to this day. In Wyoming this fly is known as the Humpy, and elk hair versions were initiated there mainly through introduction by Jack Dennis.

Jungle Cock Adams

Hook: #12-14 Mustad 94840
Thread: Black 6/0
Wing: Pair of white-striped jungle cock butt
   feathers, upright and divided
Tail: Sparse grizzly hackle fibers
Body: Dubbed muskrat fur
Hackle: Dry-fly-quality mixed brown
   and grizzly

This fly is in a display of Pat Barnes's favorite flies presented to him by the Pat Barnes Chapter of Trout Unlimited of Helena, Montana. Pat's son Charles now owns this display. The pattern originated at the Pat Barnes Tackle Shop in West Yellowstone, but who created it remains uncertain. It makes use of jungle cock butt feathers that were never in as popular use as the eye feathers.

Jungle Cock Variant

Hook: #12-14 Mustad 94840
Thread: Black 6/0
Wing: Pair of small jungle cock eye feathers, upright and divided
Tail: Brown hackle fibers
Body: Blue and yellow macaw quill fiber
Hackle: Sparse brown of variant radius

It is uncertain if Don Martinez created this pattern for use on streams in California or those around West Yellowstone. At the time of its creation, he was spending summers in West Yellowstone and winters in southern California. In any case, this pattern put to use those jungle cock eyes being too small to be placed on streamer patterns.

Killer Diller

Hook: #8-12 Mustad 94840
Thread: Black 6/0
Tail: Dyed red hackle fibers
Body: Yellow yarn or floss
Wing: Gray under red squirrel tail
Hackle: Blue dun or grizzly

Don Martinez recognized the effectiveness of this old pattern and began promoting it for use as an adult caddis and small

stonefly pattern on faster waters. He proposed changing its name to "Snake River Caddis" because of its origins and popularity on the Henry's Fork. Another Trude-style pattern, its origins go back to the early twentieth century.

Madison

Hook: #10-12 Mustad 94840
Thread: Black 6/0
Tail: Silver pheasant tippet fibers
Body: Peacock herl and white floss
Wing: White calf tail, upright and divided
Hackle: Grizzly

Created probably in the early 1940s, this pattern was offered in West Yellowstone fly shops during that decade. Its origin is unknown, but its name attests to the regional regard for the Madison River. This pattern's body is "royaled." Royaling describes the act of winding a floss central segment in a body usually formed of peacock herl. The term originates from the Royal Coachman, where the peacock herl body is royaled with red floss.

Multi Color Variant

Hook: #10-16 Mustad 94840
Thread: Black 6/0
Tail: Mixed hackle fibers in combinations such as blue dun, Rhode Island Red, and black, or badger and white
Wing: Short grizzly hackle tips
Body: Gold tinsel or black silk
Hackle: Variant radius of combinations such as (front to rear) white, dark ginger, black or blue dun, Rhode Island Red, and black

Don Martinez popularized these Ray Bergman patterns for use on Greater Yellowstone–area waters. He specifically recommended them in larger sizes as brown drake imitations. The term "multi color" refers to the multiple colors in the tail and hackle.

Pink Lady

Hook: #8-14 Mustad 94840
Thread: Black 6/0
Tail: Ginger hackle fibers
Rib: Fine flat gold tinsel
Body: Pink floss
Hackle: Light ginger
Wing: Gray duck quill sections, upright and divided

The Pink Lady is another pattern favored by eastern fly fishers that became popular on the waters around West Yellowstone. Coming from George LaBranche, it should be considered a classic. Don Martinez offered it from his shop in the 1930s. Later Bud Lilly offered it in the Trout Shop and its catalog for more than a decade.

Quack Special

Hook: #10-14 Mustad 7957B
Thread: Black 6/0
Tail: Golden pheasant tippet fibers
Body: Peacock herl and red floss
Hackle: Brown, variant radius
Wing: Trude style from white calf tail

Pat Barnes describes this fly in his 1964 Waterborn Flies catalog, but no drawing of it is given there. It is based on the Royal Coachman but modified by having oversize hackle and a Trude-style wing. In fly-fishing literature it is sometimes referred to as the "Quack Coachman."

Reuben Wood

Hook: #10-12 Mustad 3906
Thread: Black 6/0
Tip: Red floss
Tail: Barred wood duck flank fibers
Body: White chenille
Hackle: Brown
Wing: Barred mallard drake fibers

We include this pattern because it is one of the first eastern patterns used in the waters around West Yellowstone. James Blomfield identifies it as a taking pattern during his 1914 visit to fish the Madison River and hunt its surroundings. The description of his visit is the basis for his book *Rod, Gun and Palette in the High Rockies*. This pattern was named for Reuben Wood, a nineteenth-century fly-casting champion.

Rough Water Series

Hook: #10-14 Mustad 7957B
Thread: Gray size A nylon
Tail: Medium ginger hackle fibers
Body: Spun yellow caribou body hair,
　　clipped to shape
Hackle: Medium ginger

Don Martinez created this series for high visibility on turbulent southwest Montana

waters. A second version has a white body and black tail and hackle, and a third has a light blue body, light grizzly hackle, and brown tail. Inspired by the Irresistible, Don created them in 1953, two years before his death. Other than a note on use and origin in Ray Bergman's *Trout*, little information on this series is available in print.

Spider (Pat Barnes version)

Hook: #8-18 Mustad 9556
Thread: Black 6/0
Tail: Sparse grizzly hackle fibers
Body: Macaw wing quill fiber
Hackle: Brown, variant style

Pat's pattern is based on the construction of Charles DeFeo's Spiders. It is in the display of flies presented to Pat by the Pat Barnes Chapter of Trout Unlimited based in Helena, Montana, and now owned by his son Charles. Pat originally tied this pattern for the Craighead brothers, Frank and John, famed for doing grizzly bear research in the Greater Yellowstone area. The Craigheads were fly fishers.

West Yellowstone

Hook: #6-10 Mustad 94840
Thread: Tan 6/0
Tail: Forked from two fine ginger
hackle stems
Rib: Ginger hackle stem and ginger hackle
Body: Dyed yellow rabbit fur dubbing
Wing: Deer body hair, upright and divided
Hackle: Dry-fly-quality ginger

What better town to name a fly after than West Yellowstone! In the 1960s Letcher Lambouth, a Federation of Fly Fishers advocate, so named this fly in recognition of unforgettable fly-fishing experiences on nearby waters. The rib of Lambouth's pattern, a fine ginger hackle stem, protects the hackle wound just behind it.

Wulff Patterns

Hook: #8-14 Mustad 7957B
Thread: Black 6/0
Wing: Calf tail, upright and divided
Tail: Deer body hairs
Body: Peacock herl and red floss
Hackle: Dark brown neck hackle

The Royal Wulff remains a regional favorite as an attractor pattern. Its recipe is given above. The Wulff series of flies was originated by Lee Wulff while fishing New York's Au Sable River with Dan Bailey in 1929. The Gray Wulff was the first of the series. Later Lee added the White Wulff and the Royal Wulff. Dan Bailey originated the Black, Blond, Brown, and Grizzly Wulff patterns to the series after opening his shop in Livingston, Montana. He distributed them to West Yellowstone fly-fishing retailers to answer local demand for decades. Wulff patterns remain in popular use around the region.

Caddisfly Patterns

Brown Caddis

Hook: #10-12 Mustad 9671
Thread: Tan 6/0
Rib: Fine gold wire
Body: Tan poly yarn
Wing: Mixed red and gray squirrel tail hairs
Hackle: Gray hackle clipped from top
and bottom

Charlie Brooks hunted large trout, and thus he created and mainly fished wet flies. He made a few exceptions, however, when he observed large fish feeding on the surface. He conceived a pattern for use when large concentrations of caddisflies fluttering over the surface attract large fish. The result is this, his only dry caddis pattern, which can be tied in brown, tan, or gray.

Caddis Buck

Hook: #4-12 Mustad 9672
Thread: Gray 6/0
Body: Yellow chenille or yarn
Hackle: Furnace palmered over body
Wing: Deer body hair one and one-half
length of body

This fly was immensely popular on Rocky Mountain and West Coast streams during the 1960s and 1970s. It originated outside the Greater Yellowstone area, but all West Yellowstone fly-fishing retailers promoted it in these decades, particularly during giant and golden stonefly emergences. In smaller sizes it was one of the first patterns offered to simulate the October caddis that is common on many streams around West Yellowstone.

Chapman Adult Caddis

Hook: #12 Mustad 3399
Thread: Black 6/0
Body: Dubbed from muskrat or beaver fur
Hackle: Brown palmered over body
Wing: Trude style from deer body hair

This pattern is in the display of Scotty Chapman's flies that Fred LaTour prepared for Jim O'Toole. Another example of it is

in one of Scotty's fly boxes that Bill and Loretta Chapman now own. Other than these, it is doubtful that other examples exist. With its Trude-style wing and simple construction, this fly is typical of Scotty's creations at the fly-tying vise in the 1930s and 1940s.

Elk Hair Caddis

Hook: #8-18 Mustad 94840
Thread: Tan or ginger 8/0
Body: Tan or ginger dubbing
Hackle: Brown or ginger
palmered over body
Wing: Elk rump hair

This fly became legendary through promotion by Bud Lilly. Al Troth had originated it back in his days in Pennsylvania. Bud saw that the fly was versatile enough to be used to simulate moths, stoneflies, hoppers, and spruce moths as well as caddis. Its wing is based on Preston Jennings's use of elk hair. Today a thread body is favored over the original dubbed body.

Ice Soft Hackle

Hook: #8-12 TMC 3761
Thread: Fire orange 6/0
Tail: Pheasant tail fibers
Rib: Copper wire
Body: Pheasant tail fibers
Thorax: Orange Ice Dub
Wing: UV Krystal Flash
Hackle: Partridge

Arrick Swanson recommends this fly for fishing the Madison River in Yellowstone National Park during the autumn season. Its body and tail components hint at influence from the Pheasant Tail Nymph, and its hackle is a standard for soft-hackled flies. In smaller sizes this pattern simulates small caddis emergers, while larger ties simulate the emerging October caddis. It also is successfully used for mahogany dun emergers.

Jacklin's Fluttering Gray Caddis

Hook: #14-18 Dai-Riki 270
Thread: Black 8/0
Body: Dubbed hare's mask
Wing: Elk body hair trimmed of tips
Hackle: Medium blue dun

As had Dan Bailey in the 1930s, Bob Jacklin came from the East in the 1960s. He

advanced from guiding and fly tying for others to beginning his own fly-fishing retail business in the 1970s. Through his business he developed his reputation as a casting instructor, aquatic entomologist, and tackle consultant. This pattern was among his first to simulate an adult caddis. It is now a proven pattern on regional waters.

Spent Sparkle Caddis

Hook: #14-18 TMC 100
Thread: Brown or tan 8/0
Body: Tan or olive Antron dubbing
Wing: White or amber Z-Lon tied spent
Head: Dubbed natural brown hare's ear

At first this pattern appears to be a mayfly spinner, and certainly it can be used successfully in that role. But its Blue Ribbon Flies originators meant it to simulate a spent adult caddis lying on the surface. Because there is caddis activity on all area streams, having a pattern like this to simulate spent caddisflies or mayflies is a good on-stream strategy.

White Miller

Hook: #16-18 TMC 5210
Thread: White 8/0
Body: Polar bear sparkle blend dubbing
Hackle: Partridge tied soft-hackle style

White Miller patterns are "don't leave home without them" items if you intend to fish the Firehole River in June or September. It is one of the most important caddis patterns for this river, and the same can be said for the Gibbon and Madison. There are many White Miller versions out there, indicating the importance of this insect to salmonids. This one, an emerger pattern, comes from Blue Ribbon Flies. On finishing this popular pattern, Craig Mathews recommends not trimming the dubbing fibers because they help trap air bubbles that simulate those of a caddis trying to emerge.

X-Caddis

Hook: #14-18 TMC 100
Thread: Olive or tan 8/0
Shuck: Caddis amber or gold Z-Lon
Body: Antron dubbing, color matching natural
Wing: Short, fine mule deer body hair

This pattern has gained immense popularity on all regional streams since Craig Mathews and John Juracek introduced it in the late 1980s. Mule deer body hair is preferred over white-tailed deer body hair to achieve the proper set in the wings. A variation in which this hair is replaced with tan Enrico Puglisi EP Fibers begat the EPEX caddis, now achieving popularity in the region.

Damselfly and Dragonfly Patterns

Jacklin's Blue Damselfly

Hook: #10-12 Dai-Riki 730
Thread: Bright blue 70- or 140-denier
Extension and thorax: Blue 2 mm Wapsi Damselfly Foam
Hackle: Natural grizzly saddle
Body extension: ⅜-by-1½-inch piece of blue foam

The body extension of this fly is tied on a straight pin then removed to be tied onto the fly. Bob suggests using it on still and slow-moving waters during damselfly hatches. The damselfly emergence peak is late spring to early summer, but it can continue in diminishing numbers well into the summer.

Zing Damsel

Hook: #14 TMC 101
Thread: Gray 8/0
Extended body: Blue damsel body material
Wing: Transparent Medallion sheet
cut to shape
Thorax: Blue Furry Foam strip
Eyes: Monofilament melted to shape
Hackle (optional): Turn or two of
blue saddle

This is a variation of Shane Stalcup's adult damselfly pattern. Not an in-house pattern, it is sold in most West Yellowstone fly shops. It has become very popular in season because of the plentiful nearby stillwaters. The wings are tied in place using figure-eight wraps before the thorax is built. The eyes are tied in with figure-eight wraps, the thorax material is pulled over their tie-in point and trimmed, and the wings are cut to shape.

Mayfly Patterns

Almost There Baetis

Hook: #18-22 Daiichi 1140
Thread: Olive dun 8/0
Tail: Three wood duck flank fibers

Abdomen: Olive tying thread
Thorax: Beaver or gray Superfine dubbing
Wing: Blue Winged Olive EP Trigger
Point Fibers
Head: Butt end of clipped Trigger
Point Fibers

After tying in the tail and forming the abdomen from tying thread wraps, Bucky McCormick forms a dubbing ball and attaches it to form a thorax. In front of this he ties in strands of the EP Trigger Point Fibers at about their midpoint. A turn of thread to the rear helps elevate the fibers. A few thread wraps forward form a thread base, and the rear-facing portion of the fibers are clipped to form a short emerging wing. The front-facing fibers are clipped close to form the head. Bucky recommends this pattern anywhere Baetis are just emerging.

Blue Quill

Hook: #12-18 Mustad 94840
Thread: Black 6/0
Wing: Gray duck quill segments, upright
and divided
Tail: Blue dun hackle fibers
Body: Stripped peacock eye quill
Hackle: Blue dun

Through their catalogs, Bud Lilly and Pat Barnes championed this pattern for use in area waters. Earlier in the century, Don Martinez also offered a version of it. Now all West Yellowstone fly shops offer versions. All streams in the region host Baetis mayflies, and they emerge almost every month of the year. From the 1950s to the 1980s this pattern was popular for simulating their duns drifting on rivers in the West Yellowstone region.

Bradley

Hook: #12-14 Mustad 94840
Thread: Black 6/0
Wing: Brown hackle tips, upright
  and divided
Tail: Brown hackle fibers
Body: Blue and yellow macaw quill fiber
Hackle: Brown and grizzly

This is another pattern created by Don Martinez and Bob Carmichael. Carmichael praises it in Ray Bergman's *Trout*. It predates the Bradley M, but succeeds the Dunham. Don and Bob named this pattern for Bradley Lake, an excellent fishery in Grand Teton National Park. Subsequent tiers have replaced the blue and yellow macaw quill fiber to form the body with stripped peacock herl dyed yellow.

Bradley M

Hook: #8-12 Mustad 94840
Thread: Black 6/0
Tail: Brown hackle fibers
Body: Argus pheasant tail feather fiber
Wing: Brown hackle tips
Hackle: One grizzly dyed Silver Doctor blue
  and one furnace hackle

This Don Martinez pattern was a standard brown drake imitation in the Greater Yellowstone area from the late 1930s into the mid-1940s. It was in popular use on the Firehole and Madison Rivers in those days when the brown drake emergence was copious on those rivers. Since the 1959 earthquake, brown drakes have all but disappeared from the Firehole River. Only the famed early-July emergence of these mayflies from meadow reaches of the Gibbon River and minimal emergences on other upstream Madison River drainage streams remain.

Brown Drake Emerger

Hook: #8-10 Mustad 9672
Thread: Black 6/0
Abdomen: Dyed reddish-brown raffia
Wing: Golden olive marabou fibers
Thorax: Gold chenille
Wing case: Dyed reddish-brown raffia
Hackle: Soft brown

Don Martinez was the first fly fisher to comprehensively study the life cycle of Greater Yellowstone aquatic insects from an angling point of view. In fly-fishing literature, he is mainly considered as being interested in dry-fly patterns to simulate the dun stage of the mayfly life cycle and as a proponent of the Woolly Worm. However, Don, knowing the importance of the emerger stage in that life cycle, offered this pattern in season to his customers.

Cam's Skittering PMD

Hook: #14-16 TMC 2488
Thread: Olive/cream 6/0 combo thread
Shuck: Pheasant tail Z-Lon
Body: Olive/cream tying thread
Wing: Bleached deer hair
Thorax: PMD Z-Lon dubbing

Cam Coffin, current owner of West Yellowstone's Blue Ribbon Flies, has fished area waters for several decades and one of his favorite hatches are PMDs. Wind, a common occurrence during this period, can be strong enough to cause these mayfly duns to skitter along the surface and trout to chase them. The sail-like Sparkle Dun–style wing easily catches the breeze, allowing this pattern to skitter along the surface in a manner that simulates that of the natural PMD dun.

Chapman Mayfly Dun

Hook: #14-18 Mustad 3399
Thread: Black 6/0
Wing: Light blue dun hackle tips, upright and divided
Tail: Blue dun hackle fibers, somewhat longer than standard length
Body: Dubbed beaver fur
Hackle: Blue dun

This pattern is in the box of flies tied by Scotty Chapman that Bill and Loretta Chapman own. It is also in the collection framed by Fred LaTour for Jim O'Toole, Scotty's longtime fishing partner. Scotty tied many of the traditional patterns, but at times created flies for his favorite waters. This one undoubtedly saw service on waters such as Soda Butte Creek and the Firehole River.

Chocolate Dun

Hook: #10-16 Mustad 94840
Thread: Brown 6/0
Tail: Dyed brown grizzly hackle fibers
Body: Rear two-thirds dubbed brown rabbit fur with brown tying thread rib, front third fine yellow chenille
Hackle: Dark ginger and light blue dun

This is a rather obscure pattern originated by Don Martinez. Some sources believe it to be a variation of the Bradley, on which Martinez and Bob Carmichael collaborated. There is, however, little resemblance between these two patterns. As is the case with many fly patterns originating over half a century ago, information on the inspiration for this one seems lost.

Drake Mackerel Cripple

Hook: #12 TMC 2488
Thread: Tan 8/0
Shuck: Mayfly brown Z-Lon
Rib: Brown floss
Body: Tan dubbing or Antron
Wing: Silver Widow's Web
Hackle: Dyed brown grizzly

Commonly known as the summer drake or drake mackerel, *Hecuba timpanoga* is the last of the large mayflies to emerge from Greater Yellowstone streams. It is a more common inhabitant of the streams in the northeast corner of Yellowstone Park than in the Madison River drainage. It emerges August into September from these streams, and is mistakenly called a green drake by many anglers. This is Blue Ribbon Flies' cripple pattern, easy to tie and very effective. Aaron Freed, of Blue Ribbon Flies, recommends trimming the wing even with the hackle and trimming the hackle to about even with the hook point.

Dunham

Hook: #10-16 Mustad 94840
Thread: Gray 6/0
Tail: Red golden pheasant breast
feather fibers

Rib: Fine gold wire
Body: Blue and yellow macaw quill fiber
Hackle: Furnace or coch-y-bondhu with
a few turns of dyed light blue grizzly
as a facing

Ray Bergman discusses and praises this beautiful but lesser-known Don Martinez pattern in *Trout*. The Martinez, a similar pattern, is tied as above but without the option of coch-y-bondhu hackle. Blue and yellow macaw quill fiber is not used as a body material in commercially tied flies today simply because it is not available in reliable quantities.

EP Cripple

Hook: #12-22 TMC 100
Thread: Tan 6/0, or 8/0 for smallest sizes
Shuck: Amber Antron fibers
Abdomen: Natural goose or turkey biot
Wing: White EP Fibers

Paul Stimpson offers that although he calls this pattern a cripple, it can be used as an emerger, dun, or spinner. If the intended use is as a spinner, he replaces the shuck with Microfibett strands and ties in the wings at a near-horizontal position. Also, through changing size and colors, it can be used to simulate any mayfly species. Paul has used it to imitate nineteen mayfly species. The recipe given above is for the PMD version.

Extended Body Green Drake

Hook: #10 Mustad 94840
Thread: Olive 3/0
Tail: Elk body hair
Body: Dyed olive bucktail
Body beam: Elk hair forming tail
Wing: Elk body hair
Hackle: Dyed olive grizzly

All West Yellowstone fly shops offer green drake patterns. This practice began in the 1930s with Don Martinez and Eagle's Store. In those days extended bodies were called detached bodies. The extended body versions that Doug Gibson tied for Bud Lilly and his successor Jim Criner are perhaps the most elegant. Gibson, an accomplished Greater Yellowstone region guide and fly tier, also tied quill-body brown, gray, and green drake duns for Bob Jacklin.

Firehole

Hook: #10-20 Mustad 94840
Thread: Black 6/0
Wing: Wood duck flank fibers, upright and divided
Tail: Wood duck flank fibers
Body: Cream fur dubbing
Hackle: One each of black and grizzly

This is the only known pattern that Ray Bergman created as a result of his visits to the waters around West Yellowstone. He used it to simulate mayfly duns emerging from the Firehole River in the late season. Bergman's descriptions of his visit to the Firehole in *Trout* reveal appreciation and pleasure. Undoubtedly his good times resulted in creating and naming this pattern.

Foam Emerger

Hook: #8-10 TMC 100
Thread: Color matching natural 6/0
Shuck: Z-Lon fibers, color matching natural
Body: Dubbed beaver or rabbit, color matching natural
Rib (optional): Tying thread
Wing case: Polycelon strip, color matching natural
Hackle: Color matching natural

This Blue Ribbon Flies concept pattern by Paul Brown can simulate any emerging mayfly species. The gray drake formula is given and pictured above. Another example is the pale morning dun emerger consisting of brown Z-Lon shuck, orange-yellow dubbed body, gray Polycelon wing case, and dun starling hackle.

Ginger Quill

Hook: #10-16 Mustad 94840
Thread: Black 6/0
Wing: Gray duck quill sections, upright and divided
Tail: Light ginger hackle fibers
Body: Stripped peacock eye quill
Hackle: Pale ginger

Here is another fly with roots in England that was in demand at West Yellowstone fly shops from the 1930s to the 1980s. The version given above was most popular here. The original pattern, as created by F. M. Halford, featured a stripped peacock eye quill dyed red and wing of upright and divided starling quill sections. Bud Lilly featured this fly, in dry and wet versions, in his catalog into the 1980s.

Golden Quail

Hook: #10-12 Mustad 94840
Thread: Black 6/0
Wing: Pair of California quail nape feathers, upright and divided
Tail: Light ginger hackle
Body: Gold tinsel wrapped on rear half of shank, yellow dubbing on front half
Hackle: Sparse grizzly neck

Historically Don Martinez was known for popularizing dry flies for use in the Greater Yellowstone area and for promoting the Woolly Worm. This beautiful pattern won a *Field & Stream* contest award for Don. It was unusual for its day, but during the 1940s it was in popular use throughout the region from Yellowstone National Park waters to the Henry's Fork to simulate large mayfly duns. When asked how he liked it, Martinez was reputed to have replied: "Don't know, I've never tried it!"

Green Drake Wulff

Hook: #8-14 Mustad 94831
Thread: Black 6/0 or 8/0
Wing: Black calf tail, upright and divided
Tail: Dyed light olive stiff deer body hair
Rib: Yellow 3/0 thread
Body: Light olive dubbing
Hackle: Dyed golden yellow grizzly

Whether on the Henry's Fork, the Yellowstone River, or Slough Creek, major green drake emergences get the attention of fly fishers in the Greater Yellowstone region. That is because trout feed heavily on these insects when they emerge. Green drake emergences are also important on the Lewis and Lamar Rivers and on other regional waters. This is Bob Jacklin's answer for fly fishers seeking high-riding and visible green drake dun patterns.

Gulper Special

Hook: #14-22 TMC 100
Thread: Brown 6/0
Wing: White or orange poly yarn post
Tail: Grizzly hackle fibers
Body: Dubbed from gray, olive, or
   tan rabbit
Hackle: Parachute-style grizzly

The speckled dun emergence is one of the famed aspects of Hebgen Lake. Trout intercepting a floating dun or emerger here are known as gulpers because of the noise they make. Gulpers were first fished for from boats, but almost from their introduction, float tubes became preferred because the angler sitting in one offers a lower profile to feeding fish. Bud Lilly marketed this pattern by Al Troth.

Hen Spinner

Hook: #10-18 Mustad 94840
Thread: 6/0 or 8/0, color matching natural
Tail: Hackle fibers tied forked
Body: Dubbing of color matching natural
Wings: Hen hackle tips tied with
   concave side down

Doug Swisher and Carl Richards consider this to be a most effective spinner pattern.

Wide and webby, hen hackle tips proved suitable for spinner wings. Bonnie Harrop gained renown for tying and creating elegant, effective spinner patterns. Her Hen Spinner has been a Greater Yellowstone favorite for decades.

Natant Nylon Nymph

Hook: #6 Mustad 9671
Thread: Tan 6/0
Tail: Short, sparse grouse or grizzly
   hackle fibers
Body: Tan wool yarn
Wing: Square piece of nylon stocking
   material enclosing polypropylene ball
   attached to top of thorax
Hackle: Beard style of same material as tail

Charlie Brooks writes in *Nymph Fishing for Larger Trout* that this is his favorite pattern for use during Epeorus mayfly emergences. Its unusual wing construction is meant to simulate the unfurling wing of the insect. To form it correctly, place the ball in the middle of the material piece and gather the edges together, and tie it into the hook shank. Then dub the thorax around the gathered edges. The polypropylene ball provides all the buoyancy this pattern needs.

Natural Dun

Hook: #8-18 Dai-Riki 270
Thread: 6/0, color matching natural
Tail: Forked from hackle barbules for #14-18 ties, from elk hair or deer hair in larger sizes
Body: Dubbing of color matching natural
Wing: Comparadun style from deer hair
Hackle: Color matching natural, tied sparse in front of wing and clipped from bottom
Head: Same as body

Bob Jacklin experimented with this pattern design for decades. He eventually discovered that hooks designed for nymph patterns, such as suggested above, allowed the balance that makes the fly ride naturally on the water. By changing colors and sizes, any mayfly dun can be simulated through this technique.

PMD Duck Butt Dun

Hook: #14-18 TMC 100
Thread: Primrose 8/0
Tails: Yellow dyed over natural CDC
Wing: Natural elk hair tied in at one-third shank length behind eye
Body: Nature Spirit light yellow PMD dubbing
Head: Same as body

This pattern has an interesting pedigree. Its predecessors begin with the Fran Betters Haystack, which inspired the Caucci-Nastasi Comparadun, which in turn inspired the Craig Mathews Sparkle Dun. This is another pattern by Gary LaFontaine that Paul Stimpson tied for Arrick's Fly Shop.

Sidewinder Dun

Hook: #12-24 Mustad 94840
Thread: 6/0 or 8/0, color matching natural
Tail: Stiff hackle fibers or mink tail guard hairs
Body: Dubbed from fur blend in color matching natural
Wing: Gray duck quill segments

In *Selective Trout*, Doug Swisher and Carl Richards described a no-hackle mayfly dun imitation tied in this manner, but it remained for René Harrop to develop the correct wing set for it. This pattern and René's Double Sidewinder tied with a double set of wings gained extreme popularity with fly fishers throughout the region in the 1970s. Bud Lilly offered both through his mail-order catalog.

Sparkle Dun

Hook: #12-18 TMC 100
Thread: 8/0, color matching natural
Shuck (tail): Olive brown Z-Lon
Body: Natural or synthetic dubbing, color matching natural
Wing: Hollow deer hair

This Blue Ribbon pattern by Craig Mathews and John Juracek has enjoyed wide popularity due to its effectiveness, versatility, and simplicity. Its inspiration is described in their *Fly Patterns of Yellowstone*. The wing is the first component tied in, and the "sparkle" comes from the second component tied in, the Z-Lon shuck. Hollow hair must be used to form the wing, similar to that of a Comparadun, in order to achieve stability and the proper set.

Sparkle Spinner

Hook: #12-20 Mustad 94840
Thread: 6/0, color matching natural
Tail: Dun hackle fibers
Wing: White Z-Lon
Body: Dubbing of color matching natural

Craig Mathews and John Juracek suggest that Z-Lon makes a superior spinner wing because its sparkle simulates the

air bubbles trapped by the natural wing lying on the surface. The body behind the wing should be dubbed thin and the wings figure-eight wrapped into place, leaving about a third of the shank in front on which to dub over the wing base and the reminder of the body. Body colors that match that of the natural spinner such as gray, olive, or rust can be used. The size of this pattern can also be changed to match that of the natural spinner.

Teton Special

Hook: #12-14 Mustad 94840
Thread: Black 6/0
Tail: Ginger hackle fibers
Wing: Ginger hackle tips
Body: Light cream dubbing
Hackle: One ginger and one dyed light blue dun grizzly

Don Martinez, collaborating with Bob Carmichael, was the first to apply hackle tip wings to western mayfly dun patterns. This pattern could have been created when Martinez operated his Jackson Hole shop during the mid-1940s. It was distributed to West Yellowstone fly-fishing retailers and Yellowstone Park concessionaires by Rae Servatius. Its earliest description is in Ray Bergman's *Trout* and J. Edson Leonard's *Flies*.

Trico Paraspin

Hook: #18-20 TMC 9300
Thread: Black 8/0
Tail: Two clear Microfibetts
Body: Dyed black beaver fur or other fine-fibered dubbing
Thorax: Same as body
Wing: White Antron or poly yarn post
Hackle: Parachute-style grizzly

Bob Jacklin developed this pattern for Tricorythodes spinner falls on Hebgen Lake and the upper Madison River. During the spinner falls he noted that spent wings were difficult to see. He thus conceived this pattern where the parachute-style wings simulate spent spinner wings and the post wing provides visibility. Through this concept, the visibility of any spent-wing pattern can be improved. Bob has used this pattern to simulate adult midges.

Whitcraft

Hook: #12-14 Mustad 94840
Thread: Black 6/0
Wing: Pair of grizzly hackle tips, upright and divided
Tail: Rhode Island Red hackle tips or fibers
Body: Blue and yellow macaw quill fiber
Hackle: Brown and grizzly neck hackles

This pattern is the best known and probably the first offered commercially on which Bob Carmichael and Don Martinez collaborated. Both considered it to be superbly effective when properly presented. Carmichael named it after his friend Tom Whitcraft, a contemporary Grand Teton National Park superintendent. Outside of the Greater Yellowstone region, this pattern is known as the Quill Adams. The above photo shows a later variation with a hackle fiber tail.

Midge Patterns

Chapman Midge

Hook: #18-20 Mustad 3399
Thread: Black 6/0
Tail: Grizzly hackle fibers, somewhat longer than standard length
Body: Dubbed muskrat fur
Hackle: Grizzly

This is another simple pattern Scotty Chapman created. It is in the collection framed by Fred LaTour for Jim O'Toole, Scotty's longtime fishing partner. Scotty seemed to prefer fishing smaller waters, according to Jim, and one favorite was the Blacktail Ponds, on which this pattern was surely effective for resident brook trout taking midges. Hackle in the proper size for this pattern was likely more difficult to find in the days when Scotty tied compared to current times.

Cream Wiggler

Hook: #18-22 Partridge K4
Thread: Gray or tan 6/0
Body: Strip of car-washing chamois, half inch long, thick as a toothpick, and attached near middle of hook shank
Hackle: One turn of short, soft gray grouse hackle

Meant to be an adult midge pattern, this is one of Charlie Brooks's smaller patterns. It is also one of his few dry flies. He wrote in *Nymph Fishing for Larger Trout* that he first experimented with rubber hackle for the body, but settled on a chamois strip because it gave better action. He dressed the head and hackle only to let the head hang in the surface film with the body trailing.

Madison Buzzer

Hook: #18-20 Dai-Riki 125
Thread: Black 14/0
Rib: Extra-fine silver wire
Body: Black tying thread
Wing: Sparkle Dun deer hair
Hackle: Grizzly saddle

Cover the back three-quarters of the hook, including the top of the bend, with the

tying thread. Rib the body and make a thread base at the front end of the body. Tie in the wing at the thread base such that the tips extend just forward of the hook eye. Leave the butts to add buoyancy. Turn a few thread wraps in front of the wing to secure it in place. Tie in two turns of hackle behind the wing and one in front. Bucky McCormick recommends this pattern for large midges or midge clusters.

Zelon Midge

Hook: #18-24 Tiemco 100
Thread: Black 8/0
Shuck: White or dun Z-Lon
Rib: Gray thread
Body: Thin, of black dubbing
Wing: White Z-Lon tied back over body or in spent-wing position
Head: Black dubbing, thinly applied

At the end of their informative book *Fishing Yellowstone Hatches*, John Juracek and Craig Mathews included a selection of fly patterns recommended to simulate the life cycles of the insects discussed earlier in the book. This section is easily overlooked, but it provides valuable information that, based on their fly-fishing experience, will improve angling success throughout the year. This pattern is one that is highly recommended in this section. Through the years Craig and John have offered variations of the Zelon Midge.

Stonefly Patterns

Bar-X Stonefly

Hook: #4-6 Mustad 3906
Thread: Black 6/0
Tail: Dyed orange monofilament
Antennae: Dyed orange monofilament
Underbody: Orange floss
Body: Black Nymph weave of dyed brown monofilament fibers
Wing: Cut to shape from Herter's Wing Sheet
Hackle: Rhode Island Red saddle hackle or red squirrel tail

Della "Tony" Sivey was one of the renowned Montana woven body fly-tying specialists. This unusual fly was her adult stonefly pattern. She first tied on tails and antennae and wove bodies on dozens of hooks. Then she hackled and winged each in the batch. Sivey supplied these to local fly-fishing retailers, with Jim Danskin perhaps her biggest customer. As with all patterns she tied personally, this one is much sought by fly collectors.

Bird's Stonefly

Hook: #2-8 Mustad 79580
Thread: Orange 6/0
Tail: Two bear paw bristles
Rib: Trimmed brown saddle hackle

Body: Orange floss or yarn
Wing: Bucktail tied down wing
Hackle: Furnace saddle hackles, tops and bottoms trimmed flat
Antennae: Two bear paw bristles

This classic adult stonefly pattern originated by Californian Cal Bird, frequent visitor to rivers in the West Yellowstone area, rivaled the Sofa Pillow in popularity in West Yellowstone fly shops around mid-twentieth century. In those days all area fly-fishing retail shops featured it. Now it is relatively obscure due to the advent of patterns using closed-cell foam. Nevertheless, it remains one of the most effective adult stonefly patterns created, and those who have tried it swear by it.

Bitchin' Salmonfly

Hook: #2-6 Daiichi 2220
Thread: Fluorescent fire orange 6/0
Tail: Moose hair and black rubber hackle
Body: Woven black (top) and orange (bottom) poly yarn
Wing: Two layers of plastic screen-door material cut to shape under several strands of pearlescent Krystal Flash under elk mane
Legs: Black rubber hackle
Head and collar: Bullet style from dyed gray deer hair

Arrick Swanson's use of plastic screening material in the wing of this pattern is unique. The pattern is a blend of synthetic and natural materials, which is common in contemporary fly-tying circles. The result is another effective pattern, particularly during times of large stonefly activity in the area.

Dave's Adult Stone

Hook: #4-6 Mustad 79580
Thread: Rusty orange 6/0
Rib: Rusty orange tying thread or small
copper Wapsi Ultra Wire
Body: Dyed orange elk rump
Wing: Elk rump
Collar and head: Dyed orange and brown
deer hair, clipped to shape
Antennae: Goose biots

Throughout the 1970s and into the 1980s, this pattern by Dave Whitlock was a consistent seller from Bud Lilly's Trout Shop. Dave and his tiers supplied it to Bud, and along with the Sofa Pillow and Bird's Stonefly, it was the most popular large stonefly pattern when emergences on the Madison, Gallatin, and Yellowstone Rivers and the Henry's Fork were in progress. Dave now ties this pattern on a Tiemco 5263 hook.

Fluttering Stone

Hook: #8-16 Mustad 3906B
Thread: Black 3/0 monocord
Body: Twisted orange Antron yarn
Antennae: Stripped light brown
hackle stems
Wing: Elk body hair

Hackle: Dry-fly-quality brown or badger
saddle hackle

Stonefly patterns tied with extended bodies of twisted Antron yarn were popular back in the 1970s and 1980s. And there were a number of patterns named "Fluttering Stone" in those days. Frank Johnson, then living in Missoula, Montana, created this one. Bud Lilly offered it through his mail-order catalog, and it was the cover fly for the 1982 edition.

Jacklin's Early Black Stone

Hook: #14-18 Mustad 79580
Thread: Black 6/0
Egg sac: Clipped dyed black deer hair
Rib: Clipped black hackle
Body: Light brown dubbing
Wing: Mule deer body hair tied in at a
45-degree angle
Head and collar: Bullet style from black
coastal deer hair

This is Bob Jacklin's pattern for *Capnia vernalis*, a small brown stonefly common to area trout streams and often called "winter stone." They can be seen crawling along stream banks on calm, sunny days during late winter and early spring. These insects are poor fliers and thus fall or are blown onto water to become forage for trout.

Jacklin's Giant Salmonfly

Hook: #4-6 Dai-Riki 700
Thread: Fluorescent orange 3/0
Egg sac: Clipped dyed black deer hair
Rib: Two dark brown saddle hackles
Body: Orange poly yarn
Wing: Blond elk hair tied in at a
45-degree angle
Legs: Medium round black rubber legs
Head and collar: Bullet style from dyed
black deer hair

Bob ties a series of stonefly patterns in the same manner as this one. Others include Jacklin's Golden Stone, Jacklin's Early Black Stonefly, and Jacklin's Western Yellow Stone. Only material colors and size are changed in tying these patterns. Bob has recently altered this pattern by adding a clipped brown saddle hackle rib, replacing the poly yarn body with orange Jacklin's Salmon Fly dubbing, adding medium or small round black rubber legs and a collar and bullet head of dyed golden brown deer hair.

Jacklin's Golden Stone

Hook: #6-8 Mustad 79580
Thread: Rusty brown 6/0
Egg sac: Clipped dyed brown deer hair

Rib: Clipped ginger hackle
Body: Golden stonefly dubbing
Wing: Blond elk hair tied in at a
45-degree angle
Legs: Small round rubber hackle
Head and collar: Bullet style from dyed
tan elk hair

As with all Bob Jacklin's stonefly patterns, this one results from years of fly-fishing experience and associated research. Golden stoneflies are widely distributed, more so than giant stoneflies, in the streams around West Yellowstone, and are therefore an important trout food within each. Golden stonefly adult patterns in a wide variety are offered at all West Yellowstone fly-fishing retail shops.

Jacklin's Western Yellow Stone

Hook: #10-14 Mustad 79580
Thread: Yellow 6/0
Egg sac: Clipped natural deer body hair
Rib: Clipped light ginger hackle
Body: Pale yellow dubbing
Wing: Light elk hair tied in at a
45-degree angle
Head and collar: Bullet style from dyed pale
yellow elk hair

This Bob Jacklin pattern represents the adult stage of the Isoperla stoneflies so common in swifter quality streams around West Yellowstone. They emerge from springtime to midsummer. This pattern is one of Bob's series of stonefly adult patterns, which resulted from his aquatic entomology interest, uncommon fly-tying ability, and widespread fly-fishing experience.

The Jughead

Hook: #4-10 Mustad 79580
Thread: Orange or gray size A
Tail: Straw-colored elk rump hair
Rib: Clipped brown saddle hackle
Body: Orange poly yarn
Underwing: Straw-colored elk rump hair
Wing: Red fox squirrel tail
Head: Spun, trimmed antelope hair

In *Ribbons of Blue*, Pat Barnes relates that Betty Hoyt, a fly-fishing and fly-tying friend, created this pattern. Pat and Sig sold it from their Pat Barnes Tackle Shop, and it became very popular in the region. It was named for obvious reason by Lloyd Bray, a guide Pat and Sig employed.

Montana Stone

Hook: #4-6 Mustad 79580
Thread: Black 3/0
Underbody: Primary feather quill section as long as hook shank and tied on top of shank
Body: Orange poly yarn covering quill
Underwing: Sparse brown bucktail
Wing: Two dyed orange grizzly hackles tied in flat and extending just past bend

Hackle: One orange and one black hackle with fibers clipped from top and bottom of fly

Charlie Brooks concentrated on tying wet flies, so this was one of his few dry flies. He created it early in his experiences fishing Greater Yellowstone region waters when he observed large trout taking drifting adult salmonflies.

Nature Stone Dry

Hook: #2-6 TMC 5212
Thread: Orange 3/0 monocord
Tail: Dark moose body
Rib: Trimmed dyed brown grizzly hackle
Body: Orange yarn
Underwing: Dyed orange deer hair
Wing: Lacquered mallard flank feather
Collar: Tips of orange deer hair used to form head
Head: Spun orange deer hair

This is the adult pattern for the Nature Stone Nymphs Blue Ribbon Flies intro-duced in the 1970s. Its inspiration is described in the fall 1985 edition of *Fly Tyer* magazine. By changing material colors and hook size, golden and smaller stonefly spe-cies are simulated by this pattern.

Pheasant Stonefly

Hook: #4-8 Mustad 94831
Thread: Orange monocord 3/0
Tail: A few strands of moose body hair
Rib: Furnace or brown hackle
Body: Orange poly yarn
Underwing: Orange-brown dyed deer hair
Wing: Greenish-brown almond pheasant
  feather from back of ringneck rooster
Legs: Deer hair
Head: Spun deer hair clipped to shape

As with most of his dry-fly patterns, Jack Gartside found an application for pheasant feathers for creating an adult stonefly pattern. Large adult stonefly patterns have always been in great demand in West Yellowstone. Jack supplied these to help meet that demand during the stonefly activity season. He offers that he based the design of the pattern on his earlier hopper pattern.

Picket Pin

Hook: #6-12 Mustad 9672
Thread: Black 6/0
Tail: Six to eight golden pheasant
  tippet fibers
Rib: Fine gold wire counter-wrapped
  over hackle

Body: Flat gold tinsel
Hackle: Brown palmered around body
Wing: Gray squirrel tail
Collar: Gray squirrel tail shorter than wing
Head: Peacock herl

This pattern, one of the oldest created in Montana around 1910, is by Jack Boehme. It was in popular use in waters around West Yellowstone to imitate adult stoneflies. Its popularity faded after the 1930s when such tiers as Pat Barnes introduced patterns for the same purpose. Many variations of this pattern exist. Some of the more popular ones have a peacock herl body and brown hackle fiber tail.

Royal Trude Skwala (Female)

Hook: #10-14 Dai-Riki 310
Thread: Black 8/0
Egg sac: Black closed-cell foam
Body: Peacock herl royaled with red floss
Wing: White Enrico Puglisi EP Fibers
Hackle: Dyed brown grizzly saddle hackle
Legs: White and black variegated fine
  rubber legs
Indicator: Stub of EP Fibers used to
  form wings

Here is a fly with a pedigree: Both the Trude and the Royal Wulff influence its construction. Skwalas, early-season stoneflies, emerge from such streams as the Gallatin and Madison Rivers. Rowan Nyman's version of the male skwala is without an egg sac and uses brown saddle hackle in place of dyed brown grizzly.

Sofa Pillow

Hook: #4-10 Mustad 9672
Thread: Black 6/0
Tail: Dyed red goose quill section
Body: Red floss
Wing: Red or gray squirrel
Hackle: Three or four brown saddle hackles

Above is the original makeup for this major contribution to fly tying by Pat Barnes. Its roots within the West Yellowstone region include a Trude-style wing and use for the giant stonefly emergence. It was named by a customer who proclaimed on first seeing it, "That's as big as a sofa pillow!" Pat's response was "You named it!" It remains a top-selling pattern during the stonefly season everywhere in the western states.

Super Sofa Pillow

Hook: #2-6 Mustad 9672
Thread: Black 6/0
Tail: Dyed red goose quill section
Rib: Clipped brown saddle hackle
Body: Orange yarn
Underwing: Blond elk rump hair
Wing: Red squirrel tail
Hackle: Three or four brown saddle hackles

Sig Barnes is one of the great fly-tying women of all time. Her style of tying through using a treadle-operated sewing machine to produce flies for the Pat Barnes Tackle Shop was unique. She and Pat produced this version of the Sofa Pillow, meant to improve visibility and durability. Coming from its originators, it was the first credible variation of the Sofa Pillow. Now variations by the dozen of this famed fly pattern exist.

Troth Salmon Fly

Hook: #4-6 Mustad 79580
Thread: Orange size A
Tail: Black moose or elk hair
Rib: Orange tying thread
Body: Dyed orange elk rump
Underwing: Brown elk body hair
Overwing: Tips of elk hair used
   to form head
Head: Bullet style from brown elk hair

This pattern is mainly tied of elk hair. Al Troth forms the body by folding the elk hair over, giving a double thickness and increased buoyancy. The overwing provides visibility in the rough water fished during giant salmonfly activity. During the 1970s and 1980s Bud Lilly offered this pattern through his mail-order catalog.

Trude

Hook: #6-12 Mustad 94840
Thread: Black 6/0
Tail: Reddish-brown hackle fibers
Rib: Oval silver tinsel
Body: Scarlet wool yarn
Wing: Red fox squirrel tail
Hackle: Two reddish-brown neck or
saddle hackles

West Yellowstone fly-fishing retailers sold this Trude version for decades. The original version, meant to imitate an adult stonefly, was without a tail or rib and had a body of red rug yarn and a wing of reddish hair from a cocker spaniel. As we saw earlier, the Trude has had many variations. "Trude-style wing" has become as common in fly-tying circles as "tied in the round," "royaled," and "beard-style."

Yellow Sally Stonefly

Hook: #6-12 Mustad 94831
Thread: Yellow 6/0
Tail: A few ginger hackle fibers
Body: Pale yellow Spectrum (no. 3) dubbing
Underwing: A few strands of light
gray deer hair
Overwing: Overlapping mallard duck
quill segments

Hackle: Light dun clipped from top
and bottom

Yellow sally stoneflies are numerous in most Greater Yellowstone streams, large and small. Generally these hatch on the surface of the hosting stream, unlike golden and giant stoneflies, which transform to adults on land. The Madison River and the Henry's Fork feature significant yellow sally activity much of the season. Mike Lawson offers this delicate pattern based on his own experience guiding for Jim Danskin on both rivers.

Terrestrial Patterns

Al's Hopper

Hook: #4-10 Mustad 3906
Thread: Black 6/0
Rib: Rhode Island Red saddle hackle
Body: Yellow wool
Wing: Turkey quill segments about two
times the length of hook and mounted at
a 45-degree angle
Hackle: Rhode Island Red and grizzly
saddle hackle

According to Fred and Catherine Uchiyama, Al Nelson, a tailor by trade, was a perfectionist whether fly-fishing or tying flies. This is the only pattern he offered commercially, and it is similar to Joe's Hopper. Both Jim Danskin and Bud Lilly marveled at its durability and thus offered it for sale. Nelson fished area waters seasonally, and the Madison Junction Campground was his favorite home base.

Ant "B"

Hook: #12-20 TMC 100
Thread: Black 8/0
Body: Dubbed black front and rear portions, dubbed red in middle
Wing: A few Krystal Flash fibers under white EP Fibers
Legs: Small black rubber legs
Head: Black dubbing under a small foam shellback

During the late-summer season, ant swarms are common over waters around West Yellowstone. In many waters when these appear, trout key on them and ignore other food forms. Most competent fly tiers in town offer flying ant versions. Paul Stimpson offers this pattern, a constructive modification of Kelly Galloup's Ant Acid. It has proven itself on most West Yellowstone–area waters.

Beetle Bug

Hook: #8-16 Mustad 3906
Thread: Brown monocord 3/0, for #14 and smaller, brown size A for #12 and larger
Wing: White calf tail, upright and divided or spent
Tail: Brown bucktail or calf tail
Body: Brown tying thread

Hackle: Brown or light brown

In the spring 1987 issue of *Fly Tyer* magazine, Pat Barnes describes this as his "last resort fly." Here he tells of using it to take a large rainbow trout from a local stream. Pat never sold this pattern from his shop, nor did he reveal the name of the tier who created it. He never published where this fly fooled the big rainbow either.

Blue Ribbon Foam Beetle

Hook: #12-18 TMC 5210
Thread: Black 6/0
Legs: Three pairs of dark elk or moose body hair tied in before forming shellback
Body: Shellback formed from black closed-cell foam strip
Indicator: White or yellow Z-Lon

Presently there are closed-cell foam patterns for any floating trout food form. But Nick Nicklas's was likely the first beetle pattern created from closed-cell foam that moved on to broadscale fly-fishing world popularity. Simple, durable, and effective, it is a must almost anywhere when terrestrial insects are an important food form from early July to mid-October. Hundreds of versions now exist.

Chaos Hopper

Hook: #12-14 Daiichi 1270
Thread: Olive 6/0
Body: Olive tying thread
Hackle: Brown saddle
Overwing: Gray Z-Lon
Underwing: Shaped from tan ¼-inch-thick closed-cell foam
Legs: Yellow rubber legs with overhand knot
Antennae: Forward extension of legs
Head: Forward extension of underwing

According to Craig Mathews, this fly originated during one of the weekly Blue Ribbon Flies brainstorming tying sessions he held mainly during the off-season. With a name like this, any fly would attract attention. In 2003 it underwent modifications, mainly to the closed-cell foam used in the underwing and head construction, and became the Improved Chaos Hopper.

Combo Parachute Ant

Hook: #12-18 TMC 100
Thread: Black 140-denier
Rear body: Black Antron dubbing
Wing: White Para Post
Hackle: Brown
Front body: Ginger variant Antron dubbing

Arrick Swanson solves the dry ant pattern visibility problem through using a parachute wing. Pictured above is his Combo Parachute Ant. It has a dubbed black rear body segment and a dubbed ginger front body segment. After covering the hook shank with thread, dub the rear body segment and tie in the Para Post wing according to directions given in Arrick's Parachute Beetle, found later in this section. Next tie in the hackle, and finally dub the front body segment around the wing base. The Black Parachute Ant is tied through changing to black hackle, black thread, and black Antron dubbing. The Cinnamon Parachute Ant is tied through changing to brown hackle, red thread, and ginger variant Antron dubbing.

Craig's House Fly

Hook: #14-16 TMC 100
Thread: Olive dun 8/0
Body: Three strands of dyed black peacock herl
Wing: Two strands of light dun Z-Lon

Observation and experience brought the idea of a housefly pattern to Craig Mathews. Houseflies, blowflies, and deerflies abound around moving and still waters everywhere. After attaching the peacock herl strands along the hook shank, spiral them around the tying thread to add durability. Stop winding the herls at the thorax midpoint and tie in the Z-Lon strands, forming a wing at a 45-degree angle. Proceed winding the herls to hide the wing tie-in point, ending just behind the hook eye. Trim the herl, leaving a stub to form a head.

Dave's Hopper

Hook: #6-14 Mustad 9671 (original), #6-14 TMC 5253 (current)
Thread: Yellow or white 3/0 for body, Wapsi Ultra Thread 210
Tail: Dyed red deer hair
Rib: Clipped light brown or ginger hackle
Body: Cream or yellow poly yarn
Underwing: Gray (original) or yellow deer body hair
Wing: Turkey or peacock wing quill sections
Legs: Knotted golden pheasant tail segments
Head: First deer hair clump for collar and rear of head, second for front of head
Cement: Dave's Fleximent

Dave Whitlock offers that this pattern is a hybrid of Joe's Hopper and a Dan Bailey–style Muddler Minnow. After Jay Buchner showed Dave a Dick Alf hopper having ringneck cock pheasant tail barbules jointed by an overhand knot to create kicker legs, Dave tied some on his hopper and liked their looks. Photography of live adult hoppers from underwater also revealed to Dave the dominance of legs in the hopper silhouette. Thus this version became the best known commercially.

Flying Ant

Hook: #12-18 TMC 100
Thread: Red 6/0
Body: Three segments; rear of chestnut Antron, middle of red tying thread, front of rust Antron
Wing: White Para Post
Hackle: Dyed brown grizzly

During the latter part of each summer in the region, flying ants emerge on a broad basis. Trout key on their swarms, and at times feed on them almost to the exclusion of other available foods. Thus it is not surprising that flying ant patterns have been in the fly bins of past shops and remain in the fly bins of current West Yellowstone shops. Doug Gibson tied this pattern for Bud Lilly's Trout Shop.

Fraud Hopper

Hook: #6-12 Mustad 9672
Thread: Yellow 3/0
Tail: Dyed red deer hair
Rib: Clipped brown hackle
Body: Yellow art foam
Underwing: Dozen dyed golden brown deer hairs
Wing: Pellon pattern tracing cloth dyed tan with brown markings

Legs: Knotted and cemented golden
   pheasant tail fibers
Collar: Tips of deer hair forming head
Head: Flared golden brown deer hair on
   top and light yellow deer hair on bottom,
   trimmed to shape

During the 1970s Bud Lilly could not keep
up with demand for this hopper pattern
by Darwin Atkin. From Slough Creek to the
Henry's Fork, in season it was a most effective pattern. Now examples of it grace fly
collections.

Improved Killer Bee

Hook: #12 TMC 2312
Thread: Black 6/0 pre-waxed Danville
Body: Two strips of yellow 2 mm foam
Rib: Black 1 mm razor foam
Wing: White Widow's Web with two pieces
   pearlescent Krystal Flash
Hackle: Dry-fly-quality grizzly saddle
Head: One wrap of yellow foam strip
   extension that formed body

The original Killer Bee pattern came out of
Blue Ribbon Flies. When the precut body
supply became inconsistent, Aaron Freed
made a revision. He uses two yellow foam
strips to form the body, with one clipped
off at the bend and remaining over the
rear two-thirds of the shank. The other,
wrapped forward three or four turns, gives
a full body. The Widow's Web–Krystal Flash
bunch split in two with thread wraps forms
wings. Aaron suggests this popular pattern
as a great late-summer attractor.

Jacklin's Black Caterpillar

Hook: #8-10 Dai-Riki 285
Thread: Black 6/0
Tail: Black hackle fibers
Rib: Counter-wrapped fine gold wire
Hackle: Dry-fly-quality black
Body: Black medium Ultra Chenille

Hebgen Lake brown and rainbow trout in
a spawning mode begin moving upstream
into the Madison River by late August.
Realizing this and observing that black cat-
erpillars populate some of the riverbanks
this time of year, Bob Jacklin created this
pattern and presented it from out in the
river to some of these fish schooling in
shallow water. To his pleasant surprise, several of these large fish took the pattern. So
here is an alternative to the streamers and
large soft-hackle flies presented to these
fish in season. Bob also has a brown version
of this pattern.

Jacklin's Hopper

Hook: #6-14 Dai-Riki 1720
Thread: Yellow 6/0
Tail: Dyed red deer hair
Rib: Brown saddle hackle clipped to shape
Body: Fluorescent green yarn
Wing: Turkey wing quill segment
clipped to shape
Head and collar: Bullet style from light elk

Beginning in midsummer, fishing terrestrial patterns on waters around West Yellowstone is a way of life for Bob Jacklin. Within an hour's drive of town are meadow reaches on the Buffalo, Gallatin, Gardner, Gibbon, Firehole, Madison, Henry's Fork, and South Fork of the Madison, in addition to numerous smaller streams. Bob's hopper pattern results from experiences on this matchless array of streams.

Jacklin's Madison River Mouse

Hook: #6 TMC 8089
Thread: Black Danville 280-denier
Tail: Dark tan medium Ultra Chenille
Body: Deer body hair tied in
tightly and spun
Back, head, and face: ½-inch-wide strip of
gray 3 mm Fly Foam

Eyes: Large black monofilament eyes
Whiskers: Black hackle

Tie in the Fly Foam strip at the tail tie-in point above the hook bend. Spin deer hair along the hook shank and clip to a half inch in diameter, flat on the bottom, and rounded on the top surface and sides. Tie in and cement in place the monofilament eyes just behind the hook eye followed by the hackle. Drape the Fly Foam strip snugly over the spun deer hair body to form the back and the face of the mouse, then tie off at the hook eye.

Klod Hopper

Hook: #6-12 Mustad 9671 (2X) or 9672 (3X)
Thread: Dark brown 3/0
Body: Tan closed-cell foam strip, 2 mm
thick for #10-12, 3 mm for #6-8
Hackle: Brown saddle
Wing: Elk hair
Legs: Red/black rubber legs
Head: Extension of foam strip
forming body

Paul Stimpson claims not to be enthusiastic about tying hopper patterns, but he enjoys fishing them. He adapted this pattern from a cicada pattern a friend created. He has another friend named Claude, and with a phonetic change in spelling named it after him. He recommends fishing this pattern in the surface film. You can see it in the fly bins at Arrick's Fly Shop in West Yellowstone.

Madison River Stopper

Hook: #10-14 Mustad 94840
Thread: Yellow 3/0 monocord
Body: Yellow Polycelon or equivalent closed-cell foam strip
Underwing: Golden pheasant tippet strands
Wing: White-tailed deer body hair
Head: Trimmed butt of deer hair clump used to form wing

Nick Nicklas had been associated with Blue Ribbon Flies nearly as long as its founders Craig and Jackie Mathews. This is his simple pattern to simulate a grasshopper. Craig and John Juracek praise it for its effectiveness and ease in tying in *Fly Patterns of Yellowstone*.

Parachute Beetle

Hook: #10-16 TMC 100
Thread: Black 140-denier
Back: Black closed-cell foam strip, wide as hook gap
Wing: White Para Post
Hackle: Black
Body: Black closed-cell foam
Thorax: Peacock black Ice Dub

Wrap the hook shank with the tying thread, then tie in the foam along the shank, leaving room behind the eye for the post wing. The foam working portion extends to the rear. Form a shellback with the foam and tie off. Use two Para Post strips to form the wing. Tie them in on the shank at their midpoint. Pull the front and rear sections up together, and wrap their base with thread to make a rigid post. Tie in the hackle. The Ice Dub fills the space between the post and shellback.

Pat's Hopper

Hook: #4-12 Mustad 9671
Thread: Black 6/0
Tail: Dyed goose wing quill segment
Rib: Clipped brown saddle hackle
Body: Yellow floss
Underwing: Straw-colored elk rump
Wing: Turkey quill segment
Hackle: Mixed brown and grizzly saddles

In *Ribbons of Blue*, Pat Barnes proclaims that as a trout food the grasshopper is "king of the terrestrials." The lure of hoppers as a trout food began early in life for Pat. His mother encouraged him to use the naturals, even though his father was a fly fisher. This pattern was therefore his contribution to the world of hopper patterns.

Pheasant Hopper

Hook: #8-14 Mustad 94831
Thread: 3/0, same as body color
Tail: Dark moose hair
Rib: Dry-fly-quality clipped badger or furnace saddle hackle
Body: Light gray, tan, yellow, or olive poly yarn tapered back to front
Underwing: Deer hair, same as body color
Wing: Pheasant church window feather shaped with cement
Legs: Unclipped deer hair on either side of collar
Collar and head: Spun deer hair clipped to shape and same color as body

This fly is a product of Jack Gartside's many summers fishing waters around West Yellowstone. It is an excellent example of his elegant tying technique, and was featured in Bud Lilly's mail-order catalog. It was also the subject of an October/November 1978 *Fly Fisherman* magazine article.

Spent Spruce Moth (Daigle)

Hook: #12-14 TMC 100
Thread: Primrose 8/0
Body: Light cahill Antron dubbing
Underwing: Amber Z-Lon
Wing: Bleached deer body hair

The spruce moth emergence is a late-summer event on regional streams flanked by conifers. Such streams as the West Gallatin River, the Taylors Fork of the Gallatin, the West Fork of the Madison, and portions of the Madison River are prime locations for fly fishers to enjoy trout greedily responding to this event. Patrick Daigle, as one of the Blue Ribbon fly-tying crew, created this pattern. Every fly-fishing retail shop in West Yellowstone stocks imitations of this insect when their season of abundance is in progress.

Spruce Moth (Gartside)

Hook: #10-12 Mustad 94842
Thread: Cream 6/0
Body: Rabbit dubbing or poly yarn of color to simulate that of natural, usually tan or amber
Hackle: Light grizzly palmered over body, then top and bottom clipped away

Wing: Mixed light elk rump and natural deer tied in flat then flared

In the February 1980 edition of *Fly Tyer* magazine, Jack Gartside describes his first encounter with trout feeding on spruce moths floating on the West Fork of the Madison River. This pattern is the result of his efforts at the tying vise to simulate the insect that was so attractive to trout on that stream.

Stan's Hopper

Hook: #10-12 Mustad 9672
Thread: Black 6/0
Underbody: Orange or yellow chenille
Overbody/tails: Bunch of natural deer hair with tips forming tails and secured to underbody with tying thread wraps
Wings: Matched turkey quill segments
Hackle: Two grizzly and one brown saddle hackles

Stan Yamamura tied flies for Bud Lilly's Trout Shop in the early 1970s. This is his most successful pattern. His use of a hollow-hair overbody made this a more buoyant pattern than other hopper patterns of the era. He supplied it to outlets in Idaho, Wyoming, and Montana. It is still used by many fly fishers in the region.

WET FLIES
Attractor Patterns

Alexandria

Hook: #6-14 Mustad 3906
Thread: Black 6/0
Tail: Peacock swords
Tip: Scarlet floss
Rib (optional): Round silver tinsel
Body: Flat silver tinsel
Hackle: Black tied beard style
Wing: Peacock swords

This is a traditional pattern originating in England and modified for waters in the eastern states. Ray Bergman was the most renowned tier to modify it for those waters. Both Bud Lilly and Jim Danskin endorsed it as being effective on regional waters. The Alexandria was one of the first of the many eastern favorites to be in demand in West Yellowstone fly shops. It's also more proof that any pattern, in or out of style, will catch fish if presented properly.

Bar-X Woven Nymphs

Hook: #6-12 Mustad 3906
Thread: Black 6/0
Underbody: Black, brown, olive, orange, red, or yellow floss
Body: Overhand weave of monofilament and underbody material
Hackle: Black, brown, ginger, or grizzly soft badger

"The make fish take! THE FLY WITH INSEXAPPEAL!" advertised the carded woven nymphs produced by Tony Sivey's Bar-X Fly Company. She operated out of Butte, Montana, during winters and West Yellowstone during fishing season. Many of her carded nymphs were snelled, and all were famed for durability. Nymphs in larger versions featured tying thread X-patterns along the sides of underbodies. Few examples, let alone those tied by Sivey, of these unusual flies exist.

BS Halloween

Hook: #4-10 Dai-Riki 700
Thread: Black 6/0
Tail: Burnt orange marabou with optional Mylar fibers of any color
Body: Variegated black and burnt orange chenille

Hackle: Dyed burnt orange grizzly

This is perhaps Bill Schiess's most popular fly pattern. Bill, the current dean of Henry's Lake fly fishers, originated it as one of his "BS" flies. Others are the BS Brookie, the BS Green, and the BS Hot Chocolate. All were originally proven effective on Henry's Lake, but now are in popular use in most other regional stillwaters. In form they are Woolly Buggers, but in color they are unique.

California Leech

Hook: #8-16 Dai-Riki 075
Thread: Black 6/0
Tail: Rust marabou with four strands of copper Krystal Flash
Body: Rust/brown dubbing mixed with copper and river green Lite-Bright
Wing: Four strands of light olive Krystal Flash

In *Fishing Henry's Lake*, Bill Schiess describes the inspiration for this fly as one used by an unknown California fly fisher on Henry's Lake. Bill made additions and modifications to result in this pattern. Whether cast and stripped or trolled, it has become one of his favorites. Bill likes this fly in size 8 best, and other than Henry's Lake, he attests to its effectiveness on Cliff, Grebe, Hebgen, and Wade Lakes.

Featherduster Nymph

Hook: #10-16 Mustad 9672
Thread: Brown or olive 6/0
Tail: #12 and larger, pheasant tail fibers; #14 and smaller, partridge hackle fibers
Rib: Fine copper wire
Body: Natural ostrich herl
Wing case: Same as tail
Legs: Tips of fibers used for wing case

The Eagle family has the longest record of any in contributing to West Yellowstone's fly-fishing heritage. Guiding, retailing, conservation actions, preserving history, and sport fisheries law enforcement are functions family members have performed. Wally is the most accomplished fly tier in the family, and this is his most renowned contribution.

Flight's Fancy

Hook: #10-12 Mustad 94840
Thread: Black 6/0
Tail: Brown hackle fibers
Rib: Flat gold tinsel
Body: Cream floss
Hackle: Light ginger tied beard style
Wing: Sections of gray duck primary quill

This fly originated in England, and it has several variations. Don Martinez promoted English patterns such as this and Birch's Favorite for use in waters around West Yellowstone. Bud Lilly promoted Flight's Fancy for the same purpose. It was offered as an effective wet fly in the Trout Shop mail-order catalog.

Light Olive Crystal

Hook: #10 Mustad 3906
Weight (optional): 0.025-inch-diameter lead-free wire
Thread: Black 6/0
Body: Light olive crystal chenille
Hackle: Dyed brown grizzly saddle hackle

This simple pattern by Bill Schiess has proven to be a most effective impressionistic pattern. It is a shorter, tailless version of Bill's Olive Crystal Bugger. He first began using these patterns on Henry's Lake in the 1990s, but since has used them with equal success on Cliff, Elk, Grebe, Hebgen, Hidden, and Wade Lakes. Any pattern having such a record should be in all fly boxes used in the Greater Yellowstone area during damselfly emergences.

Madison Special

Hook: #10-12 Mustad 7957B
Thread: Black 6/0
Tail: Golden pheasant tippet fibers
Rib: Black tying thread
Body: Orange floss
Hackle: Brown tied beard style
Wing: Brown mottled turkey wing
    quill segments

The Madison Special was never a widely used fly or offered for sale on a large scale by West Yellowstone fly-fishing retailers. We include this pattern because it is another example of the reverence the fly-fishing world has for the Madison River. How many pattern have been created as a result of quality fly-fishing experiences on the Madison is an interesting question.

Marabou Egg Sac

Hook: #8 Mustad 90240
Thread: Black 6/0
Body: Red or orange wool yarn
Egg clumps: Three clumps of chartreuse, pink, red, salmon, or yellow marabou fibers
Hackle: Scarlet neck or saddle hackle

Gary LaFontaine's inspiration for this fly came from watching trout lying behind spawning suckers to intercept drifting eggs. He describes this inspiration in the August 1980 edition of *Fly Tyer* magazine. So popular was this pattern that Bud Lilly offered it for sale in the Trout Shop. It could also be found in his mail-order catalog during the 1980s.

Miss Take

Hook: #6-8 Mustad 9672
Thread: Brown 3/0
Tail: Three peacock sword tips
Rib: Purple wool in front of gray ostrich herl
Over-rib: Counter-wrapped gold wire
Body: Mottled brown wool
Thorax: Same as body only wrapped thicker
Hackle: Wrap of another same hackle near front of thorax

Charlie Brooks claims that this obscure pattern was a mistake, thus its name. He gave some information on its use in *Nymph Fishing for Large Trout*. Some of the materials and construction techniques he uses for it are repeated in several patterns.

Mite Patterns

Hook: #8-14 Mustad 3906
Thread: Black 6/0
Body: Ox hair or horse mane over floss using Mite weave
Hackle: Ends of ox hair used to form body in most of these patterns

The impact of Franz Pott's Mite patterns on western fly fishing is well documented. They remain popular and thus continue to be offered by all West Yellowstone fly-fishing retailers. Of these the Sandy Mite (sandy hair, orange floss), pictured above, and the Lady Mite (white hair, yellow floss) remain perhaps the most popular. Mite pattern popularity has inspired many regional tiers to offer woven nymph patterns.

Mity Mouse

Hook: #6-10 Mustad 9672
Thread: Dark olive 3/0
Hackle: Dyed brown grizzly
Rib: Reverse-wrapped red thread
Body: Peacock herl

Bill Scheiss in his *Fishing Henry's Lake* offers that this fly began as a Henry's Lake and Island Park Reservoir mainstay. But through word of its success on these waters, its use

spread to Hebgen, Wade, and Cliff Lakes. Bill credits the origin of this fly to Seldon Jones and Lynn Turman. He also identifies the Mity Mouse as the inspiration for his "Crystal" series of flies.

Queen of the Waters

Hook: #10-14 Mustad 3906
Thread: Black 6/0
Tail: Golden pheasant tippet fibers
Rib: Flat gold tinsel
Body: Orange floss
Hackle: Ginger palmered over body
Wing: Duck quill segments tied wet style

This is another pattern originating in England but brought to waters in the West Yellowstone area by fly fishers from eastern states. In fact, the Queen of the Waters enjoyed a certain popularity with fly fishers throughout the Rocky Mountain states. Bud Lilly offered this pattern in the Trout Shop and through his mail-order catalog in the early 1980s.

Selby Special

Hook: #4-12 Mustad 9672 or 79580
Thread: Black 6/0
Tail: Red yarn
Body: Medium olive chenille
Hackle: Badger saddle

The Selby family tied this Woolly Worm variation for guests at their resort on Elk Lake. In larger sizes it was trolled on that lake as well as Cliff and Hidden Lakes. In medium sizes it was presented to simulate a damselfly nymph on nearby stillwaters. In smaller sizes it was presented in nearby streams to simulate caddis pupae and stonefly and mayfly nymphs. A later variation had an orange chenille head.

Shakey Bealy

Hook: #8-12 Daiichi 1260
Thread: Rusty brown 6/0
Tail: Orange Krystal Flash
Trailing shuck: Wood duck flank feather fibers
Rib: Rusty brown tying thread
Abdomen: Amber dubbing
Thorax: Orange ostrich herl
Hackle: Hungarian partridge

Alfred Harold Beals, out of San Diego, California, was a seasonal Yellowstone Park ranger. He worked during the summer months, and in off-duty hours he chased wild trout. The Madison River became his favored water, and he could be seen on it almost daily during the evening, casting to trout. Nick Nicklas created this pattern in honor of Alfred and gave it Alfred's nickname, Shakey.

Shop Vac

Hook: #12-18 Dai-Riki 135
Bead: 7/32-inch-diameter gold
Thread: Black 8/0
Rib: Gold wire, diameter consistent with hook size
Body: Five or six ringneck pheasant tail fibers
Wing case: White Z-Lon tied in behind bead

Named for effectiveness, this is Rowan Nyman's favorite nymph pattern. Its versatility has made it very popular, as depending on size tied, it can simulate submerged life-cycle stages of midges, mayflies, or caddisflies. One of Rowan's favorite uses is as a dropper behind a floating mayfly or caddis pattern.

Soft-Hackle Patterns

Hook: #10-16 Mustad 94840
Thread: Amber, olive, orange, or tan 8/0 silk
Body: Tying thread
Hackle: Grouse

Simple, effective, and tied from readily available materials: What more could be asked for in a fly pattern? Sylvester Nemes was the most renowned proponent of these flies, and with several self-published books he gifted all fly fishers by passing on his experiences with these patterns. From Bud Lilly on to the present, all West Yellowstone fly-fishing retailers have offered or continue to offer them. Sylvester demonstrated these patterns in the town's fly-fishing shops and at FFF Conclaves held there. He was one of the first to demonstrate how effective these patterns are when presented as emerging mayflies and caddisflies in the Firehole and Madison Rivers.

Sparrow

Hook: #4-14 Daiichi 1710
Thread: Brown 6/0
Tail: Blue-shaded ringneck pheasant church window feather fibers

Underbody: Stem of feather used to form tail
Body: Mixed gray Antron and natural rabbit dubbing
Hackle: Ringneck pheasant church window feather
Head: Three or four turns of aftershaft feather

Jack Gartside considered the ringneck pheasant rooster to be the most useful bird for tying flies. The Sparrow is one of the best examples of his thoughts on this subject. He offered it to all West Yellowstone fly-fishing retailers. Because Jack created this pattern about fifty years ago, and because of his renown in the fly-fishing community, many variations of it exist, some with a tail formed from an aftershaft feather.

UV Ice Soft Hackle

Hook: #10-12 Mustad 3906B
Thread: Fire orange 6/0
Tail: Pheasant tail fiber tips of those used to wrap body
Rib: Fine copper wire
Body: Pheasant tail fibers
Thorax: Orange Ice Dub
Hackle: Partridge feather tied soft-hackle style

Arrick Swanson recommends this pattern for fly-fishing the Madison River in Yellowstone Park during the autumn run-up of Hebgen Lake brown and rainbow trout. His pattern body and tail component construction is similar to that of the famed Pheasant Tail Nymph. In smaller sizes this pattern can represent small emerging caddis species. In larger sizes it can represent emerging October caddis.

Wet Mouse

Hook: #6-12 Mustad 9671
Thread: Black 6/0
Body: Pheasant philoplumes
Collar: Pheasant, partridge, or grouse
  back feather
Head: Black tying thread

In the fall 1978 edition of *Fly Tyer* magazine, Jack Gartside offers that he was inspired to come up with this pattern by accident. Sitting in Baker's Hole Campground tying his Pheasant Hopper, he noted the soft, flexible qualities of the aftershaft, or philo-plume, feathers. He tied some on a hook with a collar as described above and took the result fishing. The fly proved greatly effective, which Gartside attributed to the lifelike qualities of the philoplume body.

Whitlock Special Woolly Worms

Hook: #2-8 Mustad 79580
Weight (optional): Lead wire
Thread: Black 6/0
Tip: Gold Mylar tinsel
Butt: Fluorescent orange chenille
Body: Dark olive chenille
Hackle: Grizzly tied to divide body into
  three segments

Topping: Peacock herl
Head: Gold Mylar tinsel

Dave's Woolly Worm versions were offered through Bud Lilly's Trout Shop. Weighted or unweighted, their purpose was to offer a more versatile pattern useful in a variety of ways. The most popular colors were those given above as well as a version tied with a golden yellow body and another with a black body, red wool tail, and brown hackle.

Woolly Worm

Hook: #2-12 Mustad 9672
Thread: Black 6/0
Tail: Red hackle fibers
Rib: Flat silver tinsel
Hackle: Grizzly saddle palmered over body
Body: Black chenille

Like it or not, this pattern has caught more salmonids than any pattern created. Don Martinez began offering it in the mid-1930s from his West Yellowstone shop. He first expressed mild scorn for it, calling it "more of a lure," and poked fun at its origin as a fly for warmwater species. His scorn for it ceased, however, after he observed that it outsold by far all of the other patterns he offered. It is now the pattern most identi-fied with him, and pictured above is how he originally tied it.

Caddisfly Patterns

Caddis Emerger

Hook: #8 TMC 2457
Bead: ⁵/₃₂-inch-diameter gold
Thread: Black 8/0
Tails: Two duck biot tips
Body: Fine red wire
Thorax: Peacock herl
Wing case: Pearlescent holographic tinsel
Hackle: Hen pheasant flank feather

Several fly fishers from outside places owned property in West Yellowstone. Typically they returned during fishing season to live and enjoy the waters surrounding town. Jim Fisher was one of these. Being an excellent fly tier, he created patterns to simulate many of the available food forms for regional salmonids. This pattern is his caddis emerger, and in it he makes use of red wire, a popular component in patterns imitating bloodworms.

Cream Caddis Larva

Hook: #8-14 Mustad 3906B
Thread: Tan 6/0
Rib: Fine copper wire or buttonhole twist thread

Body: Cream or tan fur or yarn
Hackle: Soft, short black

This is Charlie Brooks's imitation of an uncased caddis larva. In his observations of trout feeding habits, he quickly found that caddis larvae are an important trout food. He devotes much attention to tying imitations of these in his major fishing-technique books *Nymph Fishing for Larger Trout* and *The Trout and the Stream*.

Emergent Sparkle Pupa

Hook: #12-20 Mustad 94840
Thread: Color matching natural 6/0
Underbody: Dubbed Antron strands, color matching natural
Overbody: Antron strands, color matching natural
Hackle: Hen hackle fibers or deer hair
Head: Dubbed marabou fibers, color matching natural

This is probably Gary LaFontaine's most famed pattern. He first described it in *Caddisflies*. Since he introduced it in the 1970s, all West Yellowstone fly-fishing retailers have offered it, and it remains immensely popular. The version of this pattern for deep presentation is weighed with turns of copper wire spiraled around the shank before dubbing the underbody.

Gray Caddis Larva

Hook: #8-10 Mustad 3906B
Thread: Black 6/0
Rib: Peacock herl and counter-
wound gold wire
Body: Gray wool
Thorax: Collar of brown thread
Hackle: Soft, short black hackle, one turn

"Make the body somewhat thinner than a kitchen match," Charlie Brooks writes in *The Trout and the Stream*. He also recommends that the peacock herl be wound so bands of it and the wool are about the same width. This is his imitation of the cased form of Brachycentrus caddis, a major food form for trout in the Greater Yellow-stone region.

Green Caddis Larva

Hook: #8-10 Mustad 9671
Thread: Brown 6/0
Rib: Gold wire
Body: Dark shiny green wool
Thorax: Collar of brown tying thread
Hackle: Soft, short black hackle, one turn

In *The Trout and the Stream*, Charlie Brooks recommends making the body of this pattern about as thick as a wooden match.

It is his larval imitation for Rhyacophila, the caddisfly that does not build a case. It survives as a worm underneath cover on stream bottoms. Charlie's experience with this insect was mostly on the Henry's Fork and the Madison River.

Green Caddis Rockworm

Hook: #8-16 TMC 2457
Bead: Black tungsten in proportion
to hook size
Thread: Black 6/0
Rib: Dark green Sparkle Flex
Body: Dubbed chartreuse rabbit fur
Thorax: Peacock herl

This was the pattern Bob Jacklin used to take a ten-pound brown trout from the Madison River just below the Cabin Creek confluence on June 16, 2006. This fish was more than likely a Quake Lake trout forag-ing in the river. It is another example of a simple pattern placed properly to bring an unforgettable result. As one might expect, sales of this pattern have been up for Bob since he took this fish.

Jacklin's October Caddis

Hook: #6-10 Mustad 3906
Thread: Burnt orange 70- or 140-denier
Rib: Medium or fine copper wire
Body: Burnt orange wool yarn
Thorax: Cyclops copper bead
Hackle: Oversize partridge or dyed orange flank feather

This relatively new pattern by Bob Jacklin has carved a popularity notch with fly fishers coming to try late-summer and autumn Greater Yellowstone waters. Most other caddis species emerge to lay eggs in late spring and well into the summer. Being a casemaker, this caddis is widespread in Greater Yellowstone streams. Those with rocky substrate, such as the West Gallatin River, much of the Madison River, and parts of the Henry's Fork and Yellowstone River, hold good populations of it. Bob suggests a dead-drift presentation at depth works well for presenting this pattern because the naturals drift downstream to populate waters.

Little Grey Caddis Pupa

Hook: #8-10 Mustad 3906B
Thread: Olive 6/0
Egg sac: Tuft of fluorescent green yarn

Rib: Gold wire
Body: Olive green yarn
Thorax: Two strands of tan or gray ostrich herl
Wing: Ends of ostrich herl used for thorax
Hackle: Grouse body feather

Charlie Brooks offered this pattern as a pupal imitation of Brachycentrus caddisflies. It is a major food form for trout in three of his favorite streams, the Henry's Fork, the Firehole River, and the Madison River. Change the body color to olive, and you have Charlie's Little Green Caddis Pupa for Rhyacophila caddisflies, also a major food form in these waters.

Philo Caddis Pupa

Hook: #12-16 Mustad 3906B
Thread: Black 6/0
Rib: Fine gold or silver wire
Body: Dubbed from three parts feather down and gray squirrel fur to one part rabbit fur
Legs: Partridge or pheasant feather tips tied beard style
Wing and thorax: Pheasant philoplume
Antennae: Natural wood duck or dyed mallard

Jack Gartside offers that the philoplume used to simulate the wings and thorax makes this pattern effective. He prefers the gray philos from a cock ringneck pheasant for these parts because of their lifelike action in water. Jack also suggests varying the body color of this pattern depending on the caddis species to be imitated.

R. A. M. Caddis

Hook: #10-18 Mustad 7957B
Thread: Black 8/0
Weight (optional): Fine lead-free wire
Rib: Fine gold wire
Body: Light olive floss, yarn, or dubbing over optional lead-free wire turns
Hackle: White hen neck
Head: Dark brown fur dubbing

Ross Merigold is renowned for contributions to fishing the Madison River below Earthquake Lake. However, his contributions also include fly patterns that found their way into West Yellowstone's fly-fishing heritage. The R. A. M. Caddis was first described in *Fly Patterns of Yellowstone* by Craig Mathews and John Juracek. This is Ross's very popular free-living caddis larva imitation. He tended to fish this pattern deep and just before or during caddis emergences. By omitting the gold wire rib and lead-free wire underbody, it becomes his pupal stage version.

Ruff Cote

Hook: #12-16 Mustad 3906B
Thread: Black 3/0
Rib: Oval gold tinsel or wire spiraled front to back and returned counter-wrapped

Body: Full from black or brown fuzzy yarn
Hackle: Short, soft black or dark brown

This is one of Charlie Brooks's two cased caddis imitations. The other, his Skunk Hair Caddis, is more difficult to tie than this one. According to Charlie, these two flies are equally effective under the same presentation conditions. He named this fly after a pattern in Izaak Walton's *Compleat Angler*.

Cranefly, Leech, and Scud Patterns

Giant Cranefly Larva

Hook: #6-10 TMC 5262
Thread: Black 6/0
Weight: Lead or 0.015-inch fuse wire for smaller ties, 0.025-inch wire for larger ties
Gills: About six fibers from ringneck cock pheasant brown tail feather
Rib: Gold wire
Body: Dubbed light olive rabbit fur
Thorax: Dubbed dark olive rabbit fur

Through using an insect seine on their favorites, Craig Mathews and John Juracek have determined the presence of the giant cranefly larva on the bottom of many regional streams. They have done the same for the smaller summer cranefly larva that they tie similarly with component changes of gray muskrat fur dubbing for the body and thorax, and gray-blue pheasant back feathers for the gills.

Grass Shrimp

Hook: #8-16 Mustad 3906B
Thread: Tan 3/0
Rib: Brown, olive, or orange buttonhole twist
Underbody: Light green yarn
Hackle: Light ginger
Overbody: Light gray yarn

Charlie Brooks created this pattern to simulate scuds inhabiting submerged grasses in slow-moving or still waters. His Sow Bug is tied in a similar manner, but with a tail made from tips of the quill segment forming the overbody. Its underbody is made of cream or light gray fur or yarn.

Lazy Leech

Hook: #6-8 Mustad 3906
Thread: Tan 3/0
Tail: Gold marabou fibers tied to end of chamois strip body
Body: Chamois strip (2 inches long by ¼ inch wide) attached to hook shank behind hook eye
Hackle: Gold marabou fibers tied beard style

While visiting the Widow's Pool in Centennial Valley, Charlie Brooks met a wildlife biologist who recommended that presenting patterns that simulate leeches would considerably increase his success. After experimenting with numerous materials to simulate the undulating motion of a swimming leech, Charlie settled on chamois, as suggested by Darwin Atkin. The result was this effective pattern.

Otter Shrimp

Hook: #10-18 Mustad 3906
Thread: Olive 6/0
Tail: Grouse body feather fibers
Body: Grayish otter fur with a "smidgen" of brown seal mixed in, then dubbed to form body
Hackle: One or two turns of grouse body feather

This is Charlie Brooks's version of Ted Trueblood's Otter Nymph. He offers that it can be weighted with lead or solder wire for deeper presentations. He recommends it for lakes, ponds, and weedy streams. In *Nymph Fishing for Larger Trout*, he gives the instructions for forming the body. With respect to what a "smidgen" is, Charlie states "Don't ask!"

Damselfly and Dragonfly Patterns

Assam Dragon

Hook: #4-10 Mustad 9672
Thread: Brown 3/0
Weight: 0.025-inch-diameter non-lead or fuse wire
Body: Rabbit skin strip, ⅛ inch wide by 4 inches long, tightly spiraled around hook shank
Hackle: Two turns of large grouse or brown dyed grizzly

Charlie Brooks originally tied this pattern with a sealskin strip. He placed a glue layer on the wire wraps before spiraling the sealskin strip over them to form the body. Charlie recommended fishing this pattern deep with slow, sharp pulls along sandy or silty stillwater bottoms to simulate a swimming dragonfly nymph. He named it after a dragon that the people of Assam, India, claimed was eating their children. A tiger was doing this deed, but the Assamese didn't want to admit that their hunting skills were not up to bagging it.

Beaver Pelt

Hook: #2-8 Mustad 3906B
Thread: Brown 3/0
Weight: 0.025-inch-diameter lead wire
Body: Dubbed full from beaver fur
Hackle: Long, soft natural black hackle or greenish ringneck pheasant rooster rump feather

Charlie Brooks realized that dragonfly nymphs were an important early-season food item for trout in stillwaters and slowly moving streams. Thus he put effort into simulating these nymphs. This is his impressionistic pattern for them and likely more conveniently tied than the Assam Dragon, which requires a sealskin strip. As with his Assam Dragon, he presented the Beaver Pelt with a full-sinking line along the bottom of stillwaters and slowly moving streams.

Dave's Damsel Nymph

Hook: #8-10 Mustad 9672
Thread: Light olive 6/0
Tail: Barred olive hen marabou
Rib: Gold wire
Body: Dyed light olive Swiss straw over light olive SLF Dubbing
Thorax: Same as body
Wing case: Dyed light olive Swiss straw
Legs: Barred olive hen back
Eyes: Small gold bead chain

Damselfly emergences are common on many stillwaters around West Yellowstone and in season an important food form for trout. This was the basis of demand for this pattern by Dave Whitlock. Bud Lilly recommended it to Trout Shop customers for success when damselfly nymphs became active in stillwaters from Henry's Lake to smaller waters such as the Widow's Pool and Grebe Lake. Their use is also productive in the several meadow reaches of area streams.

Fair Damsel

Hook: #6-10 Mustad 9672
Thread: Olive 6/0
Tail: Dyed brown grizzly hackle tips, forked
Rib: Oval gold tinsel
Body: Mottled brown yarn
Thorax: Mottled brown yarn slightly larger in diameter than body

Charlie Brooks experimented with damselfly patterns until he created this initial version in the 1970s. It is meant to simulate the nymphal stage of Argia, a damselfly common in many waters around West Yellowstone. He used it mostly on slower stretches of the Madison River and the Henry's Fork. Later he created a version with dyed brown grizzly hackle at the front and rear of the thorax and gold-ribbed body

Green Damsel

Hook: #8-10 Mustad 9672
Thread: Black or olive 3/0
Tail: Three peacock swords
Rib: Oval gold tinsel
Body: Green yarn
Thorax: Same as body only thicker
Hackle: Dyed green grizzly tied in at rear and front of thorax

This was among the first of the damselfly nymphs that Charlie Brooks created, and he altered it over the years. Being a hunter of large trout, he fished Henry's Lake and Hebgen Lake from his home on Targhee Pass. This pattern was always with him during these visits. So was his Fair Damsel, tied in a similar size but with brown yarn and dyed brown grizzly hackle.

Henry's Lake Nymph

Hook: #4-10 Mustad 9671
Thread: Black 6/0
Tail: Gray squirrel tail
Shellback: Gray squirrel tail
Body: Medium yellow chenille
Antennae: Tips of gray squirrel tail used to form shellback

This is one of the oldest flies tied for fishing Henry's Lake as well as named for that lake. In *Montana Trout Flies* George Grant notes that it is in widespread use on Montana stillwaters. Here he offers that it simulates scuds in smaller sizes and damselflies and dragonflies in larger sizes.

Pink Petuti

Hook: #6-10 Mustad 79580
Thread: Black 6/0
Body: Light green wool yarn
Hackle: Greenish ringneck pheasant
  rooster body feather wrapped soft-
  hackle style

The name Pat Barnes gave this fly was meant to hide its purpose. He also offered little information on it. It is described briefly in *Ribbons of Blue*, where he relates using it very effectively during damselfly emergences, and it is further evidence that only properly presented simple patterns are needed for successful fly fishing. Soon after Pat created this pattern, he remembers using it on Hidden Lake with superb results. This lake remains a superb coldwater fishery.

P. W. Nymph

Hook: #10-14 Mustad 3906
Thread: Black 6/0
Weight: Fuse wire (no. 2)
Tail: Mallard flank feather fibers
Body: Yellow floss ribbed with peacock herl
Thorax: Peacock herl
Wing case: Mallard flank feather
Hackle: Mallard flank feather tips

Pat Barnes relates in *Ribbons of Blue* that the Martinez Black dominated the nymph pattern market in West Yellowstone fly shops for years. Looking for a nymph pattern for deeper presentations, he took ideas from clients Buck and Margaret Voorhees to satisfy this desire. His first use of this pattern was to simulate a dragonfly nymph, but soon it became successful when used to simulate other nymphs.

X-mas Tree

Hook: #6-12 TMC 5263
Thread: Olive 3/0
Tail: Olive marabou
Body: Olive/red crystal chenille
Hackle: Brown saddle

Arrick Swanson touts this fly as a Hebgen Lake favorite. However, it also has a reputation for producing on other area stillwaters, especially when damselflies emerge. This includes the famed Henry's Lake emergence and relatively obscure but important damselfly emergences such as those on Elk Lake, Hidden Lake, and Smith Lake.

Mayfly Patterns

Brooks Hendrickson Nymph

Hook: #10-12 Mustad 3906B
Thread: Black 6/0
Tail: Wood duck flank fibers
Rib: Gold wire
Body: Rear two-thirds muskrat fur dubbing, front third brown seal dubbing
Hackle: Speckled grouse tied beard style
Wing case: Gray duck quill section

This obscure pattern by Charlie Brooks has a single reference: *Perrault's Standard Dictionary of Fishing Flies*. Nothing exists on the purpose for which Charlie intended this pattern. Keith Perrault canvassed West Yellowstone tiers, including Charlie, in the 1970s for their fly patterns. In 1984 he published his dictionary of about sixteen thousand fly patterns, perhaps the most complete collection of flies to that date.

Brown Drake Nymph

Hook: #8-10 Mustad 9672
Thread: Black 6/0
Tail: Wood duck flank fibers
Rib: Fine oval copper wire
Abdomen: Dyed reddish brown raffia
Back: Golden olive marabou fibers
Thorax: Light yellow chenille
Wing case: Dyed reddish brown raffia
Hackle: Soft brown

Brown drake nymphs inhabit high-quality stream margins and stillwaters, where they burrow into sand or gravel bottoms. Living in West Yellowstone and Jackson, Wyoming, Don Martinez had ample opportunity to encounter all brown drake life-cycle stages. They are present in abundance in Gibbon River meadows above the falls and in lesser numbers in nearby Duck Creek. He tied this pattern for use on each aforementioned stream and other waters hosting brown drakes. Examples of this pattern can now be found only in private collections.

Gray May

Hook: #8-10 Mustad 3906B
Thread: Gray 6/0
Tail: Several dyed light olive grizzly
  hackle fibers
Body: Full from gray yarn
Hackle: One and a half turns of dyed olive
  soft grizzly

This all-purpose nymph by Charlie Brooks was one of the last patterns he created. Due to failing health, he did not fish it as comprehensively as his other patterns. In larger sizes the gray may simulate the *Siphlonurus occidentalis* common in many regional trout streams and a major spring-time emergence.

Ida May

Hook: #10-12 Mustad 3906B
Thread: Black 3/0
Tail: None or dyed olive grizzly
  hackle fibers
Rib: Single peacock herl counter-ribbed
  with fine gold wire
Body: Black fuzzy yarn
Hackle: Dyed olive hen grizzly

When Charlie Brooks first fished the Last Chance–Harriman reach of the Henry's

Fork, he encountered a dense green drake emergence. This and successive encounters inspired this pattern. Its name, Ida May, is a truncated form of "Idaho Mayfly," and Charlie revealed its effectiveness in his books and magazine articles. Along with his Brooks Montana stonefly nymph, it became his most renowned pattern.

March Brown Nymph

Hook: #10-14 Mustad 3906B
Thread: Burnt orange 3/0
Tail: Three pheasant tail fibers
Rib: Large flat dark brown nylon thread
Body: Amber Australian possum dubbing
Wing case: Dark turkey tail segment
Legs: Hungarian partridge body feather
Thorax: Same as body only heavier
Head: Same as body

Bob Jacklin first tied this pattern to simulate March brown mayfly nymphs emerging from New Jersey and New York streams. When he used it in streams around West Yellowstone, he observed that it was an excellent golden stonefly nymph imitation. He has offered it for decades from his shop, and it has accounted for many large trout.

Martinez Black Nymph

Hook: #8-14 Mustad 3906B
Thread: Black 6/0
Tail: Spotted guinea flank feather fibers
Body: Black seal fur (or substitute)
Wing case: Strip of green raffia
Hackle: Speckled gray partridge

Along with the Woolly Worm, this pattern was the most renowned concession Don Martinez made to wet-fly fishing. It is still in popular use on waters in the Greater Yellowstone region to simulate mayfly and stonefly nymphs. Many fly fishers, including Pat Barnes, knew it as the Greenback Nymph. Barnes and Charlie Brooks both proclaimed its effectiveness in their books.

Martinez Blue Dun Nymph

Hook: #8-10 Mustad 3906B
Thread: Black 6/0
Tail: Blue dun hackle fibers
Rib: Oval gold tinsel
Body: Dubbed muskrat fur
Hackle: Wet-style blue dun
Wing: Gray squirrel tail

Don Martinez preferred to create dry-fly patterns. But when he created wet flies, they were also effective and therefore

became popular. This one remained popular for more than half a century and is still found in the fly bins of West Yellowstone shops. Bob Carmichael, Don's colleague working out of Jackson Hole, proclaimed in J. Edson Leonard's *Flies* that this pattern was his top-selling wet fly.

Martinez Mahogany Nymph

Hook: #8-14 Mustad 3906B
Thread: Black 6/0
Tail: Hungarian partridge hackle fibers
Rib: Fine oval silver tinsel around abdomen
Abdomen: Dubbed dark brown wool
Wing case: Dyed orange raffia over thorax
Thorax: Same as abdomen only thicker
Hackle: Collar-style Hungarian partridge

This nymph is not as well known as the Black Nymph and Blue Dun Nymph created by Don Martinez. The reason for this is uncertain, but Terry Hellekson in *Fish Flies: The Encyclopedia of the Fly Tier's Art* speculates that the shortage of partridge hackle is the reason. Examples of this pattern can be seen in the Don Martinez collection of flies in the Butte, Montana, visitor center.

Philo Mayfly Emerger

Hook: #14 Mustad 94840
Thread: Tan 8/0
Tail: Partridge hackle fibers
Body: Blended squirrel and hare's
    ear dubbing
Wing: Pheasant aftershaft feather
    (philoplume)
Legs: Partridge hackle fibers

Jack Gartside was a master at using philo-plumes for various fly-tying purposes. He uses them to form an unfurling wing in this pattern. To do this he splits his tying thread, places the philoplume inside the split portion, spins the result, then wraps it in front of the body such that fibers extend to above the hook bend. Next he trims the fiber from the bottom of the shank and adds the partridge hackle fiber legs on either side to complete the pattern.

Velma May

Hook: #10 Mustad 9672
Thread: Olive 3/0
Tail: Dyed green grizzly hackle fibers
Rib: Gray ostrich herl
Body: Purple wool
Counter-rib: Fine gold wire

Thorax: Mottled brown wool
Hackle: Dyed green grizzly hackle fibers

This lesser-known pattern by Charlie Brooks is described in *Nymph Fishing for Larger Trout*. He claims that it proved effective in the Firehole and Madison Rivers and the Henry's Fork, and speculates that it is taken for nymphs of large mayfly species. Typically Charlie's flies prove to be more effective than originally intended.

Midge Patterns

Midge Pupa

Hook: #14-22 Mustad 94840
Thread: Black 6/0
Body: Antron dubbing
Hackle: One turn of starling behind head
Head: No more than two turns of dark
    dubbing to contrast with body

Unlike other aquatic insects, midges hatch year-round, and trout key on the pupal stage whether in still or moving water. Craig Mathews, John Juracek, and the Blue Ribbon Flies crew have a record of winter-time fishing, and this pattern is one of their favorites for use then or for any part of the season. Craig and John suggests varying the body color (olive, black, green, or red) to match that of the midges emerging at a given location and in season.

Serendipity

Hook: #14-22 TMC 2487
Thread: Black, brown, gray, dark green, light green, or red 8/0
Body: Twisted Z-Lon fibers, color matching tying thread
Head and wing: Spun and trimmed deer hair

Blue Ribbon Flies and Ross Merigold did much to popularize this pattern of uncertain origin. By the 1990s it was as popular as any pattern created regionally. Originally a midge pupa pattern, it also became effective when used to simulate a caddis pupa. In some newer versions a glass or brass bead replaces the trimmed deer hair head. Nick Nicklas's Three Dollar Bridge Serendipity is a popular variation of this pattern.

Stonefly Nymph Patterns

Bitch Creek Nymph

Hook: #2-10 Mustad 9672
Thread: Black 6/0
Tail: White rubber hackle
Body: Orange chenille
Overbody: Black chenille
Thorax: Black chenille

Hackle: Brown saddle palmered over thorax
Antennae: Same as tail

There are many backroom stories on the origin of this pattern, but Tony Sivey has the best claim to creating it. It is an immensely popular pattern, having been offered in fly shops throughout western states for nearly six decades. By the 1960s versions with bodies formed through the Montana Nymph weave appeared, and these now make up essentially all those sold.

Brooks Montana Stone

Hook: #4-10 Mustad 9672
Thread: Black 3/0
Weight (optional): 0.015-inch-diameter lead or fuse wire
Tail: Crow or raven primary fibers, forked
Rib: Gold wire
Body: Black fuzzy yarn
Hackle: Two turns of one natural grizzly saddle and one dyed brown grizzly saddle, each with fibers stripped from one side
Gills: Light gray or white ostrich herl wrapped at hackle base

This may be Charlie Brooks's most enduring pattern, and it is still offered in the fly bins of all West Yellowstone fly shops. His Yellow Stone Nymph is constructed in a similar manner. Cinnamon turkey primary fiber tails, body of mottled brown yarn, and an antique gold yarn–gold wire rib make the difference.

Chapman Golden Stone Nymph

Hook: #6-10 Mustad 3665
Thread: Tan 6/0
Tail: Ginger hackle fibers
Rib: Dyed light brown flat monofilament
Body: Slender, of gold yarn
Thorax: Gold yarn, slightly
   thicker than body
Hackle: Ginger neck hackle around thorax
Antennae: Dyed brown goose biot pair

I observed this pattern in a box of flies tied by Scotty Chapman and owned by his son Bill. It is tied in the simple style Scotty adopted for most patterns he created. His vast experience on Yellowstone Park drainages revealed the importance of golden stoneflies as a salmonid food form.

Chapman Stonefly Nymph

Hook: #4-10 Mustad 79580
Thread: Black 6/0
Weight (optional): 0.015-inch-diameter
   lead or fuse wire
Body: Peacock herl reinforced with
   tying thread
Hackle: Soft brown

As his Yellowstone National Park fly-fishing experiences accumulated, Scotty Chapman

moved from tying traditional patterns to creating his own. He tied flies for several decades, beginning in the 1930s. This one is described in Datus Proper's *What the Trout Said*. Simple and effective, it is proof that complicated patterns are not needed to fool trout. Scotty realized this truth decades ago, but many fly fishers will never come to accept it.

Giant Nature Stone

Hook: #2-6 TMC 5263
Thread: Black 6/0
Weight: Fuse wire (no. 4)
Tail: Brown goose quill pointers
Rib: Number 21(Transparent Black)
   Swannundaze
Abdomen: Dyed brown Australian possum
   and black seal fur mix
Belly: Dyed orange angora strip
Wing cases: Chocolate brown latex cut to
   shape, front end longer for pulling over
   thorax to form pronotum
Thorax: Same as abdomen
Legs: Dyed amber pheasant church
   window feathers
Head: Black tying thread
Antennae: Same as tail

This recipe is for the Blue Ribbon Flies Giant Black Nature Stone. The Blue Ribbon Orange Stone Nymph is tied in the same manner but of material colors to simulate the golden stone nymph. Both of these popular patterns are among the most elegant offered as stonefly nymph imitations.

Golden Rubberlegs

Hook: #2-6 TMC 5263
Thread: Brown 6/0
Weight: 0.025-inch-diameter fuse wire
Body: Brown-yellow variegated chenille
Legs: Pumpkin and black Sili Legs
Antennae: Same as legs

Arrick's Fly Shop has been operating for more than a quarter century at full service in West Yellowstone. Arrick Swanson opened the shop after several years of experience fly-fishing regional waters. This pattern is based on the globally popular Rubberlegs. Arrick's simulation of a golden stonefly nymph was born from on-the-stream experience and experimentation with fly-tying materials. It has proven successful on all regional waters hosting golden stoneflies.

Jacklin's Giant Stonefly Nymph

Hook: #4 Dai-Riki 270
Thread: Black 6/0
Tail: Cut from thin-walled bicycle tire inner tube
Underbody: 0.020-inch-diameter lead or fuse wire

Body and abdomen: Wrapped from tapered strip of thin-walled bicycle tire inner tube
Abdomen and head undersides: Dubbed tan Australian possum fur
Legs: Cut from thin-walled bicycle tire inner tube then knotted to form joints
Wing case: Cut from thin-walled bicycle tire inner tube
Top of head: Wing case material extension
Eyes: Monofilament bead eyes
Antennae: Black dyed monofilament

Bob Jacklin's Giant Stonefly Nymph results from thirty years of observation and experimentation. As well as being fished, many examples are displayed as artwork.

Montana Black Nymph

Hook: #4-8 Mustad 9672
Thread: Black 6/0
Tail: Opposing brown hackle tips
Body: Black chenille
Thorax: Montana Black Nymph weave of black chenille over yellow chenille
Hackle: Brown saddle palmered over thorax

Every West Yellowstone fly-fishing retail business from the mid-twentieth century to the present has featured this pattern. In the West it is perhaps the most venerated giant stonefly nymph created. Who created it is obscure, but it has inspired a long line of stonefly nymph imitations. Having been offered for decades by regional fly-fishing retailers, these imitations include the Bitch Creek Nymph, the Soufal, and the Brooks Montana Stone.

Montana Forked Tail

Hook: #6 Mustad 9672
Thread: Black 6/0
Tail: Grizzly hackle tips, divided
Body and thorax: Dark brown mohair yarn
Hackle: Black or dark brown saddle
Wing case: Goose quill segment

During the 1970s and 1980s the Fenwick Rod Company operated its fly-fishing school on the east side of Targhee Pass. Charlie Brooks's home was nearby. The Madison River is to the north and the Henry's Fork is to the south, thus this is hallowed territory in the fly-fishing world. Ed Mueller was an instructor at the school and a local guide. This was his pattern for simulating stonefly nymphs in regional streams.

Soufal

Hook: #2-6 Mustad 79580
Thread: Black 6/0
Weight: 0.025-inch-diameter fuse or lead wire
Tails and antennae: Dyed black goose biot pairs
Body and thorax: Black yarn
Hackle: Black saddle
Wing case: Goose quill segment

Tony Sivey's Soufal was one of the first locally produced stonefly nymph patterns to achieve regional popularity. Tony was also the first local fly tier to befriend Bob Jacklin on his arrival in West Yellowstone in the late 1960s. This fly was featured in Bud Lilly's catalog for years, and was also promoted by Charlie Brooks, Dan Bailey, and Jim Danskin.

Sunken Stone

Hook: #4-8 TMC 5263
Thread: Black 3/0
Egg sac: Black poly yarn
Body: Bright orange rabbit dubbing
Wing: Deer hair

For years the late Nick Nicklas tied flies and guided for Blue Ribbon Flies. This was one of his most effective patterns. Tie in the poly yarn egg sac over the hook point. The first deer hair clump should be tied in to extend just beyond the egg sac. Bind down all butts of the deer hair clumps. Dub the body material over the butts of the hair and slightly forward. Repeat to give four sections of deer hair wing. In the last section, tie in the wing as is done with the Elk Hair Caddis, and clip the butts over the hook eye. A so-called improved version is tied with a foam body.

Thunderbug

Hook: #2-6 Mustad 9672
Thread: Black 6/0
Tail: Black bear hairs, one-third body length
Rib: Copper, gold, or silver wire
Body: Muskrat or beaver fur dubbing
Thorax: Same as body only thicker
Legs: Pick out hairs from bottom of thorax

Two highly renowned fly-fishing personalities recommend this pattern: Pat Barnes and Charlie Brooks. Both recommend it as a fly to be fished deep in moving water. The Thunderbug seems similar to two other patterns, the Fledermouse and the Muskrat Nymph, whether in use or in construction. Some fly-tying authors refer to it as the Thunderberg.

Whit's Stone Nymph

Hook: #4-6 Mustad 79580
Thread: Rusty orange 6/0
Tail: Dyed orange goose biots
Rib: Rusty orange tying thread
Abdomen: Dark stone nymph Dave Whitlock Dubbing
Legs: Formed from ringneck rooster church window feather

Wing case: Peacock herl, church window feather segments, or dark brown Swiss straw
Head: Rusty orange tying thread
Antennae: Goose biots

The customer could see various nymph patterns by Dave Whitlock in the fly bins of Bud Lilly's Trout Shop. The dark stone pattern by Dave, pictured above, was one of the most popular of these. When stonefly nymphs emerged on regional streams, this one carved its own popularity niche. The golden stone version uses brown stone nymph Dave Whitlock Dubbing. Dave now ties this pattern on a Tiemco 5263 hook.

Willard Fly

Hook: #2-4 Mustad 79580
Thread: Black 6/0
Weight: 0.030-inch-diameter lead-free wire
Body: Large black chenille
Hackle: Black saddle hackle
Collar: Brown saddle hackle

Will Godfrey suggests bending the rear half of the hook downward before tying this pattern. The result is a pattern that better resembles the wiggling motion of a drifting stonefly nymph. Will created this pattern for use when giant stonefly nymphs move toward shorelines with intent to emerge. He notes successful use of his pattern in the Madison River between Earthquake and Hebgen Lakes, in the river below Earthquake Lake, and in the Yellowstone River's Black Canyon. For decades Will has been a major contributor to West Yellowstone's fly-fishing history.

Streamer Patterns

Baker's Hole Bugger

Hook: #2-8 Mustad 79580
Weight: 0.030-inch-diameter lead-free wire
Thread: Hot orange 6/0
Tail: Yellow and brown marabou, copper or root beer Krystal Flash
Rib: Red Wapsi Ultra Wire
Body: Variegated brown and yellow medium chenille
Hackle: Palmered grizzly saddle
Head: Hot orange tying thread

Here is Arrick Swanson's pattern inspired by Baker's Hole and the autumn upstream run of brown trout out of Hebgen Lake. If you intend to fish this famed run at the Baker's Hole Campground, be aware that the Madison River winds in and out of Yellowstone National Park. Thus it is prudent here to use this pattern tied on a barbless hook and weighted with lead-free wire.

Bitchin' Bugger

Hook: #4-8 TMC 5263
Thread: Black 6/0
Tail: Black marabou with pearl Krystal Flash and white rubber hackle

Body: Overhand weave of black chenille on top and orange chenille on bottom
Thorax: Black chenille
Hackle: Brown saddle palmered over thorax
Legs: White rubber hackle

This pattern by Arrick Swanson combines Tony Sivey's revered Bitch Creek Nymph and the Woolly Bugger concept. What would Tony have thought on seeing this! It is common practice to combine past and contemporary tying concepts these days. This example of such a combination has resulted in an effective pattern.

Blew on Blue Soft Hackle

Hook: #8 Tiemco 3769
Thread: Aqua blue UNI-Stretch
Tail: Pearl blue Krystal Flash
Rib: Fine gold or silver wire
Body: Aqua blue tying thread
Thorax: Blue steely Ice Dub
Hackle: A few turns of ruffed grouse

The Blew on Blue Soft Hackle is unusual in its use of bright blue components in tying soft-hackle patterns in a streamer mode. It was created to attract brown and rainbow trout migrating during autumn to spawning areas in streams around West Yellowstone. Craig Mathews credits Bucky McCormick with creating this soft-hackle pattern after they researched its effectiveness in different colors. The pattern has proved particularly effective during bright, sunny autumn days when these fish tend to lie deep and refuse large streamer patterns.

Black Ugly

Hook: #2-4 Mustad 79580
Thread: Black 6/0
Tail: Black marabou
Rib: Black tying thread
Shellback: Six to eight peacock herls
Body: Black chenille
Wing: Black bucktail separated to left and right sides by shellback
Head and collar: Spun and trimmed dyed black deer hair

Information on the purpose of this Pat Barnes pattern appears to be lost. Pat's son Charles remembers nothing of its purpose or use. The only description of its construction is given in *Perrault's Standard Dictionary of Fishing Flies*.

Blue Ribbon Sculpin

Hook: #1-6 Mustad 79580
Thread: Gray size A
Rib: Gold wire
Body: Red yarn
Wing: Rabbit fur strip
Fins: Hen pheasant flank feathers
Head: Ram's wool of various colors

Fly tiers at Blue Ribbon Flies were among the first to use ram's wool to fashion heads on sculpin patterns. These patterns were offered in a variety of colors. During the 1980s and 1990s sculpin patterns with heads tied in this manner established a record of popularity that still stands. An early version of this fly was tied with a deer hair head and featherwing. This version was featured in Bud Lilly's 1982 Trout Shop catalog.

Cross-Eyed Zonker

Hook: #2-4 Daiichi 2220
Thread: White and red size A
Underbody: Lead tape
Body: Gold or silver Mylar tubing
Head: Gold or silver X-cone
Wing: Rabbit strip, color of choice
Gills: Red Estaz

Every West Yellowstone fly-fishing retail business offers streamer patterns for early- and late-season fishing. Many of these such as the Black Ugly, Blue Ribbon Sculpin, South Branch Chub, Vint's Special, and Woolhead Sculpin are in-house patterns, those originating through tying activities of each business. Such is the case for this pattern by Arrick Swanson.

Fuzzy Wazzie

Hook: #2-10 Mustad 90240
Thread: Black 6/0
Rib: Fine oval silver tinsel
Body: Slender, of black floss
Thorax: Gray philoplume
Hackle: Soft natural black saddle
Facing hackle: Turn and a half of barred
    teal flank

Paul Brown created this pattern for fishing the Madison River's famed fall run of brown and rainbow trout out of Hebgen Lake. Presented on a sink-tip line into runs and holes, it is deadly. Brown was one of several schoolteachers who made contributions to West Yellowstone's fly-fishing heritage. A renowned fly tier, he fished all area major waters and became a fly-rod design consultant.

Light Spruce Fly

Hook: #1-10 Mustad 79580
Thread: Black 6/0
Tail: Four or five peacock swords
Body: Aft quarter red floss, front three-
    quarters peacock herl
Wing: Two silver badger hackles
Hackle: Collar formed of silver
    badger hackle

This classic streamer pattern has been highly recommended by West Yellowstone fly-fishing retailers from the 1940s on. Pat Barnes, Jim Danskin, Bob Jacklin, Vint Johnson, Craig Mathews, and Bud Lilly all featured it in their shops. In general, most recommended the Light Spruce Fly over the dark version. Bud Lilly featured both in his mail-order catalog and specified that they were most effective in the spring and fall. Both the light and the dark versions remain area favorites.

Little Yellow Muddler

Hook: #10 Mustad 79580
Thread: Yellow 70-denier
Tail: Dyed yellow mottled turkey
    quill segment
Rib: Fine gold wire
Body: Gold flat tinsel
Underwing: Gray squirrel tail
Wing: Dyed yellow mottled turkey
    quill segment
Collar: Tips of deer hair forming head
Head: Natural gray white-tailed deer body
    hair dyed yellow with an olive cast, spun
    and clipped to shape

This is Bob Jacklin's variation of Don Gapen's Muddler Minnow. He started tying and using it in size 10 in the 1970s for brook trout in the Widow's Pool and Yellowstone Park's Duck Creek. He is certain that it imitates a baitfish species having an olive cast that resides in these and other waters having good aquatic vegetation.

Major Pitcher

Hook: #10 Mustad 3906
Thread: Black 6/0
Tail: Lemon wood duck fibers
Hackle: Furnace palmered over body
Body: Yellow floss rear, red floss front
Wing: White duck quill strips and
    narrow Silver Doctor blue swan strip
    outside each wing

This fly was created and named to honor Major John Pitcher, appointed by President Theodore Roosevelt in 1901 as acting superintendent for Yellowstone National Park. The basis for this appointment was Roosevelt's respect for his friend Pitcher's commitment to conserving and protecting the park's wildlife and natural features. Pitcher did not let Roosevelt down.

Marabou Muddler

Hook: #2-10 Mustad 9672 or 79580
Thread: Gray size A
Tail: Dyed red bucktail
Body: Gold or silver sparkle chenille
Wing: Marabou of any color or color
    combination, tied full
Overwing: Peacock herl fibers
Head and collar: Spun deer hair
    clipped to shape

For decades this fly was one of the most popular streamers offered by West Yellowstone fly-fishing retailers. It was offered in versions having wings of single, double, and triple colors of marabou. Dan Bailey and Dave Whitlock supplied versions, and many retailers tasked their own tiers with producing Marabou Muddlers by the dozens. The recipe given here is for the Dan Bailey version.

Missouri Muddler

Hook: #2-8 Mustad 79580
Thread: Gray 3/0
Tail: Blue dun marabou
Tag: Red floss
Body: Embossed gold tinsel
Hackle: White hackle fiber beard
Wing: White marabou
Shoulders: Short red and yellow marabou
Topping: Six to eight peacock herls with
    equal number of light blue ostrich herls
Head: Spun deer hair clipped to shape

This fly is described in Pat and Sig Barnes's 1964 Waterborn Flies catalog. It is claimed here that the action of the marabou tail helps make it effective. Pat originally used it for large browns and rainbows on the Missouri River, but found it to also be effective for the trout in the waters around West Yellowstone.

Peacock Doctor

Hook: #4-8 Mustad 79580
Thread: Black 6/0
Body: Flat silver tinsel
Underwing: Red bucktail under medium blue bucktail or calf tail
Overwing: Six to eight peacock swords

Pat Barnes relates in a display of his favorite flies, owned now by his son Charles, that he "fished this pattern extensively during Prohibition days." Pat was a teenager in those days, and one of his favorite places to fish was Meadow Lake, known today as Ennis Lake. Back then, most Montana fly fishers preferred to present wet flies, and Pat was no exception. This pattern was one of his favorites for trolling the lake.

Pheasant Muddler

Hook: #6-10 Mustad 38941
Thread: Primrose 6/0
Tail: Short clump of rusty cock pheasant tail or back feathers
Body: Gold braided Mylar
Underwing: Dyed yellow deer body hair
Wing: Matched pheasant back or rump feathers tied Hornberg style
Head: Spun and clipped deer hair with collar forming gills

In the fall 1978 edition of *Fly Tyer* magazine, Jack Gartside describes this pattern as constructed with a broad silhouette in order to simulate baitfish hosted by Yellowstone region waters. He also used it to simulate grasshoppers and in the autumn found it attractive when fished deep to trout migrating from Hebgen Lake up the Madison River to spawn.

Royal Coachman Bucktail

Hook: #2-12 Mustad 9671
Thread: Black 6/0
Tail: Golden pheasant tippet fibers
Body: Peacock herl royaled with red floss
Wing: White bucktail
Hackle: Brown saddle hackle tied beard style

According to Bud Lilly in *A Trout's Best Friend*, Vint Johnson began a run for this pattern in the 1930s by recommending it for fishing Yellowstone Park waters. In *Trout*, Ray Bergman states that Don Martinez tied those he used with some success on the Madison River. Bud continued this pattern's popularity by offering it in his mail-order catalog and in the Trout Shop.

Soft Hackle Streamer

Hook: #2-6 Mustad 3406
Thread: Olive, red, or white 6/0
Body: None
Hackle: Blood marabou wound as hackle in white or any dyed color with a few strands of pearl Flashabou
Collar: Mallard flank feather folded and wound on as hackle just in front of marabou

This Jack Gartside classic is an ultimately effective streamer for any season. Jack describes his inspiration for it as the autumn brown and rainbow trout ascending the Madison River from Hebgen Lake in his booklet *The Soft Hackle Streamer*. Within he also gives tying instructions, which are repeated above. As with any popular pattern, this one has undergone several variations, including a brass bead just behind the eye to run deeper, two colors in the wing, and a variety of feathers as facing. These include peacock body feathers, various golden pheasant feathers, and schlappen dyed various colors.

South Branch Chub

Hook: #6-10 Mustad 79580
Thread: Black 6/0
Rib: Fine gold wire
Body: Flat gold tinsel
Wing: White under black segments of monga ringtail topped with a barred teal flank feather
Cheek: Jungle cock nails

Originally Bob Jacklin tied this fly for the South Branch of the Raritan River brook trout in his native New Jersey. This was a favorite stream in his youth, thus he so named this fly. He brought it to West Yellowstone when he came in 1967 and soon found that it was very effective for taking local rainbow and brown trout.

Troth Bullhead

Hook: #2/0-6 Mustad 36890
Thread: Black size A
Weight: Lead or fuse wire in proportion
  to hook size
Tail: Tips of black ostrich herl over brown
  and white bucktail used to form wing
Body: Cream yarn
Gills: Red yarn
Collar: Tips of deer hair used to spin head
Head: Spun deer hair

For years Bud Lilly's catalog featured this fly in the section on streamer patterns. Besides tying flies, Al Troth guided for Bud and made photographic contributions to his mail-order catalog. The catalog recommended this pattern for all local rivers. It was particularly effective during brown trout migrations.

Vint's Special

Hook: #2-10 Mustad 9672
Thread: Black 6/0
Tail: Red wool
Rib: Wide silver tinsel
Body: Yellow or red yarn
Wing: Red squirrel tail tied Trude style
Hackle: Brown saddle

This Vint Johnson pattern is among the first created in West Yellowstone, and over the years most fly-fishing retailers in town have stocked it. Some sources suggest that the hackle and tail were added later. The pattern given above is as described by Charlie Brooks. It is also known as the Trude Streamer and Red Squirrel Tail Streamer.

Whitlock Multicolored Marabou Muddler #1

Hook: #2-6 Mustad 79580
Thread: Fluorescent orange 6/0 nylon
Butt: Fluorescent orange thread
Body: Gold Mylar braided tubing tied in
  with fluorescent red tying thread
Wing: Stacked white, yellow, orange, and
  brown marabou plumes
Overwing: Several peacock herls
Head: White, yellow, orange, brown, and
  black deer hair clipped to shape
Eyes: Orange and black doll eyes
Cement: Dave's Fleximent

The Multicolored Marabou Muddler #2 is tied in the same manner using pink tying thread; pearl and silver Mylar braided tubing for the body; white, yellow, and medium olive marabou for the wing; white, yellow, and olive deer hair for the head; and yellow and black doll eyes. Dave Whitlock's Multicolored Marabou Muddlers became immensely popular with Bud Lilly's Trout Shop customers, especially during the brown trout migration season.

Woolhead Sculpin

Hook: #2-8 TMC 9395
Thread: Brown or olive 6/0
Rib: Gold wire
Body: Olive yarn
Wing: Olive rabbit fur strip
Fins: Dyed orange sage grouse feathers
Head: Clumps of brown, gray, and/
or olive wool tied onto shank then
trimmed to shape

Craig Mathews and John Juracek first
described the use of wool to form streamer
heads and mouse patterns in a 1985 issue
of *Fly Fisherman* magazine. They offered it
as an alternative to spinning hollow hair
for these purposes but do not claim credit
for this use of wool. Certainly, wool is less
buoyant than hollow hair. Their Woolhead
Sculpin is likely the most popular of fly
patterns using the Woolhead technique,
and its color variations rival spun hollow-
hair versions.

Yellow Perch

Hook: #1/0-6 Mustad 3665A
Thread: Black 8/0
Tail: Yellow hackle fibers
Rib: Flat gold tinsel
Body: Yellow floss
Hackle: Scarlet hackle tied beard style
Wing: Two dyed yellow grizzly hackles
Topping: Peacock herls
Shoulders: Jungle cock eye

Bud Lilly popularized this famed eastern
pattern by Lew Oatman for use in West
Yellowstone–area waters. It can be seen
in his catalogs from the 1970s. Featherwing streamers were commonly used for
decades here, and were particularly popular early and late in the angling season.

SOURCES

Back, Howard. *The Waters of Yellowstone with Rod and Fly.* 1st Lyons Press ed. New York: Lyons Press, 2000.

Barnes, Antrim E. "Pat." "Goofus Bug Evolution." *American Angler,* Spring 1990.

Barnes, Antrim. E. "Pat," and Dave Schors. *Ribbons of Blue.* Helena, MT: Farcountry Press, 2001.

Bergman, Ray. *Trout.* New York: Alfred A. Knopf, 1981.

Blomfield, James. *Rod, Gun and Palette in the High Rockies.* Chicago: W. E. Wroe, 1914.

Brooks, Charles. *Fishing Yellowstone Waters.* Piscataway, NJ: Winchester Press, 1984.

———. *The Henry's Fork.* Piscataway, NJ: Winchester Press, 1986.

———. *Larger Trout for Western Fly Fisherman.* Piscataway, NJ: Winchester Press, 1983.

———. *The Living River.* Garden City, NY: Nick Lyons Books, 1979.

———. *Nymph Fishing for Larger Trout.* New York: Crown Publishers, 1976.

———. *The Trout and the Stream.* New York: Crown Publishers, 1974.

Brown, C. J. D. *Fishes of Montana.* Bozeman, MT: Big Sky Books, Montana State University, 1971.

Chittenden, H. M. *The Yellowstone National Park: Historical and Descriptive.* 4th ed. Cincinnati, OH: Robert Clarke Company, 1904.

Diem, Kenneth L., and Lenore L. Diem. *A Community of Scalawags, Renegades, Discharged Soldiers and Predestined Stinkers?* Moose, WY: Grand Teton Natural History Association, 1998.

Dunbar, Jan. *It Is All True, or It Ought to Be: West Yellowstone Remembered.* Middleton Springs, VT: P. S., A Press, 2002.

Eagle, S. P., and Ed Eagle. *West Yellowstone's 70th Anniversary, 1908–1978.* West Yellowstone, MT: Eagle Company, 1978.

Flick, Art. *Art Flick's Master Fly-Tying Guide.* New York: Crown Publishers, 1972.

Grant, George F. "Don Martinez: Western Dry Fly Master." *The American Fly-Fisher* 9, no. 2 (Spring 1982).

———. *The Master Fly Weaver.* Portland, OR: Champoeg Press, 1981.

———. *Montana Trout Flies.* Portland, OR: Champoeg Press, 1981.

Green, Dean F. *A History of Island Park.* Ashton, ID: Gateway Publishing, 1990.

Gresswell, Robert E. "Yellowstone Lake—A Lesson in Fishery Management." *Proceedings of Wild Trout II, Yellowstone National Park, September 24–25, 1979,* 143–47. Published by Trout Unlimited and Federation of Fly Fishermen, 1980.

Haines, Aubrey L., ed. *Journal of a Trapper.* Lincoln and London: University of Nebraska Press, 1965.

———. *The Yellowstone Story.* Boulder, CO: Yellowstone Library and Museum Association and Colorado Associated University Press, 1977.

Hellekson, Terry. *Fish Flies: The Encyclopedia of the Fly Tier's Art.* Salt Lake City, UT: Gibbs-Smith, 2005.

Herter, George Leonard. *Professional Fly Tying and Tackle Making: Manual and Manufacturer's Guide.* 9th ed. Waseca, MN: Brown Publishing Company, 1953.

Hewitt, Edward R. *Telling on the Trout.* New York: Scribner's, 1926.

———. *A Trout and Salmon Fisherman for Seventy-Five Years.* New York: Scribner's, 1948.

Holt, John. *River Journal: Madison*. Portland, OR: Frank Amato Publications, 1993.

Jacklin, Bob, and Gary LaFontaine. *Fly Fishing the Yellowstone in the Park*. Helena, MT: Greycliff Publishing, 2001.

Jaeger, M. E. , R. W. Van Kirk, and T. Kellogg. "Distribution and Status of Yellowstone Cutthroat Trout in the Henry's Fork Watershed." *Intermountain Journal of Sciences* 6, no. 3 (September 2000): 197–216.

Jennings, Daryl E. "Other Uses of Aquatic Systems." *Proceedings of Wild Trout II, Yellowstone National Park, September 24–25, 1979*, 148–51. Published by Trout Unlimited and Federation of Fly Fishermen, 1980.

Jones, R. D., et al. *Fishery and Aquatic Management Report in Yellowstone National Park, Technical Report for Calendar Year 1978*. U.S. Department of the Interior, Fish and Wildlife Service, July 1979.

———. *Fishery and Aquatic Management Report in Yellowstone National Park, Technical Report for Calendar Year 1978*. U.S. Department of the Interior, Fish and Wildlife Service, July 1980.

———. *Fishery and Aquatic Management Report in Yellowstone National Park, Technical Report for Calendar Year 1983*. U.S. Department of the Interior, Fish and Wildlife Service, May 1984.

———. *Fishery and Aquatic Management Report in Yellowstone National Park, Technical Report for Calendar Year 1989*. U.S. Department of the Interior, Fish and Wildlife Service, August 1990.

Juracek, John, and Craig Mathews. *Fishing Yellowstone Hatches*. West Yellowstone, MT: Blue Ribbon Flies, 1992.

Lavender, David. *Land of Giants*. Garden City, NY: Doubleday & Company, 1958.

Lilly, Bud, and Paul Schullery. *Bud Lilly's Guide to Western Fly Fishing*. New York: Lyons & Burford, 1987.

———. *Bud Lilly's Guide to Fly Fishing the New West*. Portland, OR: Frank Amato Publications, 2000.

———. *A Trout's Best Friend*. Boulder, CO: Pruett Publishing Company, 1988.

Marcoux, Ronald G. "Montana's Madison River—A Continuum of Management Challenges." *Proceedings of Wild Trout II, Yellowstone National Park, September 24–25, 1979*, 82–85. Published by Trout Unlimited and Federation of Fly Fishermen, 1980.

Mathews, Craig, and John Juracek. *Fly Patterns of Yellowstone*. West Yellowstone, MT: Blue Ribbon Flies, 1987.

Mathews, Craig, and Clayton Molinaro. *The Yellowstone Fly-Fishing Guide*. Guilford, CT: Lyons Press, 1997.

McClane, A. J. *The Wise Fishermen's Encyclopedia*. New York: W. H. Wise & Co., 1953.

Proper, Datus. *What the Trout Said*. New York: Lyons and Burford, 1986.

Schiess, William. *Fishing Henry's Lake*. Jerome, ID: 3KB Publications, 1997.

Schullery, Paul. *American Fly Fishing*. New York: Nick Lyons Books, 1987.

Schwiebert, Ernest. *Remembrances of Rivers Past*. New York: MacMillan Company, 1972.

———. *Trout*. New York: E. P. Dutton, 1978.

Simon, J. R. *Yellowstone Fishes*. Yellowstone National Park, WY: Yellowstone Library and Museum Association, 1939.

Sloat, Mathew R., Robert G. White, and Bradley B. Shepard. "Status of Westslope Cutthroat Trout in the Madison River Basin: Influence of Dispersal Barriers and Stream Temperature." *Intermountain Journal of Sciences* 8, no. 3 (September 2002): 153–78.

Smith, A. T., and H. Van Dyke. "Yellowstone Park and the Nation." *The Outlook* 145 (January 19, 1927): 77–80.

Staples, Bruce A. *Trout Country Flies*. Portland, OR: Frank Amato Publications, 2003.

Staples, Bruce A. *Fly Fishing the Greater Yellowstone Backcountry*. Guilford, CT: Stackpole Books, 2017.

Sturgis, William Bayard. *Fly-Tying*. New York: Scribner's, 1940.

Swisher, Doug, and Carl Richards. *Selective Trout*. New York: Crown Publishers, 1971.

Tollefson, Greg. "The Pat Barnes Saga." *Fly Line*, 1992

Townshend, D. "Up Our Way: Around the West Fork of the Madison River." Layout and design by the Madisonian, Ennis, MT, 1998.

Varley, J. D. "A History of Fish Stocking Activities in Yellowstone National Park between 1881 and 1980." National Park Informational Paper 35, Yellowstone National Park, WY, 1981.

Varley, John, and Paul Schullery. *Freshwater Wilderness*. Yellowstone National Park, WY: Yellowstone Library and Museum Association, 1983.

———. *Yellowstone Fishes*. Mechanicsburg, PA: Stackpole Books, 1998.

Vincent, E. Richard. "Effect of Stocking Catchable Trout on Wild Trout Populations." *Proceedings of the Wild Trout Management Symposium at Yellowstone National Park, September 25–26, 1974*, 88–91. Published by Trout Unlimited, 1975.

Waterman, Charles. *Mist on the River: Remembrances of Dan Bailey*. Livingston, MT: Yellowstone Press, 1986.

Whitney, Arthur N. "Creel, Size, Seasons and Angling Methods—The Manager's Point of View." *Proceedings of the Wild Trout Management Symposium at Yellowstone National Park, September 25–26, 1974*, 64–66. Published by Trout Unlimited, 1975.

Whittlesey, Lee H. *Yellowstone Place Names*. Helena, MT: Montana Historical Society Press, 1988.

BOOKS ON FLY FISHING IN THE WEST YELLOWSTONE AREA

Back, Howard. *The Waters of Yellowstone with Rod and Fly*. 1st Lyons Press Ed. New York: Lyons Press, 2000.

Brooks, Charles. *Fishing Yellowstone Waters*. Piscataway, NJ: Winchester Press, 1984.

———. *Larger Trout for Western Fly Fisherman*. Piscataway, NJ: Winchester Press, 1983.

———. *The Living River*. Garden City, NY: Nick Lyons Books, 1979.

———. *Nymph Fishing for Larger Trout*. New York: Crown Publishers, 1974.

———. *The Trout and the Stream*. Piscataway, NJ: Winchester Press, 1984.

Hughes, Dave. *The Yellowstone River and Its Angling*. Portland, OR: Frank Amato Publications, 1992.

Jacklin, Bob, and Gary LaFontaine. *Fly Fishing the Yellowstone in the Park*. Helena, MT: Greycliff Publishing, 2001.

Juracek, John, and Craig Mathews. *Fishing Yellowstone Hatches*. West Yellowstone, MT: Blue Ribbon Flies, 1992.

Lawson, Mike. *Spring Creeks*. Mechanicsburg, PA: Stackpole Books, 2003.

Lilly, Bud, and Paul Schullery. *Bud Lilly's Guide to Western Fly Fishing*. New York: Lyons & Burford, 1987.

Mathews, Craig, and John Juracek. *Fly Patterns of Yellowstone*. West Yellowstone, MT: Blue Ribbon Flies, 1987.

Mathews, Craig, and Clayton Molinaro. *The Yellowstone Fly-Fishing Guide*. Guilford, CT: Lyons Press, 1997.

Staples, Bruce A. *Trout Country Flies*. Portland, OR: Frank Amato Publications, 2003.

———. *Yellowstone Park River Journal*. Portland, OR: Frank Amato Publications, 1996.

Suggested Reading

Everman, B. W. 1892 "A Reconnaissance of Streams and Lakes of Western Montana and Northwest Wyoming." *Bulletin of the U.S. Commission of Fish and Fisheries for 1891*, 11: 60 pgs.

Jordan, D. S. 1891 "A Reconnaissance of Streams and Lakes of Yellowstone National Park, Wyoming, in the Interests of the U.S. Commission of Fish and Fisheries." *Bulletin of the U.S. Commission of Fish and Fisheries for 1890*, 9: 42–63.

Muttkowski, Richard A. "The Ecology of Trout Streams in Yellowstone National Park." *Roosevelt Wild Life Annals* 2 (1920): 151–240.

Smith, H. M., and W. C. Kendall. "Fishes of the Yellowstone National Park." U.S. Department of Commerce, Bureau of Fisheries Document 904, Washington, D.C., 1921.

INDEX